Principles of health and safety at work

Third international edition

Allan St John Holt BA FIOSH RSP
Hascom Network Limited

Published by IOSH Services Limited

Foreword

Principles has established itself as the standard introductory text for the trainee health and safety practitioner. The publication also provides an excellent reference source for the line managers and supervisors who have day-to-day responsibilities for health and safety at work. In one convenient volume *Principles* encompasses all the subject areas needed for study: safety management techniques, workplaces and work equipment, occupational health and hygiene, and compliance.

For this third international edition, safety expert Allan St John Holt has thoroughly revised an already comprehensive text. The latest edition provides coverage of key topics and recognises that good health and safety practice is not merely about achieving legal minimum standards. In addition to the substantial revisions, new sections on the Internet and the ILO have been incorporated.

I recall using *Principles* as my primary reference material when starting my health and safety studies. It remains as valuable a source of information now as it was then, and I am pleased to commend it to those starting out in any role that involves the improvement of health and safety standards and practices at work.

Eleanor Lawson
IOSH President
2002–2003

About the author

Allan St John Holt is one of Britain's best-known safety experts. He has also lectured widely in the USA, Canada, the Asia Pacific region and Australia on health and safety matters. Twice President of IOSH and a Fellow of the Institution, he is a Registered Safety Practitioner. Allan founded the profession's examining body, NEBOSH, in 1979.

Non-executive chairman of the consultancy Hascom Network Ltd, he has been Global Director of Environment, Health and Safety for Bovis Lend Lease and is currently Head of Safety, Royal Mail Group.

An Ambassador of Veterans of Safety International, he was inducted into the Safety and Health Hall of Fame International in 1997 for services to international safety management and in 2000 received the Distinguished Service to Safety Award of the US National Safety Council. A magistrate in Southampton since 1987, Allan was elected Honorary President of the Southampton Occupational Safety Association in 1991.

Introduction

Many people around the world believe, wrongly, that 'getting health and safety right' is about complying with local and national regulations. As a result, information on the subject is typically presented in a legal context. But the law in most countries sets only a minimum standard. Compliance is important, of course, but we should be aiming higher than that, and looking towards continuous improvement.

This book sets out basic information that students, managers and professionals in several disciplines need to know. It should be useful to anyone seeking to improve conditions at work, giving a solid foundation for learning, and a professional desk reference.

Comments from many readers have been used to enhance the book, and thanks are due to all who have suggested improvements. Since the last edition, substantial revisions and additions have been made. Sections have been added on the Internet, the ILO and other topics relevant to an international audience. The text has been augmented with checklists and examples.

I am confident that the book will be a practical help to readers in all countries who wish to gain an understanding of the fundamentals of health and safety management.

Allan St John Holt
Southampton, 14 February 2003

Publishing history

First international edition   February 1995
Second international edition   May 1998
Third international edition   March 2003

ISBN 0 9013 5733 2

Allan St John Holt has asserted his right under the Copyright, Designs and Patents Act 1988 to be identified as the author of this work.

Publisher's note

IOSH and IOSH Services Limited assume no liability for the contents of this book, in whole or in part, nor for interpretations or concepts advanced by the author. The objective of the book is to provide a summary of basic principles, and thus to provide a means for better informed management and health and safety practitioners.

Printed in England by the Lavenham Press Limited

CONTENTS

PART 1 – Safety management techniques

PART 2 – Workplaces and work equipment

PART 3 – Occupational health and hygiene

PART 4 – Compliance

INDEX

PART 1
Safety management techniques

ACCIDENT PREVENTION

Introduction

Few of the things we do in life are free from risk or uncertainty. As Benjamin Franklin observed as long ago as 1789: "Nothing in this world can be said to be certain, except death and taxes." Nevertheless, we order our affairs in the reasonable expectation that things usually turn out as planned. Nobody goes to work prepared to die that day, but sadly some people do. Accident prevention is aimed at spotting what could go wrong and preventing it from doing so, or at least minimising the consequences. Since the subject first received significant attention – from lawmakers about two hundred years ago and from research over the past hundred years – we have learned a good deal about the 'accident phenomenon'.

Accidents are the direct results of unsafe activities and conditions, both of which can be controlled by management. Management is responsible for the creation and maintenance of the working environment, into which workers must fit and interact. Control of this environment is discussed elsewhere in this book. Control of workers and their behaviour is more difficult. They have to be given information, and taught to understand that accidents are not inevitable but are caused.

Workers need training to develop skills, to recognise the need to develop and comply with safe systems of work, and to report and correct unsafe conditions and practices. Their health and safety awareness and attitudes require constant improvement, and the social environment of the workplace must be one which fosters good health and safety practices and conditions, not one which discourages them. Such an environment is known as a **positive safety culture**.

A primary requirement of management is to appreciate the need to concentrate on the nature of the accident phenomenon, rather than its outcome, the injury or damage/loss. Also, there is a need for awareness that the primary cause of an accident is not necessarily the most important feature; secondary causes, usually system failures, will persist unless action is taken. Thus, a 'simple' fall from a ladder may be dismissed as 'carelessness', but this label may hide other significant factors, such as lack of training, maintenance, adequate job planning and instruction, and no safe system of work. These topics will be discussed in this Part.

Three statements must be adopted by management in order to achieve success by planning rather than by chance:
1. Accidents have causes.
2. Steps must be taken to prevent them.
3. Accidents will continue to happen if these steps are not taken.

Accident prevention objectives

Moral objectives derive from the concept that a duty of reasonable care is owed to others. Greater awareness of the quality of life at, and as affected by, work has focused popular attention on the ability of employers to handle a wide variety of issues, previously seen only as marginally relevant to the business enterprise. Environmental affairs, pollution, product safety and other matters are now commonly discussed, and there is a growing belief that it is simply morally unacceptable to put the safety and health of others, inside or outside the workplace, at risk, for profit or otherwise. Physical pain and hardship resulting from death and disability is impossible to quantify. Moral obligations are now more in the minds of employers and business stakeholders than ever before.

A dimension of the moral objective is morale, which also interlinks with the following two objectives. Worker morale is strengthened by active participation in accident prevention programmes, and weakened following accidents. Adverse publicity affects the fortunes of an organisation both internally in this way and externally, as reduced public confidence may weaken local community ties, market position, stakeholder confidence, market share and reputation generally.

Legal objectives are given in local and/or national statute law, which details steps to be taken and carries

2

the threat of prosecution or other enforcement action as a consequence of failure to comply. Civil law enables injured workers and others to gain compensation as a result of a breach of statutory duties or because a reasonable standard of care was not provided under the circumstances.

Economic objectives are to ensure the continuing financial health of a business and avoid the costs associated with accidents. These include monetary loss to employers, to the community and society from worker injuries, damage to property and work interruptions. Some, but not all, of these costs are insurable and are known as **direct costs**. Increased premiums will be a consequence of claims, so an increase in overheads is predictable following accidents. **Indirect costs** include uninsured property damage, delays, overtime costs, management time spent on investigations, and decreased output from the replacement worker(s).

Basic terms

An **accident** is an incident plus its consequences; the end product of a sequence of events or actions resulting in an undesired consequence (injury, property damage, interruption and/or delay). The **incident** is that sequence of events or actions. An incident does not necessarily have a definable start or finish. (Think about a road bulk tanker overturning and spilling its contents onto the road and down drains. Can you say when the incident started or finished?) Thus, an **injury** is a consequence of failure – but not the only possible one.

An accident can be defined more fully as 'an undesired event, which results in physical harm and/or property damage, usually resulting from contact with a source of energy above the ability of the body or structure to withstand it'. The idea of energy transfer as part of the definition of an accident is a relatively recent one, and one which helps us to understand the accident process.

Hazard means the inherent property or ability of something to cause harm – the potential to interrupt

or interfere with a process or person, which is or may be causally related to an accident, by itself or with other variables. Hazards may arise from interacting or influencing components, eg two chemicals interacting to produce a third.

Risk is the chance or probability of loss, an evaluation of the potential for failure. It is easy to confuse the terms 'hazard' and 'risk', and many writers have done so. The terms are often incorrectly used, sometimes interchanged. A simple way to remember the difference is that 'hazard' describes potential for harm, while 'risk' is the likelihood that harm will result in the particular situation or circumstances.

Another way of defining risk is that it is the probability that a hazard will result in an accident with definable consequences. In a wider sense, we can look at 'risk' as the product of the severity of the consequences of any failure and the likelihood of that failure occurring. Thus, an event with a low probability of occurrence but a high severity can be compared against an event likely to happen relatively often but with a comparatively trivial consequence. Comparisons between risks can be made using simple numerical formulae (see Part 1 Section 3).

Accident ratio studies

There have been several studies on the frequency of the possible outcomes of incidents, and an interest in this was one of the influences on H. W. Heinrich, an American safety specialist whose *Industrial Accident Prevention* was first published in 1931 and which became the first widely-available textbook for health and safety practitioners. In it, he developed the Domino Theory of accident causation and distinguished between unsafe acts and unsafe conditions as major causative agents (see below). Seventy years ago, he found that less than 10 per cent of all 'accidents' result in personal injury. From a study of 75,000 reported accidents, he saw that, on average, for every disabling injury there were 29 less serious injuries and 300 accidents involving no personal injury at all. Much depends on the definitions chosen, but the principle was new then and holds good today.

ACCIDENT PREVENTION

Heinrich's work on the outcomes of incidents was repeated by Frank Bird (1969) and in the UK by Tye & Pearson (1974/75) and, most recently, by the UK's Health and Safety Executive (HSE) Accident Prevention Advisory Unit. The results of frequency outcomes are usually represented in the shape of a triangle:

The frequencies shown are taken from recent HSE work in five industries, including construction, food and transport. They will vary between employers according to the nature of the hazards and risk levels. 'Non-injury accidents' need to be measured, and conventionally this is done by recording incidents resulting in property damage rather than people damage.

The main conclusions that can be drawn from this work are:

- Injury incidents are less common than non-injury incidents
- There is a consistent relationship between all loss-producing incidents
- Non-injury incidents could have been injury incidents, and the outcome in each case is mostly determined by chance

Overall, because the consequences of incidents are usually distributed randomly throughout a range of outcomes (with death at one end of the range through to property damage and 'near miss' at the other), we cannot distinguish usefully between those which result in injury and those that do not. Therefore, it is important to look at all incidents as sources of information on what is going wrong; relying on injury records only allows a look at a minority of incidents which happened to result in a serious injury consequence. Each incident can offer information as to its cause, and limiting study to those resulting in physical injury wastes opportunity to gain more information about system and control failures. Furthermore, this is why prevention efforts need to be aimed at loss prevention as a whole.

Accident causes

Immediate or **primary** causes of accidents are often grouped into unsafe acts and unsafe conditions. This is convenient, but can be misleading as accidents typically include both groups of causes at some stage in the chain of causation.

Unsafe acts can include:
- Working without authority
- Failure to warn others of danger
- Leaving equipment in a dangerous condition
- Using equipment at the wrong speed
- Disconnecting safety devices such as guards
- Using defective equipment
- Using equipment the wrong way or for the wrong tasks
- Failure to use or wear personal protective equipment
- Bad loading of vehicles
- Failure to lift loads correctly
- Being in an unauthorised place
- Unauthorised servicing and maintenance of moving equipment
- Horseplay
- Smoking in areas where this is not allowed
- Drinking alcohol or taking drugs

Unsafe conditions can include:
- Inadequate or missing guards to moving machine parts
- Defective tools or equipment
- Inadequate fire warning systems
- Fire hazards
- Ineffective housekeeping
- Hazardous atmospheric conditions
- Excessive noise
- Exposure to radiation
- Inadequate illumination or ventilation

These are all deviations from required safe practice,

but they must be seen as the symptoms of more basic underlying **indirect** or **secondary** causes which allow them to exist and persist.

Indirect causes include:
- Management system pressures
  - financial restrictions
  - lack of commitment
  - lack of policy
  - lack of standards
  - lack of knowledge and information
  - restricted training and selection for tasks
- Social pressures
  - group attitudes
  - trade customs
  - tradition
  - societal attitudes to risk-taking
  - 'acceptable' behaviour in the workplace

Accidents in the EU

During 1998* there were 4.7 million occupational accidents leading to more than three days' absence from work. This gives an incidence rate of 4,089 accidents per 100,000 people at work. Deaths were 5.0 per 100,000 people, with a total of 5,476 people killed at work. A further 3,100 fatalities occurred between home and work. Of the total of nearly 8,600 work-related deaths, 59 per cent were due to road or transport accidents. More details can be obtained from the website of the European Agency for Safety and Health (www.osha.eu.int). The site links to Member State sites where national legislation and guidance can be found.

People employed for less than two years were found to be between 1.2 and 1.3 times more likely to have an accident than the average worker, irrespective of whether they had a temporary or permanent contract.

In some sectors, the figure was much higher than this. For example, staff in hotels and restaurants who had been permanently employed for less than two years were 47 per cent more likely to have an accident, relative to their industry average. Similarly,

temporary employees in construction were 65 per cent more likely to be injured than other workers in their sector.

For all people aged between 18 and 24, and for everyone working night shifts of at least 20 hours a week, the risk of an accident was 1.4 times the average.

Fishing was the most dangerous occupation at 2.43 times the EU occupational average. Other high-risk sectors included construction (1.41 times the EU average), health and social welfare (1.34), and agriculture (1.32).

Other than accidental injuries, work-related health problems affected 7.7 million people in 1998/99, 53 per cent of the cases involving musculoskeletal disorders. These were commonest in the health and social welfare sector followed by construction and transport. Eighteen per cent of cases were related to stress, depression or anxiety. In education and the health and social welfare sectors, the incidence of these problems was twice the EU average.

*Eurostat – Statistics in Focus – Population and Social Conditions – No 16/2001 *Accidents at Work in the EU 1998-1999* – Catalogue No KS-NK-01-016-EN-C.

The world picture

It is remarkably difficult to assemble an accurate picture of occupational accidents around the world. There are many reasons for this: there is no common agreement even on what constitutes 'an accident' for the purposes of recording information or on the types of incident that should be reported to, or collected by, enforcing authorities, and there is underreporting for a range of reasons on a huge scale. Nevertheless, the International Labour Organisation (ILO) makes regular estimates on the best information available to it, and the following table was presented at the 16th International Conference of Labour Statisticians (Geneva, October 1998) by the ILO's Jukka Takala. Note that the world labour force is estimated at 2.7 billion people.

ACCIDENT PREVENTION

TABLE 1: Annual fatal occupational accidents in the world (NB: estimates)

Region	Fatality rate $F_r/10^5$	Employment E, million	Fatalities F_r x E
Established Market Economies	5.3	366,437	19,662
Formerly Socialist Economies of Europe	11.1	140,282	15,563
India	11.0	334,000	36,740
China	11.1	614,690	68,231
Other Asia and Islands	23.1	339,840	80,586
Sub-Saharan Africa	21.0	218,400	45,864
Latin America and the Caribbean	13.5	195,000	26,374
Middle Eastern Crescent	22.5	186,000	41,850
World	**14.0**	**2,394,667**	**334,870**

Priorities in prevention

Basic principles should be observed in setting up strategies for control and management of health and safety at work. These are:

1. If possible, avoid a risk altogether by eliminating the hazard.
2. Tackle risks at source – avoid the quick temporary fix, or putting up a sign where a better physical control could be used (eg quieten machines rather than provide personal protective equipment or erect warning signs).
3. Adapt work to the individual when designing work areas and selecting methods of work.
4. Use technology to improve conditions.
5. Where options are available, give priority to protection for the whole workplace rather than to individuals (eg protect a roof edge rather than supply safety harnesses).
6. Ensure that everyone understands what they have to do to be safe and healthy at work.
7. Make sure that health and safety management is accepted by everyone, and that it applies to all aspects of an organisation's activities.

More information on strategies is given in Part 1 Section 2.

Principles of accident prevention

In summary, these are: the systematic use of techniques to identify and remove hazards, the control of risks which remain, and the use of techniques to influence behaviour and encourage safe attitudes. They are the primary responsibility of management, and are discussed in the next Sections.

Section 2 covers techniques of health and safety management, including the central role of the management organisation and policy needed to put them into practice, Section 3 explores the assessment of risk, and Section 4 looks at successful written health and safety policies. Detailed treatments of practical aspects are contained in Parts 2 and 3 of this book.

REVISION

Three accident prevention objectives:
- Moral/morale
- Legal
- Economic

Definitions: accident, incident, hazard, risk

ACCIDENT PREVENTION

Accident causes are immediate or indirect, and involve unsafe acts and/or conditions

Three principles of accident prevention:

- Use techniques to identify and remove hazards
- Use techniques to assess and control remaining risks
- Use techniques to influence behaviour and attitudes

TECHNIQUES OF HEALTH AND SAFETY MANAGEMENT

Introduction

Health and safety management is concerned with, and achieved by, all the techniques which promote the subject. Some are described in other Parts, some will be considered in Sections later in this Part. Safety management is also concerned with influencing human behaviour, and with limiting the opportunities for mistakes to be made which could result in harm or loss. To do this, safety management must take into account the ways in which people fail (ie fail to do what is expected of them and/or what is safe). The techniques are aimed at the recognition and elimination of hazards, and the assessment and control of those risks which remain.

Objectives

The practical objectives of safety management are:
- Gaining support from all concerned for the health and safety effort
- Motivation, education and training so that everyone can recognise and correct hazards
- Achieving hazard and risk control by design and purchasing policies
- Operation of a suitable inspection programme to provide feedback (see Part 1 Section 10)
- To ensure hazard control principles form part of supervisory training
- Devising and introducing controls based on risk assessments
- Compliance with regulations and standards

To achieve these objectives, a safety policy statement is required. The design of this policy and other relevant considerations are discussed in Part 1 Section 4.

Benefits

Successful safety management can lead to substantial cost savings, as well as a good accident record. Some companies have become well known for the success of their safety management system. Du Pont claims several of its plants, each with more than 1,000 employees, have run for more than 10 years without recording a single lost-time injury accident. Du Pont has 10 principles of safety management, which are worthy of study:

1. All injuries and occupational illnesses are preventable.
2. Management is directly responsible for doing this, with each level accountable to the one above and responsible for the level below.
3. Safety is a condition of employment, and is as important to the company as production, quality or cost control.
4. Training is required in order to sustain safety knowledge, and includes establishing procedures and safety performance standards for each job.
5. Safety audits and inspections must be carried out.
6. Deficiencies must be corrected promptly, by modifications, changing procedures, improved training and/or consistent and constructive disciplining.
7. All unsafe practices, incidents and injury accidents will be investigated.
8. Safety away from work is as important as safety at work.
9. Accident prevention is cost-effective; the highest cost is human suffering.
10. People are the most critical element in the health and safety programme. Employees must be actively involved, and complement management responsibility by making suggestions for improvements.

Key elements

The five key elements of successful health and safety management are:
- Policy
- Organisation
- Planning and implementation
- Monitoring
- Reviewing and auditing performance

It is important to appreciate that the five elements exist independently, not just in a cycle to be reviewed at

TECHNIQUES OF HEALTH AND SAFETY MANAGEMENT

intervals. Thus, policy needs to be kept under continuous review for relevance, applicability, and other factors which will change over time. The reader interested in a complete treatment of this topic is referred to the following guidance documents: HSG65 – *Successful Health and Safety Management*, HSE Books, UK, British Standards BS 8800, and OHSAS 18000.

Policy

Successful health and safety management demands comprehensive health and safety policies which are effectively implemented and which are considered in all business practice and decision-making. Effective policies contain commitments to continuous improvement and avoid references to 'compliance' alone, because that can foster a culture of 'doing just enough' to satisfy minimum legal requirements. At the heart of the policy must be acceptance of successful health and safety management as a key business aim of the organisation, equal in importance to more obvious aims such as profit and financial viability.

Some jurisdictions require written safety policy statements to be created by all employers, except for the smallest organisations. Written policies are the centre-pieces of good health and safety management. They insist, persuade, explain, and assign responsibilities. An essential requirement for management involvement at all levels is to define health and safety responsibility in detail within the written document, and then to check at intervals that the responsibility has been adequately discharged. This process leads to **ownership** of the health and safety programme, and it is based on the principle of accountability discussed in Part 1 Section 4.

Organisation

To make the health and safety policy effective, both management and employees must be actively involved and committed. Organisations which achieve high standards in health and safety create and sustain a 'safety culture' which motivates and involves all members of the organisation in the

control of risks. They establish, operate and maintain structures and systems which are intended to:

- Secure **control** – by ensuring managers lead by example, by the setting of performance standards and measuring against them, and by the appointment of a key senior person at the highest level to oversee and be responsible for the implementation of aspects of the policy. The visible accountability of individuals is an important aspect of control – performance reviews and appraisals should contain measures on individual safety performance
- Encourage **co-operation** – both of employees and their safety representatives. The reinforcement of shared objectives and a heightened awareness of health and safety goals is an important aspect of the maintenance of a good safety culture
- Secure effective **communication** – by providing information about hazards, risks and preventive measures. Visible behaviour of key senior people is an important tool and motivator in its own right – regular safety tours demonstrate interest and active involvement
- Achieve **co-ordination** of their activities – internally between departments and other operating areas, and with other organisations which interface with them
- Ensure **competence** – by assessing the skills needed to carry out all tasks safely, and then providing the means to ensure that all employees (including temporary ones) are adequately instructed and trained. The European Union Framework Directive encourages this by requiring employers to recruit, select, place, transfer and train on the basis of assessments and capabilities, and to ensure that appropriate channels are open for access to information and specialist advice when required. Competence is not simply a question of training – it also involves the application of knowledge, skills and appearance

Planning and implementation

Planning ensures that health and safety efforts really

TECHNIQUES OF HEALTH AND SAFETY MANAGEMENT

work. Success in health and safety relies on the establishment, operation and maintenance of planning systems which:

- **Identify** objectives and targets which are attainable and relevant
- **Set performance standards** for management, and for the control of risks which are based on hazard identification and risk assessment, and which take legal requirements as the accepted minimum standard
- **Consider and control** risks both to employees and to others who may be affected by the organisation's activities, products and services
- Ensure **documentation** of all performance standards
- **React** to changing internal and external demands
- **Sustain** a positive safety culture

Organisations which plan and control in this way can expect fewer injuries (and claims resulting from them), reduced insurance costs, less absenteeism, higher productivity, improved quality and lower operating costs.

Monitoring

Just like finance, production or sales, health and safety has to be monitored to establish the degree of success. For this to happen, two types of monitoring system need to be operated. These are:

- **Active** monitoring systems – intended to measure the achievement of objectives and specified standards before things go wrong. This involves regular inspection and checking to ensure that standards are being implemented and that management controls are working properly
- **Reactive** monitoring systems – intended to collect and analyse information about failures in health and safety performance when things do go wrong. This will involve learning from mistakes, whether they result in accidents, ill health, property damage incidents or 'near misses'

Information from both active and reactive monitoring

systems should be used to identify situations that create risks and enable something to be done about them. Priority should be given to the greatest risks. The information should then be referred to people within the organisation who have the authority to take any necessary remedial action, and also to effect any organisational and policy changes which may be necessary.

Reviewing and auditing performance

Auditing enables management to ensure that their policy is being carried out and that it is having the desired effect. Auditing complements the monitoring programme. Economic auditing of a company is well established as a tool to ensure economic stability and it has been shown that similar systematic evaluation of performance in health and safety has equal benefits. It is a feature of good governance.

An audit is not the same as an inspection. Essentially, the audit assesses the organisation's ability to meet its own standards on a wide front, rather than providing a 'snapshot' of a particular site or premises.

The two main objectives of an audit are:

- To ensure that standards achieved conform as closely as possible to the objectives set out in the organisation's safety policy
- To provide information to justify continuation of the same strategy, or a change of course

The best health and safety audit systems are capable of identifying deviations from agreed standards, analysing events leading to these deviations and highlighting good practice. They look especially at the 'software' elements of health and safety such as systems of work, management practices, instruction, training and supervision, as well as the more traditional 'hardware' elements which include machinery guarding and the use of personal protective equipment.

People problems

In all control measures, reliance is placed on **human**

TECHNIQUES OF HEALTH AND SAFETY MANAGEMENT

behaviour to carry out the solutions, so a major task of health and safety management is to assure safe behaviour by motivation, education, training, and the creation of work patterns and structures which enable safe behaviour to be practised. In a major study in 1977, it was found that supervisors in the construction industry gave a variety of reasons for their inactivity on health and safety matters. In order of frequency, the most common responses were:

● Resource limitations
● Seen as outside the boundaries of their duties
● Acceptance of hazards as inevitable
● Influences of the social climate
● Industry tradition
● Lack of technical competence
● Incompatible demands on their time
● Reliance on the worker to take care
● Lack of authority
● Lack of information

It can be seen that much of the inactivity of **supervision** can be corrected by establishing a favourable environment, with clear responsibilities given and accountability practised, together with necessary training in the complex nature of the accident phenomenon and in solutions to health and safety problems. Supervisors' and workers' attitudes to safety generally reflect their perception of the attitudes of their employer.

Attempts to motivate the individual meet with greatest success when persuasion rather than compulsion is used to achieve agreed health and safety objectives. Consultation with workers, through representatives such as trade unions, and locally through the formation of **safety committees**, is generally a successful strategy, provided that an adequate role is given to those being consulted. The importance of consulting employees on matters affecting their health and safety has been recognised in the law of many countries.

Benefits of safety committees include the involvement of the workforce, encouragement to accept safety standards and rules, help in arriving at practicable solutions to problems, and recognition of hazards which may not be apparent to management.

At an **individual level**, an appreciation of some of the more common reasons why people fail to carry out tasks safely is useful for management. People may actually decide to act wrongly – sometimes in the belief that non-observance of safety rules is expected of them by managers, supervisors or work colleagues. Few deliberately decide to injure themselves, but a deliberate decision to err may be made, for example after a poor estimate of the risk of injury in an activity. Others err because of traps – design of equipment so that the correct action cannot be taken because of physical inability to do so. Valves placed out of reach, dials too far away to be properly read, poor ergonomic design of workstations – all contribute to the likelihood that mistakes will be made. Under these circumstances, it is not surprising that motivational aids such as posters are found to be relatively ineffective in producing safe behaviour. More information on human factors can be found in Part 1 Section 12, and on ergonomics in Part 3 Section 9.

Recent work in the USA, confirmed by studies in the UK at the University of Manchester Institute of Science and Technology (UMIST), has shown that a behaviour-based approach to health and safety management can be an effective tool for increasing safety on construction sites and elsewhere, despite some practical problems of implementation. The technique involves sampling, recording and publicising the percentage of safe (versus unsafe) behaviours, as noted by specially-trained observers drawn from workforce and management. This gives more data on potential system and individual failures than could be obtained from a study of accident records. The attraction of the technique is that it offers **measurement** of potential for harm, independent of the accident record. Disadvantages may include the need to achieve an altered safety climate inside management and workforce to adopt the techniques, and employee suspicion of hidden motives for the observations.

REVISION

Six objectives of health and safety management:

■ To gain support from all concerned
■ Motivation, education and training

TECHNIQUES OF HEALTH AND SAFETY MANAGEMENT

- Achieving hazard control
- Operating inspection programme
- Devising and introducing risk controls
- Compliance with regulations and standards

Five key elements of health and safety management:

- Policy
- Organisation
- Planning and implementation
- Monitoring
- Review and auditing

Two monitoring systems:

- Active
- Reactive

Introduction

There are at least two senses in which risk assessment has been carried out subconsciously over a long period. Firstly, we all make assessments many times each day of the relative likelihood of undesirable consequences arising from our actions in particular circumstances. Whether to cross a road by the lights or take a chance in the traffic is one such example. In making a judgment, we evaluate the chance of injury and also its likely severity, and in doing so we identify a hazard and evaluate the risk.

The second sense of risk assessment is based on legal requirements for employers to make judgments about what might be reasonable precautions to take under particular circumstances to safeguard employees and third parties. In doing this, we make a balanced judgment about the extent of the risk and its consequences against the time, trouble and cost of the steps needed to remove or reduce it.

The difference between these informal assessments and those required by laws made in Europe in response to the Framework Directive is that the significant results must be recorded by most employers, and information based on them is to be given to employees in a much more specific way than before. For readers working in jurisdictions not subject to risk assessment requirements, it is recommended that the exercise should be undertaken voluntarily.

Those carrying out formal assessments report that some activities were being viewed afresh for the first time, and that the exercise was a useful one as it forced challenges to long-held assumptions about the safety of traditional work practices – which often did not stand up to the scrutiny. 'We've always done it that way' is neither an assessment nor a defence!

Benefits

Risk assessments are carried out to enable control measures to be devised. We need to have an idea of the relative importance of risks and to know as much about them as we can in order to take decisions on controls which are both appropriate and cost-effective.

Types of risk assessment

There are two major types of risk assessment, which are not mutually exclusive. The first type produces an objective probability estimate based on known risk information applied to the circumstances being considered – this is a **quantitative** risk assessment. The second type is subjective, based on personal judgment backed by generalised data on risk – the **qualitative** assessment. Except in cases of specially high risk, public concern, or where the severity consequences of an accident are felt to be large and widespread, qualitative risk assessments are adequate for the purpose, and much simpler to make. The legal requirements refer to this type of assessment unless the circumstances require more rigorous methods to be used.

What to assess

Items of work equipment will require appropriate and probably individual risk assessment. So will tasks of various kinds. Where there is similarity of activities, and the hazards and risks associated with them, although carried out in different physical areas or workplaces, a general risk assessment can be made which covers their common and basic features. This is known as a 'generic' or 'model' assessment, and may be included or referred to in the safety policy document.

There are likely to be situations in specific areas or on specific occasions when such an assessment will not be sufficiently detailed, and those circumstances should be indicated in the policy to alert to the need to take further action. There may also be work situations where hazards associated with particular situations will be unique, so that a special assessment must be made every time that the work is done. A method statement may be required (see Part 1 Section 5). Examples where this holds true include demolition work, the erection of steel structures and asbestos removal.

RISK ASSESSMENT

Contents of risk assessments

The written record should contain a statement of the significant hazards identified, the control measures in place and the extent to which they control the risk(s) (cross-references can be made to manuals and other documents), and the population exposed to the risk(s).

As it will be necessary to review for changed circumstances over time, it would be prudent to include in the documentation a note of the date the assessment was made and the date for the next regular review.

In 1994 the UK Health and Safety Executive (HSE) published guidance entitled *Five Steps to Risk Assessment*, a leaflet setting out the most basic steps in the process and providing a specimen format for recording the findings of assessments. The leaflet has since been updated and reissued. The simplistic approach presented has much to commend it. Comments contained in the text give useful pointers to the approach to risk assessment which will bring benefits to the organisation carrying out this simple but powerful analysis:

"An assessment of risk is nothing more than a careful examination of what, in your work, could cause harm to people so that you can weigh up whether you have taken enough precautions or should do more..."

A more sophisticated approach will often be required where hazards and risks are changing frequently, as in the construction industry, and also where clients, work partners and other external organisations seek evidence of more detailed analysis than *Five Steps to Risk Assessment* is likely to provide. There is no shortage of more complicated commercial systems, often computer-based so as to enable rapid review and quick updating in changing conditions.

Risk assessments should record the hazards, the control measures in place, what more needs to be done to control the hazards, and details of those exposed to the hazard. Following the assessment, a re-evaluation of the remaining, or **residual**, risk should be made. Advice on acceptable levels of residual risk can be obtained from a variety of sources.

Estimates of occupational health risks and decisions on acceptable controls for them are more difficult, not least because the hazards are less easy to detect and measure, and because their effects can take a considerable time to become apparent.

Hazard evaluation

The hazards to be identified are those associated with machinery, equipment, tools, procedures, tasks, processes and the physical aspects of the plant and premises – in other words, everything. Evaluation of the hazards is achieved by assembling information from those familiar with the hazards, such as insurance companies, professional societies, government departments and agencies, manufacturers, consultants, trade unions, old inspection reports (both internally and externally produced), accident reports and standards.

Some hazards may not be readily identifiable and there are techniques which can be applied to assist in this respect. These include inductive analysis techniques, which predict failures – Failure Modes and Effects Analysis (FMEA) is one of these; Job Safety Analysis (JSA) is another. Inductive analysis assumes failure has occurred and then examines ways in which this could have happened by using logic diagrams. This is time-consuming and, therefore, expensive, but it is extremely thorough. MORT (Management Oversight and Risk Tree) Analysis is an example of an analytical technique which is not difficult to use.

Ranking hazards by risk

There may be occasions when a priority list for action will be called for. Techniques for producing a ranking vary from the very simple to the very complex. What is looked for is a priority list of hazards to be controlled, on a 'worst first' basis. There is no need to introduce numbers into a risk assessment, but many organisations find it useful to do so in order to show a 'before' and 'after' risk reduction within the assessment.

The following system offers a simple way to determine the relative importance of risks. It takes account of the consequence (likely severity) and the probability of the event occurring. Estimation of the first is easier than the second, as data may not be available for all hazards. Estimates derived from experience can be used. It is possible to carry out ranking using a simple formula, where risk = severity estimate x probability estimate. These estimates can be given any values, as long as they are consistently used. The simplest set of values provides a 16-point scale:

SEVERITY RATING OF HAZARD	VALUE
Catastrophic – Imminent danger exists, hazard capable of causing death and illness on a wide scale	1
Critical – Hazard can result in serious illness, severe injury, property and equipment damage	2
Marginal – Hazard can cause illness, injury or equipment damage, but the results would not be expected to be serious	3
Negligible – Hazard will not result in serious injury or illness, remote possibility of damage or injury beyond minor first-aid case	4

PROBABILITY RATING OF HAZARD	VALUE
Probable – Likely to occur immediately or shortly	1
Reasonably probable – Probably will occur in time	2
Remote – May occur in time	3
Extremely remote – Unlikely to occur	4

The categories are capable of much further refinement. Words like 'time' can be defined, increasing if necessary the number of categories. Many organisations increase the categories to take account of numbers exposed to the hazard as well as the duration of exposure. However, the more precise the definitions, the more it will be necessary to possess accurate predictive data.

It should also be noted that ranking systems of this kind introduce their own problems, which must be addressed, or at least be known to the user. One is that long-term health hazards may receive inadequate evaluation because of lack of data. Another is that hazards of low severity but high frequency can produce the same risk score through multiplication as high severity, low frequency ones. Although the scores may be the same, the response to them in terms of priority for correction may be very different. Access to good data and evaluation and categorisation by experts are possible cures.

Decision-making

This process requires information to be available on alternatives to the hazard, as well as other methods of controlling the risk. Factors which will influence decision-making are training, possibility of replacement of equipment or plant, modification possibilities and the cost of the solutions proposed. **Cost/benefit analysis** will be used formally or informally at this point.

Cost/benefit analysis requires a value to be placed on the costs of improvements suggested or decided on. These will include the cost of reducing the risk, eliminating the hazard, any capital expenditure needed, and any ongoing costs applicable. An estimate of the payback period will be needed. Decisions on action to be taken are often based on this – a three to five-year payback period is often associated with health and safety improvements. The use of these techniques will direct an organisation's resources to where they will be most effective.

Introduction of corrective and preventive measures

The concept of **progressive risk reduction** encourages the setting of improving objectives of risk

RISK ASSESSMENT

reduction year by year. It is easy to become 'safety complacent' believing that 'doing just enough' is doing it safely. But hazards and risks often change over time, as materials degrade and begin to fail, and lack of maintenance results in temporary fixes becoming permanent ones, and in deviations from good work practices because 'we haven't had any accidents here for years'.

It is necessary to be aware that some corrective measures are better able to produce the desired results than others, and that some are very ineffective indeed as controls. The **safety precedence sequence** shows the order of effectiveness of measures:

1. **Hazard elimination** (eg use of alternative work methods, design improvements, change of process).
2. **Substitution** (eg replacement of a chemical with another with less risk).
3. **Use of barriers**:
   – isolation (removes hazard from the worker, puts hazard in a box)
   – segregation (removes worker from the hazard, puts worker in a box).
4. **Use of procedures**:
   – limiting exposure time, dilution of exposure
   – safe systems of work, which depend on human response.
5. **Use of warning systems**:
   – signs, instructions, labels, which depend on human response.
6. **Use of personal protective equipment**:
   – depends on human response, used as a sole measure only when all other options have been exhausted – PPE is the last resort.

Personal protective equipment is discussed in Section 6 of Part 3. This should only be used if there is no immediately feasible way to control the risk by more effective means, and as a temporary measure pending installation of more effective solutions. PPE always involves at least one positive human act before it can be effective – that of making use of it.

Disadvantages of PPE include:
- Interference with the ability to carry out the task

- PPE may fail and expose the worker to the full effect of the hazard
- Continued use may mask the presence of the hazard and may result in no further preventive action being taken

Training is a control measure, but at second-hand. When the control measures have been identified, training is given in what needs to be done to put the controls into action, or to keep them effective.

Risk and design

Wherever design can have an influence on health, safety or the environment, knowledge of the relative effectiveness of some measures compared with others is very important for the designer. In order of preference and effectiveness, the major choices open to designers are to:

- Avoid the hazard by design alone. Examples are ergonomic tool design, work station layouts, and giving thought to the way maintenance will be carried out
- Combat the hazard at source – an erection sequence can be specified in advance, rather than letting the erectors work out for themselves what the designer had in mind
- Protect the entire population affected by the hazard – by specifying adequate edge protection in high storage areas which will be accessed; communal protection with fixed barriers incorporated into the design reduces the need for personal protective equipment by contractors and maintenance staff
- And only then rely solely on personal protective equipment to minimise risk

Specifying safer chemicals or finishes, and producing designs which do not require noisy or dusty work processes are further examples of the influence which designers can have on the wellbeing of workers.

Monitoring

Risk assessments must be checked to ensure their

validity, or when reports indicate that they may no longer be valid. It is important to remember that fresh assessments will be required when the risks change as conditions change, and also when new situations and conditions are encountered for the first time. Other information relevant to risk assessments will come from monitoring by way of inspection (see Section 2), air quality monitoring and other measurements (see Part 3 Section 3), and health surveillance.

Health surveillance

Risk assessments will identify circumstances where health surveillance will be appropriate. Requirements for such surveillance now extend beyond exposure to substances hazardous to health. Generally, there will be a need if there is an identifiable disease or health condition related to the work, there is a valid technique for its identification, there is a likelihood that the disease or condition may occur as a result of the work, and that the surveillance will protect further the health of employees. Examples where these conditions may apply are hand-arm vibration including vibration white finger, and forms of work-related upper limb disorders (WRULDs).

Information to others

Co-operation and sharing of information between employers sharing or acting as host at a workplace is essential – control measures will never be successful or sufficient if full information on hazards and risks is not available. Risk assessments will form the basis of that information. In formal circumstances of contracts, there may be a contractual or legal requirement to exchange risk assessment data. The information given to others about risks should include the health and safety measures in place to address them, and be sufficient to allow the other employers to identify anyone nominated to help with emergency evacuation.

REVISION

Two types of risk assessment:
- Qualitative
- Quantitative

Individual risk = severity x probability

Six contents of risk assessments:
- Hazard details
- Applicable standards
- Evaluation of risks
- Existing preventive measures
- What, if anything, needs to be done to reduce risks further to an acceptable level
- Review dates/feedback details

THE HEALTH AND SAFETY POLICY

Introduction

Without active support, any attempt at organised accident prevention will be useless – or even worse than useless – since there may be an illusion that health and safety matters are under control, resulting in complacency. Avoidance of accidents requires a sustained, integrated effort from all departments, managers, supervisors and workers in an organisation. Only management can provide the authority to ensure this activity is co-ordinated, directed and funded. Its influence will be seen in the policy made, the amount of scrutiny given to it, and the ways in which violations are handled.

The safety policy

The most effective means of demonstrating management commitment and support is by issuing a safety policy statement, signed and dated by the most senior member of the management team, and then ensuring that the detailed requirements of the policy are actively carried out by managers, supervisors and workers. Lack of firm management direction of this kind encourages the belief that 'safety is someone else's business'.

An essential requirement for management involvement at all levels is to define health and safety responsibility in detail within the written document, and then to check at intervals that the responsibility has been adequately discharged. This is **accountability** – the primary key to management action. It is not the same thing as responsibility; accountability is responsibility that is evaluated and measured, possibly during appraisal sessions.

Safety policy contents

The statement itself is an expression of management intention, and as such does not need to contain detail. What is usually referred to as 'the safety policy' will contain this statement of the employer's intention together with the details of the organisation set up to make it happen (responsibilities at each level within the operation), and the arrangements (how, in detail, health and safety will be managed).

It is important to distinguish between a health and safety policy and a safety manual – these are not the same, but are often found combined. The safety policy will refer to the manual for details on technical points. The main problem is that the likelihood of a document being read and used is proportional to its length and complexity. Current opinion is that safety policies should be shorter rather than longer, and accompanied by explanatory manuals.

The safety policy should provide all concerned with concise details of the organisation's health and safety objectives and the means of achieving them, including the assignment of responsibility and detailed arrangements for each workplace. Organisations with several workplaces in different locations find it convenient to express management philosophy in an overall statement, leaving a detailed statement and policy to be written and issued at local level.

Risk assessments can form part of the organisation's safety policy, as they form the basis for deciding on the control measures – the arrangements – and detailing the responsibilities within the organisation. However, they are usually kept and issued separately.

The employer's statement

In the employer's opening statement, there should be commitment to the following seven aims as a minimum:

1. To identify the hazards to employees and third parties affected by the work, and control the attendant risks adequately.
2. To maintain healthy and safe working conditions, including provision of safe plant and equipment.
3. To work, through continuous improvement, to prevent accidents and work-related ill health.
4. To ensure that employees are competent to do their work and provide them with appropriate and adequate training.

International Principles of Health and Safety at Work | Allan St John Holt

5. To ensure the safe transport, storage, handling and use of hazardous substances.

6. To consult with employees on health and safety issues affecting their wellbeing, giving them necessary information, instruction and supervision.

7. To review and revise the safety policy at regular intervals as necessary.

The statement should be signed by the most senior person with corporate responsibility for health and safety, and dated. Nothing less than this will convey the necessary authority to the contents.

Organisation and arrangements

Responsibilities of management and supervisors at all levels amount to the details of the **organisation** for health and safety that should be present. At every level managers and workforce alike should have set out for them a precise summary of their duties for their own and others' health and safety at work.

Opinion varies about the amount of detail which the **arrangements** within a health and safety policy should contain. The following list of the main headings of matters which are often detailed within the safety policy is offered as a guide only:

- Role and functions of health and safety professional staff
- Appointment of a competent person required by the Management Regulations
- Allocation of finance for health and safety
- Systems used to monitor safety performance (not just injury recording)
- Identification of main hazards likely to be encountered by the workforce, including eg process noise, asbestos, manual handling, hand-arm vibration
- Arrangements for making risk assessments
- Any circumstances when specific risk assessments will be required
- Arrangements (or cross-references) for dealing with specific risk assessments
- Safety training policy, details of arrangements

- Induction training
- Young persons' training and risk assessment
- Design safety
- Fire arrangements and risk assessments
- Emergency evacuation summary and practice arrangements
- Arrangements for maintaining mechanical and electrical work equipment and systems
- COSHH implementation, assessments, review, information to employees
- Occupational health facilities, including first aid
- Environmental monitoring policy and arrangements
- Purchasing policy (eg on safety, noise, chemicals)
- Methods of reporting accidents and incidents
- Methods used to investigate accidents and incidents
- Arrangements for the use of contractors
- Personal protective equipment policy, requirements, availability
- Worker consultation arrangements (eg safety committees)
- Listed health and safety rules (eg wearing of PPE, drugs and alcohol, horseplay)

Other considerations

Safety policies, as written statements of the intentions of management, acquire a quasi-legal status. Among other things, they serve as a record of the intended standard of care to be provided by the employer. This offers a useful method of evaluating an organisation in terms of health and safety, especially because its standards, beliefs and commitments are on view and potentially measurable. Therefore, the document will be useful when evaluating contractors and their competence (see Part 1 Section 8). Others may wish to use it for different purposes – to gauge the record of a possible business partner, and, importantly, for the purpose of establishing an employer's self-assessed standard of care as a prelude to making a civil claim for damages. Claimants may be able to use any extravagant wording or undertakings to further claims, as they can demonstrate what should have been available or shown in their case.

THE HEALTH AND SAFETY POLICY

Revision of safety policies should be done at regular intervals to ensure that the organisation and arrangements are still applicable and appropriate to the needs. After changes in structure, senior personnel, work arrangements, processes or premises, the hazards and their risks may change. After incidents and accidents, one of the objectives of the investigation (see Part 1 Section 9) will be to check that the arrangements in force had anticipated the circumstances and foreseen the causes of the accident. If they had not, then a change to the policy will be required. The revision mechanism should be written into the policy.

Circulation/distribution of the policy is important – it must be read and understood by all those affected by it. How this is best achieved will be a matter for discussion. In some organisations, a complete copy is given to each employee. In others, a shortened version is given out, with a full copy available for inspection at each workplace. Members of the management team should be familiar with the complete document. If it is likely to be revised frequently, a loose-leaf format will be advisable. This is especially true if the names and contact phone numbers of staff are printed in it, as these may change frequently.

REVISION

Safety policies contain:
- A general statement of management philosophy and commitment
- Details of the organisation (responsibilities)
- Risk assessment methods and significant findings
- The arrangements in force to control the risks
- The signature of the most senior member of management
- The date of the last revision

SAFE SYSTEMS OF WORK

Introduction

It has been estimated that at least a quarter of all fatal accidents at work involve failures in systems of work – the way things are done. A safe system of work is a formal procedure which results from a systematic examination of a task in order to identify all the hazards and assess the risks, and which identifies safe methods of work to ensure that the hazards are eliminated or the remaining risks are minimised.

Many hazards are clearly recognisable and can be overcome by separating people from them physically, eg using guarding on machinery (see Part 2 Section 2). There will often be circumstances where hazards cannot be eliminated in this way, and elements of risk remain associated with the task. **Where the risk assessment indicates this is the case, a safe system of work will be required**.

Some examples where safe systems will be required as part of the controls are:
- Cleaning and maintenance operations
- Changes to normal procedures, including layout, materials and methods
- Working alone or away from the workplace and its facilities
- Breakdowns and emergencies
- Control of the activities of contractors in the workplace
- Vehicle loading, unloading and movements

Developing safe systems

Some safe systems can be verbal only – where instructions are given on the hazards and the means of overcoming them – for short duration tasks. These instructions must be given by supervisors or managers – leaving workers to devise their own method of work is not a safe system of work. The law requires a suitable and sufficient risk assessment be made of all the risks to which employees and others who may be affected by them are exposed. Although some of these assessments can be carried out using a relatively unstructured approach, a more formal analysis can be used to develop a safe system of work. Sometimes these may be

carried out as a matter of policy, with the task broken down into stages and the precautions associated with each written into the final document. This can be used for training new workers in the required method of work. The technique is known as **job safety analysis**.

For all safe systems, there are five basic steps necessary in producing them:
- Assessment of the task
- Hazard identification and risk assessment
- Definition of safe methods
- Implementing the system
- Monitoring the system

Task assessment

All aspects of the task must be looked at, and should be put in writing to ensure nothing is overlooked. This should be done by supervisory staff in conjunction with the workers involved, to ensure that assumptions of supervisors about methods of work are not confounded by reality. Account must be taken of: **what is used** – the plant and equipment, potential failures of machinery, substances used, electrical needs of the task; **sources of errors** – possible human failures, short cuts, emergency work; **where the task is carried out** – the working environment and its demands for protection; and **how the task is carried out** – procedures, potential failures in work methods, frequency of the task, training needs.

Hazard identification and risk assessment

Against a list of the elements of the task, associated hazards can be clearly identified, and a risk assessment can be made (a review of risk assessment can be found in Part 1 Section 3). Where hazards cannot be eliminated and risks reduced, procedures to ensure a safe method of work should be devised.

Definition of safe methods

The chosen method can be explained orally as already

SAFE SYSTEMS OF WORK

mentioned. Simple written methods can be established, or a more formal method known as a permit-to-work system can be used. All of these involve: setting up the task and any authorisation necessary; planning of job sequences; specification of the approved safe working methods including the means of getting to and from the task area if appropriate; conditions which must be verified before work starts – atmospheric tests, machinery lockout; and dismantling/disposal of equipment or waste at the end of the task.

Implementing the system

There must be adequate communication if the safe system of work is to be successful. The details should be understood by everyone who has to work with it, and it must be carried out on each occasion. It is important that everyone appreciates the need for the system and its place in the accident prevention programme.

Supervisors must know that their duties include devising and maintaining safe systems of work, and making sure they are put into operation and revised where necessary to take account of changed conditions or accident experience. Training is required for all concerned, to include the necessary skills, and awareness of the system and the hazards which it is aimed to eliminate by the use of safe procedures. Part of every safe system should be the requirement to stop work when a problem appears which is not covered by the system, and not to resume until a safe solution has been found.

Monitoring the system

Effective monitoring requires that regular checks are made to make sure that the system is still appropriate for the needs of the task, and that it is being fully complied with. Checking only after accidents is not an acceptable form of monitoring. Simple questions are required: Do workers continue to find the system workable? Are procedures laid down being carried out? Are the procedures still effective? Have

there been any changes which require a revision of the system?

A system devised as above which is not followed is **not** a safe system of work – the reasons must be found and rectified. Safe systems of work are associates of, not substitutes for, the stronger prevention techniques of design, guarding and other methods which aim to eliminate the possibility of human failure.

Permit-to-work systems

Written permit-to-work systems are normally reserved for occasions when the potential risk is high, and where at the same time the precautions needed are complicated and require written reinforcement. These systems will often be found where the activities of groups of workers or multiple employers have to be co-ordinated to ensure safety.

When permits to work are used in the workplace, their use should be covered specifically during induction training of all employees and contractors, and during preliminary discussions with contractors.

Permit-to-work systems normally use preprinted forms, listing specific checks and/or actions required at specific stages of the task. These may include isolation of supply systems and the fitting of locking devices to controls. Most permits are only designed to cover work lasting up to 24 hours, and require an authorisation signature for any time extension. The sequence of operation for a permit-to-work system is shown in Figure 1.

An experienced, trained and authorised person will pre-assess the hazards and risks involved in the work to be done, and will then complete and sign a certificate giving authority for the work to proceed under controlled conditions specified on the permit. No-one should be in a position to authorise a permit for themselves to do work.

A permit will include details of the work to be done and what is involved, including all precautions required and emergency procedures, who is to do it

FIGURE 1: Permit-to-work system operation

TASK SEQUENCE	COMMENTARY
Request for permit to work is made	
Hazards are assessed	
Type of permit is selected	
Permit is raised, and precautions are stated	Possible precautions include: Isolation of equipment and areas Use of protective devices and clothing Firefighting equipment and fire watchers Removal of waste generated
Initial precautions taken	
Precautions are verified by the issuer and recipient	
Sampling and testing carried out	Testing for: Toxic concentrations Flammable concentrations Lack of oxygen
Permit issued to competent person in charge of the work	
Work carried out in accordance with permit and precautions detailed in it	
Work conditions monitored	Continued monitoring of tested conditions: Sampling Spot checks Dose monitoring
Work is completed and area handed back	
Permit is cancelled	
Record is kept of permit issue	

and when, and any limits on the work area or equipment. The permit-to-work system will usually require written acknowledgement by the person who will do the work, or is in charge, and will also allow for signed confirmation that the workplace or the equipment has been restored to safety, for any time extension which may be permitted, and for the cancellation of the permit. There will also usually be some system for keeping a record that a permit has been issued.

A crucial point of principle is that no permit should be issued unless the persons issuing and receiving it have personally satisfied themselves that the permit is properly made out, and have visited the scene of the work and verified that the specified precautions are in place. Safe systems of work depend on people to carry them out and are, therefore, fallible. It is wise to remember that proceeding on assumptions is dangerous: 'assume' makes an ass out of you and me.

SAFE SYSTEMS OF WORK

FIGURE 2: General permit to work

To:	Company:
Location:	
EVERY ITEM MUST BE COMPLETED OR DELETED AS APPROPRIATE	

A. JOB DETAILS

1. Area or equipment to which this permit applies	2. Work to be done

B. ISOLATIONS (specify where necessary)

		Initials & Comments
1. Circuit breaker locked out/fuses withdrawn/isolator locked off	YES/NO	
2. Circuit tested and confirmed to be dead	YES/NO	
3. Mechanical or physical isolation	YES/NO	
4. Valves closed/locked off/spades inserted	YES/NO	
5. Pipelines drained/purged/disconnected/vented to atmosphere	YES/NO	
6. Documented isolation procedure attached	YES/NO	
7. Other	YES/NO	

C. PRECAUTIONS (to be taken as indicated, additional to those specified on other permits)

1. Protective clothing   YES/NO   Type:
2. Respiratory equipment   YES/NO   Type:
3. Protected electrical equipment   YES/NO   Type:
4. State additional precautions required (if none, state none)

5. Atmosphere tests are not/are required at intervals of   and results must be recorded overleaf

D. ADDITIONAL PERMITS AND SIGNATURES REQUIRED BEFORE WORK STARTS

1. Confined space entry YES/NO	6. In my opinion, the engineering precautions are adequate
2. H.V. electrical YES/NO	
3. Hot work YES/NO	
4. Excavation YES/NO	Signed (Engineer) Date
5. Other YES/NO	
	7. In my opinion, the precautions against special hazards within my knowledge are adequate
	Signed (Specialist) Date

E. ISSUE AND RECEIPT BEFORE WORK STARTS

1. Issue	**2. Receipt**
I have examined the area specified and permission is given for the work to start, subject to the conditions hereon, under the control of	I have read and understood the conditions of this permit
	Signed Date
	3. This permit is valid from hours to hours
Signed Date	(maximum 24 hours)

F. CLEARANCE AND CANCELLATION AFTER WORK

1. Clearance	**2. Cancellation**	YES	NO	
All workers under my control have been withdrawn. The permitted work is/is not complete	Work complete			I have notified those affected. This permit is cancelled
	Isolations removed			
	Area/Equipment is safe to use			
Signed	Signed			
Time Date	Time Date			

An example of a general purpose permit is shown in Figure 2. This permit can be used for circumstances where a more specialised version is not required. For example, it could be used for work on or near overhead crane installations, or for work on pipelines with hazardous contents. There are many different types of specialised permit. Some common examples are:

- Electrical permits to work – a useful example of this type of permit is contained in Appendix 1 of the HSE booklet HSG85 – *Electricity at Work: Safe Working Practices*
- Hot work permits
- Permits to enter premises or confined spaces
- Permits to work on pressurised systems
- Permits to excavate – in contaminated ground, or where there are congested or buried services

Method statements

The key feature of method statements is that they provide a sequence for carrying out an identified task; some work activities must be done in sequence to ensure safety. In such cases, it is necessary not only to know what the control measures are, but also to carry the work out in a particular order. Examples of activities where method statements are commonly called for include demolition work, asbestos removal and structural steel erection.

Method statements usually contain more detail than risk assessments, and normally include the following information:

1. Originator and date.
2. Identification of individual(s) who will be responsible for the whole operation and for compliance with the method statement. Key personnel responsible for particular operations may also be named.
3. Training requirements for personnel carrying out tasks which have a competency requirement. (Examples are crane and fork-lift drivers, testing and commissioning staff.)
4. Details of access equipment which will be used, safe access routes and maintenance of emergency routes.

5. Equipment required to carry out the work, including its size, weight, power rating, necessary certification.
6. Locations and means of fixing the stability of any lifting equipment to be used.
7. Material storage, transportation, handling and security details.
8. Detailed work sequence including hazard identification and risk control measures, including co-operation between trades which may be required, limitations for part completion of works and any temporary supports or supplies required.
9. Details of all personal protective equipment and other measures such as barriers, signs, local exhaust ventilation, rescue equipment, fire extinguishers, gas detection equipment.
10. Any environmental limitations which may be applicable, such as wind speed, rain, temperature.
11. Details of measures to protect third parties who may be affected.
12. The means by which any variations to the method statement will be authorised.

REVISION

Five steps in devising a safe system:
- Assessment of the task
- Identification of the hazards and assessment of the risks
- Definition of safe method
- Implementation of the safe system
- Monitoring the system

Formal safe systems may be required for:
- Cleaning tasks
- Maintenance work
- Changes to routine
- Working alone
- Working away from normal environment
- Breakdowns
- Emergencies
- Contractors' vehicle operations

HEALTH AND SAFETY TRAINING

Introduction

Training for health and safety is not an end in itself, it is a means to an end. Talking in general terms to employees about the need to be safe is not training; workers and management alike need to be told what to do for their own health and safety and that of others, as well as what is required by statute. A knowledge of what constitutes safe behaviour in a variety of different occupational situations is not inherited but must be acquired, either by trial and error or from a reputable source of expertise. Trial and error methods are likely to extract too high a price in modern industry, where the consequences of forced and unforced errors may be very serious, even catastrophic.

Experience and research also shows that knowledge of safe behaviour patterns, gained by instruction, films, videos, posters and booklets, does not guarantee that safe behaviour will be obtained from individuals. Training is, therefore, never a substitute for safe and healthy working conditions and good design of plant and equipment. Because humans are fallible, the need is to lessen the opportunities for mistakes and unsafe behaviour to occur, and to minimise the consequences when it does.

Safety training may be a part of other training in work or organisational procedures for reasons of time or cost, and there is merit in combined training as it serves to emphasise the need to regard health and safety generally as an integral part of good business management.

Training in any subject requires the presence of three necessary conditions before it commences: the active **commitment**, support and interest of management, necessary finance and organisation to provide the **opportunity** for learning to take place, and the availability of suitable **expertise** in the subject. The support of management demonstrates the presence of an environment into which the trained person can return and exercise new skills and knowledge. The management team also demonstrates support by setting good examples; it is pointless to train workers to obey safety rules if supervisors are known to ignore them.

Trainers must not only be knowledgeable in their subject, but also be qualified to answer questions on the practical application of their knowledge in the working environment, which will include a familiarity with organisational work practices, procedures and rules.

Training needs

Organisational

New employees are known to be more likely to have accidents than those who have had time to recognise the hazards of the workplace. Formal health and safety training is now required by law to form part of the induction programme. Training must also take place when job conditions change and result in exposure to new or increased risks. It must be repeated periodically, where appropriate, and be adapted to any new circumstances.

There may also be opportunities for self-instruction, perhaps using modern technology to assist, eg computer-based interactive learning programmes. The key points which should be covered in induction training are:

- Review and discussion of the organisation's overall safety programme or policy, and the policy relating to the work activities of the newcomers
- Safety philosophy: safety is as important as production or any other organisational activity, accidents have causes and can be prevented, prevention is the primary responsibility of management, each employee has a personal responsibility for his or her own safety and that of others
- Local, national and organisational health and safety rules or regulations will be enforced, and those violating them may be subject to some form of discipline
- The health and safety role of supervisors and other members of the management team – includes taking action on, and giving advice about, potential problems, and they are to be consulted if there are any questions about the health and safety aspects of work

- Where required, the wearing or use of personal protective equipment is not a matter for individual choice or decision – its use is a condition of employment
- In the event of any injury, no matter how trivial it may appear, workers must seek first aid or medical treatment and notify their supervisor immediately. For any work involving repetitive, awkward, heavy physical or timed movements, workers should be specifically instructed to report any adverse physical symptoms immediately. (These will need to be recorded and investigated without delay.)
- Fire and emergency procedure(s)
- Welfare and amenity provision
- Arrangements for joint consultation with workers and their representatives should be made known to all newcomers. A joint approach to health and safety problems, as well as the regular reviewing of work practices, procedures, systems and written documentation, is an essential part of a good health and safety programme. (But joint or balanced participation should not be used as a method of removing or passing off the prime responsibility of management at all levels to manage health and safety at least as efficiently as other aspects of the organisation.)

Job-specific

Job and task training should include skills training, explanations of applicable safety regulations and organisation rules and procedures, a demonstration of any personal protective equipment which may be required and provided for the work (including demonstration of correct fit, method and circumstances of use, and cleaning procedures), and the handing over of any documentation required, such as permit-to-work documents, safety booklets and chemical information sheets. There should also be a review of applicable aspects of emergency and evacuation procedures. Use of risk assessment findings is proving popular and worthwhile as a training aid, and by this management can also fulfil the requirement to bring risk assessment findings to the notice of those

affected by them. This training may be carried out by a supervisor, but it should be properly planned and organised by the use of checklists.

The need for training following job and process changes must not be overlooked. Introduction of new legislation may require additions to be made to the training programme, as will introduction of new technology. The programme should allow for refresher training as necessary.

Supervisory and general management training at all levels is necessary to ensure that responsibilities are known and the organisation's policy is carried out. Management failures which have come to light following investigations into disasters, plant accidents and other health and safety incidents have been concentrated in the following areas:

- Lack of awareness of the safety systems, including their own job requirements for health and safety
- Failure to enforce health and safety rules adequately or at all
- Failure to inspect and correct unhealthy or unsafe conditions
- Failure to inform or train workers adequately
- Failure to promote health and safety awareness by participation in discussions, motivating workers and setting an example

It is not sufficient simply to tell supervisors they are responsible and accountable for health and safety; they must be told the extent of the responsibilities and how they can discharge them.

Key points to cover in the training of supervisors and managers are:

- The organisation's safety programme and policy
- Legal framework and duties of the organisation, its management and the workforce
- Specific laws and rules applicable to the work area
- Safety inspection techniques and requirements
- Causation and consequences of accidents
- Basic accident prevention techniques
- Disciplinary procedures and their application

HEALTH AND SAFETY TRAINING

- Control of hazards likely to be present in the work area, including machinery safety, fire, materials handling, hazards of special equipment related to the industry, use of personal protective equipment, and techniques for motivating employees to recognise and respond to organisational goals in health and safety

Senior managers should be given essentially the same information, as this gives them a full appreciation of the tasks of subordinates, makes them more aware of standards of success and failure, and equips them to make cost-beneficial decisions on health and safety budgeting. External assessment of the training given to management at all levels is desirable. This can be done by training to the appropriate syllabi of national or international professional organisations, and encouraging those trained to take a relevant examination.

Individual

Training needs of individuals at all levels are likely to emerge over time, usually through performance appraisal. They can arise from a variety of inputs, eg because of observed inappropriate behaviour, from requests from the individual, following promotion or relocation, or following an accident. The main objective is to achieve competence in the individual.

Examples of specialised training needs

First-aid training has been proved to be a significant factor in accident prevention, as well as obviously beneficial in aiding accident victims. People trained in first aid are more safety conscious and are less likely to have accidents. Project FACTS – First Aid Community Training for Safety – was launched in 1970 in Ontario, Canada, and arranged for the training of 5,500 people in industry, schools and among the public in the community of Orillia, Ontario. Results showed that first-aid training throughout the workforce can cut accident rates by up to 30 per

cent. A second project based on industry alone found that employees not trained in first aid had accident rates double that of trained employees of similar age, sex, job and employer.

Apart from the above, and legal requirements which may exist, the need for first-aid training in the workplace depends on a number of factors. These include the nature of the work and the hazards, what medical services are available in the workplace, the number of employees, and the location of the workplace relative to external medical assistance. Shift working may also be taken into account; also the ratio of trained persons present to the total number of workers.

Driver training and certification may be a requirement for particular classes of vehicle, according to national or local regulations in force, and in these cases the detail of the training programme may be defined in law. A common cause of death at work (and away from work) is the road traffic accident. As the loss of a key worker can have a severe impact on the viability of an organisation, training for all workers who drive should be considered. Defensive driver training has been found to be effective and cost-beneficial in reducing numbers of traffic accidents, and has been extended to members of workers' families, particularly those entitled to drive the employer's vehicles.

Fire training – to the extent that all workers should know the action to be taken when fire alarms sound – should be given to all employees and included in induction training. Knowledge of particular emergency plans and how to tackle fires with equipment available may be given in specific training at the workplace. At whatever point the training is given, the following key points should be covered:
- Evacuation plan for the building in case of fire, including assembly point(s)
- How to use firefighting appliances provided
- How to use other protective equipment, including sprinkler and other protection systems, and the need for fire doors to be unobstructed
- How to raise the alarm and operate the alarm system from call points

- Workplace smoking rules
- Housekeeping practices which could permit fires to start and spread if not carried out, eg waste disposal, flammable liquid handling rules
- Any special fire hazards peculiar to the workplace

Fire training should be accompanied by practices, including regular fire drills and rehearsals of evacuation procedures. No exceptions should be permitted during these exercises.

Reinforcement training will be required at appropriate intervals, which will depend on observation of the workforce (training needs assessment), on the complexity of the information needed to be held by the worker, the amount of practice required, and the opportunity for practice in the normal working environment. Assessment will also be needed of the likely severity of the consequences of behaviour which does not correspond with training objectives when required to do so. If it is absolutely vital that only certain actions be taken in response to plant emergencies, then more frequent refresher training will be needed to ensure that routines are always familiar to those required to operate them.

REVISION

Six types of health and safety training needs:
- New employee induction
- Job-specific for new starters
- Supervision and management
- Individual
- Specialised
- Reinforcement

MAINTENANCE

Introduction

'Maintenance' can be defined as work carried out in order to keep or restore every facility (part of a workplace, building and contents) to an acceptable standard. It is not simply a matter of repair; some mechanical problems can be avoided if preventive action is taken in good time. Health and safety issues are important in maintenance because statistics show the maintenance worker to be at greater risk of accidents and injury. This is partly because these workers are exposed to more hazards than others, and partly because there are pressures of time and money on the completion of the maintenance task being achieved as quickly as possible. Often, less thought is given to the special needs of health and safety in the maintenance task than is given to routine tasks which are easier to identify, plan and control.

Maintenance policy

Whether for equipment or for premises and structures, maintenance can be:

1. Planned preventive – at pre-determined intervals.
2. Condition-based – centred on monitoring safety-critical parts and areas, maintaining them as necessary to avoid hazards.
3. Breakdown – fix when broken only. This is not appropriate if a failure presents an immediate risk without correction. Breakdown maintenance needs an effective fault-reporting system.

Maintenance standards are a matter for each organisation to determine; there must be a cost balance between intervention with normal operations by planned maintenance and the acceptance of losses because of breakdowns or other failures. From the health and safety aspect, however, defects requiring maintenance attention which have led or could lead to increased risk for the workforce should receive a high priority. Linking inspections with maintenance can be useful, so that work areas and equipment are checked regularly for present and possible future defects. Some work equipment items may be subject to statutory maintenance requirements, eg portable

electrical equipment. The manufacturer's instructions in this respect should be complied with as well.

Maintenance accidents

These are caused by one or more of the following factors:

- Lack of perception of risk by managers/supervisors, often because of lack of necessary training
- Unsafe or no system of work devised, eg no permit-to-work system in operation, no facility to lock off machinery and electrics before work starts and until work has finished
- No co-ordination between workers, or communication with other supervisors or managers
- Lack of perception of risk by workers, including failure to wear protective clothing or equipment
- Inadequacy of design, installation, siting of plant and equipment
- Use of contractors who are inadequately briefed on health and safety aspects, or who are selected on cost grounds and not for competence in health and safety

Maintenance control to minimise hazards

The safe operation of maintenance systems requires steps to be taken to control the above factors. These steps can be divided into the following phases:

Planning – identification of the need for the class of maintenance appropriate, and arranging a schedule for this to meet any statutory requirements. A partial list of items for equipment and structural issues for consideration includes air receivers and all pressure vessels, boilers, lifting equipment, electrical tools and machinery, fire and other emergency equipment, and structural items subject to wear, such as floor coverings.

Evaluation – the hazards associated with each maintenance task must be listed and the risks of each considered (frequency of the task and possible consequences of failure to carry it out correctly). The tasks can then be graded and the appropriate type and degree of management control applied to each.

Control – the control(s) for each task will take the above factors into account, and will include any necessary review of design and installation, training, introduction of written safe working procedures to minimise risk (which is known as a safe system of work), allocation of supervisory responsibilities, and necessary allocation of finances. Review of the activities of contractors engaged in maintenance work will be required in addition.

Monitoring – random checks, safety audits and inspections, and the analysis of any reported accidents for cause which might trigger a review of procedures constitute necessary monitoring to ensure the control system is fully up to date. The introduction of any change in the workplace may have maintenance implications and should, therefore, be included in the monitoring process.

Planned preventive maintenance

The need for maintenance of any piece of equipment should have been anticipated in its design. Lubrication and cleaning will still be required for machinery, but the tasks can be made safer by consideration of maintenance requirements at an early stage of design and, later, at installation.

A written plan for preventive maintenance is required, which documents the actions to be taken, how often this needs to be done, all associated health and safety matters, the training required (if any) before maintenance work can be done, and any special operational procedures such as permits to work and locking-off.

Condition-based maintenance

Safety-critical features will have been identified during the risk assessment process, and appropriate

arrangements are needed to ensure that inspection at agreed intervals actually takes place, and is recorded. This type of maintenance can easily become breakdown maintenance unless the system is followed scrupulously, giving a reason for the regular audit of maintenance practice and review of risk assessments justifying it.

Breakdown maintenance

The number of failures which require this will be reduced by planned maintenance, but many circumstances (such as severe weather conditions) can arise which require workers to carry out tasks beyond their normal work experience, and/or which are more than usually hazardous by their nature. Records of all breakdowns should be kept to influence future planned maintenance policy revisions, safety training and design.

REVISION

Maintenance accidents are due to:

- Inadequate design
- Lack of perception of risk
- Lack of a safe system of work
- Communication failures
- Failure to brief and supervise contractors

Maintenance accidents can be prevented by:

- Planning
- Evaluation
- Controls
- Monitoring

Three types of maintenance:

- Planned preventive
- Condition-based
- Breakdown

MANAGEMENT AND CONTROL OF CONTRACTORS

Introduction

Anyone entering premises for the purposes of carrying out specialised work for the client, owner or occupier must be regarded as a 'contractor' – to whom duties are owed and, indeed, who owes duties with regard to health and safety matters. Because of this, the same kinds of control measures must be applied to **all** who work on premises who are not in the direct employment of the occupier – caterers, window cleaners, agency staff, equipment repairers and servicers. The list of potential 'contractors' is long and must be written down as a first control task.

Analysis of investigations into accidents involving contractors shows that financial pressures, whether real or perceived, are nearly always present. The making and acceptance of the low bid in competitive tendering is often at the expense of health and safety standards. Other major factors include:

- A transient labour force which never gets properly or fully trained
- The small size of most contracting companies, which claim not to be aware of legislation or safe practices
- The inherent danger of the work and work conditions
- Pressure of work
- Poor management awareness of the need for safety management

Research has shown that the effective control of any activity requires ownership of responsibility for the activity and where it occurs, and acknowledgement of legitimate decision-making authority and compliance with its decisions. In relation to the presence of contractors, it is, therefore, necessary that health and safety decisions are made by, or have received the advice of, those people who are competent to make them.

Co-operation, co-ordination of activities and sharing of relevant information can only be achieved if all parties contribute to the risk assessment process for a particular activity. It is not sufficient to rely on generic assessments, as conditions are likely to vary significantly away from a standard or baseline condition. It follows that the assessment process can take account of standard arrangements but must be capable of reflecting actual conditions as well. Problems can arise when contracts are placed by and awarded to those not familiar with local working conditions and requirements for health and safety, which, in turn, may not be met through ignorance and lack of adequate specification before a price is agreed.

The practice of selecting contractors on the basis of their 'competence' in health and safety terms as well as on their ability to do the work adequately is one deserving wider recognition. Furthermore, it is the actual competence of those individuals selected to do the work (and supervise it) on the client's site which is critical, and so the dangers which can result from subcontracting below a contractor originally approved as competent should not be overlooked.

In recent times, outsourcing has extended to areas traditionally the sole province of the employer/client, including equipment maintenance, catering and facilities management. This Section discusses the general principles of managing the contracting relationship, however, long-term arrangements for managing contractors may stretch to the secondment of staff to contractors and other semi-merged positions, and these are not discussed here.

A control strategy

There are six parts to a successful control strategy. The extent to which each part is relevant will depend on the degree of risk and the nature of the work to be contracted. The parts are:

- Identification of suitable bidders
- Identification of hazards within the specification
- Checking of (health and safety aspects of) bids and selection of contractor
- Contractor acceptance of the client's health and safety rules
- Control of the contractor on site
- Checking after completion of contract

MANAGEMENT AND CONTROL OF CONTRACTORS

Identification of suitable contractors

It is clearly necessary to work out a system aimed at ensuring that a contractor with knowledge of safety standards and a record of putting them into practice is selected for the work.

1. Each contractor wishing to enter an 'approved list' should be asked to provide his/her safety policy and sample risk assessments. Arrangements will be required for vetting these for adequacy. It is important to recognise that smaller contractors may well have much less sophisticated systems than the client, and that this is not necessarily 'bad'. Requests for policy and assessments can place a significant burden on contractors, which may add significantly to the workload and the pressure faced normally. Therefore, the depth of enquiry and the adequacy of the response should be tempered against the known hazards and risks to be controlled; a certain amount of discretion should be exercised relative to the significance of the contract and the risks likely to be associated with the work. In some jurisdictions, the law may not require small businesses to produce complex (or any) health and safety documentation. In such cases, the observation of actual work practices and conditions on other contracts is likely to give a better understanding of competence than relying purely on paperwork.

2. Subject to the foregoing, a prequalification questionnaire should be completed by each contractor, providing necessary information about his/her policy on health and safety, including details of responsibility, experience, safe systems of work and training standards.

3. At this stage, it should be possible to identify potentially 'competent' contractors for approval, but feedback will be required to identify any who do not in practice conform to their own stated standards. This means that the list will require regular scrutiny and updating, especially in relation to contractors used by the employer regularly.

Specification

A checklist should be followed which will give a pointer to most, if not all, of the common health and safety problems which may arise during the work. These should be communicated to the contractor in the specification before the bid is made, and the received bid checked against them to ensure that proper provision is being made for the control of risk and that the contractor has identified the hazards. Suitable headings for a checklist for construction work include:

- Special hazards and applicable national or local regulations and codes of practice (asbestos, noise, permits to work)
- Training required for the contractor's employees, which the client may have to provide
- Safe access/egress to, from, on the site, and to places of work within the site
- Electrical and artificial lighting requirements
- Manual/mechanical lifting
- Buried and overhead services
- Fire protection
- Occupational health risks, including noise
- Confined space entry
- First aid/emergency rescue
- Welfare amenities
- Safe storage of chemicals
- Personal protective equipment
- Documentation and notifications
- Insurance and special terms and conditions of the contract

The process of drawing up the specification should include appropriate consultations with the workforce to ensure that they are fully aware of the proposed work and have a chance to comment on those aspects of it which may affect their own health and safety.

Checking the bids

When the bids are returned, it should be possible to distinguish the potentially competent at this stage. An 'approved list' of contractors, scrutinised at intervals, can save the need for carrying out a complete selection process as described on every occasion.

MANAGEMENT AND CONTROL OF CONTRACTORS

Safety rules

A basic principle of control is that as much detail as possible should be set down in the contract. An important condition should be that the contractor agrees to abide by all the provisions of the client's safety policy which may affect his/her employees or the work, including compliance with any local health and safety rules.

Often, the contractor may delegate the performance of all or part of the contract to other subcontractors. In these cases, it is essential to ensure that the sub-contractors are as aware as the original contractor of the site rules and safety policy. A condition which can be attached to the contract is that the contractor undertakes to:

- Check the 'competence', in turn, of any sub-contractor he/she intends to use
- Inform them, in turn, of all safety requirements
- Incorporate observance of them as a require-ment of any future subcontract
  and
- Require the subcontractor to do likewise if he/she, in turn, subcontracts any work

Written orders containing detailed terms and condi-tions such as the above should be the basis of the contract and should be acknowledged by the con-tractor before work starts. The loan of tools and equipment by the client should be avoided unless part of the original contractual arrangement.

Areas of concern should be covered by general site rules and by the client's safety policy. They should be communicated to the contractor in the form of site rules. For construction work on a client's premises, they should cover at least the following topics:

- Materials storage, handling, disposal
- Use of equipment which could cause fires
- Noise and vibration
- Scaffolding and ladders, access
- Cartridge-powered fixing tools
- Welding equipment – and use of client's elec-tricity supply
- Lifting equipment – certificated, adequate
- Competency of all plant operators

- Vehicles on site – speed, condition, parking restrictions
- Use of lasers, ionising radiations
- Power tools – voltage requirements
- Machinery brought on site
- Site huts – location, ventilation, gas appliances
- Use of site main services
- Electricity – specialised equipment required?
- Firefighting rules
- Waste disposal procedures
- Use of client's equipment
- Permit-to-work systems in force
- Hazardous substances in use on site by client
- Basic site arrangements, times, reporting, first aid, fire
- Site boundaries and restricted areas

Practical control of contractors

A reminder of the key questions at the heart of the issue:

- Does the level of risk from contractor activi-ties match the extent of contractor manage-ment in the organisation?
- Is there an appropriate balance between the level of client supervisory activity and the level of self-management by the contractor?
- Are contractors adequately assessed for per-formance and is that information fed back to those placing work orders?

The following measures are essential for all contrac-tor operations, however large or small the contract. They should be carried out by the client, or a compe-tent agent authorised to act on the client's behalf.

1. **Appointment/nomination** of a person or team to co-ordinate all aspects of the con-tract, including health and safety matters.

2. **A pre-contract commencement meeting** held with the contractor and subcontractors as necessary to review all safety aspects of the work. The contractor should also be asked to appoint a liaison person to ease later commu-nication problems which may arise. Also, communication paths should be developed to

MANAGEMENT AND CONTROL OF CONTRACTORS

pass on all relevant safety information to those doing the work. Any permitted borrowing of equipment should be formally discussed at this time.

3. **Arrangement of regular progress meetings** between all parties, where health and safety is the first agenda item.

4. **Regular (at least weekly) inspections of the contractor's operations** by the client.

5. **Participation in any safety committees** on site by contractors should be a condition of the contract.

6. **Provision by the contractor of written method statements in advance** of undertaking particular work, as agreed. This applies particularly to construction work, where activities may include demolition, asbestos operations, work which involves disruption or alteration to main services or other facilities which cause interruption to the client's activities, erection of falsework or temporary support structures, and steel erection. An **essential** feature, but one often missing, is the stipulation that, in the event of the need for a deviation from the method statement, no further work will be done until agreement has been reached and recorded in writing between the client and the contractor on the method of work to be followed in the new circumstances.

7. The **formal reporting** to the client by the contractor of all lost-time accidents and dangerous occurrences, including those to subcontractors.

8. The client must **set a good example** by the following of all site rules.

9. Adequate **safety propaganda** material, including posters and handbooks should be provided.

10. No machinery should be allowed on site until **documentation on statutory inspections** has been provided, including details of driver training and experience.

11. The contractor's **safety training programme** should be monitored by the client.

Contract completion

The contractor should leave the work site clean and tidy at the completion of the contract, removing all waste, materials, tools and equipment. This should be checked. Checking on the quality of the contracted work is seldom overlooked, but the actual performance and behaviours of contractors should be reviewed at the same time.

REVISION

Six parts to the control plan for contractors:

- Questionnaire to identify potentially safe contractors
- Hazard identification within the specification
- Check the bid and select contractor
- Put health and safety rules in the contract
- Control the contractor on site
- Check safe completion of work

ACCIDENT INVESTIGATION, RECORDING AND ANALYSIS

Introduction

"We... are still unable to see a worker safely through a day's work. Why? Because we have not thoroughly analysed our accident causes. As a result of inadequate accident reporting we have had insufficient data to target in on unsafe tools, machines, equipment or facilities. We also continue to place all of our safety bets on 'human performance' to avoid hazards that are not being identified. We cannot expect to reduce our accident experience by a solitary approach of attempting always to change human behaviour to cope with hazards. If there is a hole in the floor, we cannot reliably expect to avoid an accident by training all of the people to walk around the hole. It is far simpler to cover the hole." (David V. MacCollum, past President, American Society of Safety Engineers)

The hardest lessons to be learned in accident prevention come from the investigation of accidents and incidents which could have caused injury or loss. Facing up to those lessons can be traumatic for all concerned, which is one reason why investigations are often incomplete and simplistic. Nevertheless, the depth required of an investigation must be a function of the value it has for the organisation and other bodies which may make use of the results, such as enforcement agencies. Conducting one can be expensive in time. After the investigation, a standard system of recording and analysing the results should be used.

Investigation of accidents

Purpose

The number of purposes is large; the amount of detail necessary in the report depends on the uses to be made of it. Enforcement agencies look for evidence of blame, claims specialists look for evidence of liability, trainers look for enough material for a case study. From the viewpoint of prevention, the purpose of the investigation and report is to establish whether a recurrence can be prevented, or its effects lessened, by the introduction of safeguards, procedures, training and information, or any combination of these.

The procedure

There should be a defined procedure for investigating all accidents, however serious or trivial they may appear to be. The presence of a form and checklist will help to concentrate attention on the important details. Supervisors at the workplace where the accident occurred will be involved; for less serious accidents, they may be the only people who take part in the investigation and reporting procedure. Workers' representatives may also be involved as part of the investigating team.

The equipment

The following are considered as essential tools in the competent investigation of accidents and damage/loss incidents:
- Report form, possibly a checklist as a routine prompt for basic questions
- Notebook or pad of paper
- Tape recorder for on-site comments or to assist in interviews
- Camera – instant-picture cameras are useful (but further reproduction of them may be difficult, expensive or of poor quality). Digital cameras are becoming very popular, but the evidential value of their images has yet to be tested in court
- Measuring tape, which should be long and robust, like a surveyor's tape
- Special equipment in relation to the particular investigation, eg meters, plans, video recorder

The investigation

Information obtained during investigations is given verbally, or provided in writing. Written documentation should be gathered to provide evidence of policy or practice followed in the workplace, and witnesses should be talked to as soon as possible after the accident. The injured person should also be seen promptly.

Key points to note about investigations are:
- Events and issues under examination should not be prejudged by the investigator

ACCIDENT INVESTIGATION, RECORDING AND ANALYSIS

- Total reliance should not be placed on any one sole source of evidence
- The value of witness statements is proportional to the amount of time which passes between the events or circumstances described and the date of a statement or written record (theorising by witnesses increases as memory decreases)
- The first focus of the investigation should be on when, where, to whom and the outcome of the incident
- The second focus should be on how and why, giving the immediate cause of the injury or loss, and then the secondary or contributory causes
- The amount of detail required from the investigation will depend on a) the severity of the outcome and b) the use to be made of the investigation and report
- The report should be as short as possible, and as long as necessary for its purpose(s)

The report

For all purposes, the report which emerges from the investigation must provide answers to the following questions (only the amount of detail provided should vary in response to the different needs of the recipients):

- What was the immediate cause of the accident/injury/loss?
- What were the contributory causes?
- What is the necessary corrective action?
- What system changes are either necessary or desirable to prevent a recurrence?
- What reviews are needed of policies and procedures (eg risk assessments)?

It is not the task of the investigation report to allocate individual blame, although some discussion of this is almost inevitable. Reports are usually 'discoverable'; this means they can be used by the parties in an action for damages or criminal charges. It is a sound policy to assume that accident investigation reports will be seen by insurers, legal representatives and experts acting on behalf of the injured party. They will

be entitled to see a factual report, and this will include anything written in it which might later prove embarrassing – so it should certainly not contain comments on the extent of blame attaching to those concerned, or advice given to management.

It is appropriate, necessary and quite proper that professional advice is given, but it should be provided in a covering letter or memorandum suitably marked 'Confidential'.

Whether the report is made on a standard form or specially written, it should contain the following:
- A summary of what happened
- An introductory summary of events prior to the accident
- Information gained during investigation
- Details of witnesses
- Information about injury or loss sustained
- Conclusions
- Recommendations
- Supporting material (photographs, diagrams to clarify)
- The date and the signatures of the person or persons carrying out the investigation

Accident recording

Which injuries and incidents should be investigated and recorded? All those which can give information useful to prevent a recurrence of the incident giving rise to loss or injury. Regulations may also define requirements, although reporting requirements are usually limited to the more serious injuries, and those incidents with the most serious consequences or potential consequences. Counting only these may mask the true extent of injuries and losses by ignoring the potential consequences of incidents which by chance have led to relatively trivial injuries or damage.

Standardised report forms kept at each workplace should be used, and returned to a central point for record-keeping and analysis. It is important that supervisory staff at the workplace carry out preliminary investigations and complete a report, as they should be accountable for work conditions and need

ACCIDENT INVESTIGATION, RECORDING AND ANALYSIS

to have personal involvement in failure (accidents and damage incidents). This demonstrates their commitment and removes any temptation to leave 'safety' to others who may be seen as more qualified.

Lessons learned

Following investigation of an incident, it is always appropriate to make sure that everyone in the organisation is aware of the basic findings so that they are able to place the incident in the context of their own work areas and apply any relevant lessons to practices, procedures, training and the like. The checklist in Figure 1 may be helpful as a reminder.

FIGURE 1: Post-investigation checklist

Have all relevant people been advised of the nature of the incident, issues identified and solutions emerging from it?	YES	NO
Was the written procedure for investigation of the incident adequate?	YES	NO
Were the people assigned tasks able to perform them as required?	YES	NO
Were senior management informed promptly of what happened?	YES	NO
Has an accurate record of the investigation been maintained?	YES	NO

Accident analysis

The incoming reports will need to be categorised and statistics collected so that meaningful information on causes and trends can be obtained. There are several ways of doing this, including sorting by: the nature of the injury or body part involved; age group; trade; work location or work group; or type of equipment involved. Selection of categories will depend on the workplace hazards, but uniformity will assist in making comparisons between works and national or industry group figures. One classification which will be found particularly helpful is breakdown by cause.

The following gives heading examples; these can be further broken down if required:

- Falls
  - from a height
  - on the same level, including trips and slipping
- Struck
  - by moving object
  - by vehicle
  - against fixed or stationary object
- Manual handling or moving of loads
- Machinery
- Contact with harmful substances
- Fire or explosion
- Electricity
- Other causes

Each of these categories or, more usually, the aggregate numbers are converted into totals for a period, annually or at more frequent uniform intervals. Presenting the information in pictorial form will make it easier to understand; bar charts and pie charts are examples. Statistics used for comparison purposes are expressed in recognised ways using simple formulae to produce rates rather than raw numbers. Comparisons are best restricted to period-on-period within the same department or organisation, rather than between the organisation and national or international rates. An exception could be for an organisation sufficiently large to generate a statistically significant sample for comparison with national figures. Local comparative use of statistics can help with goal-setting.

Benchmarking is becoming popular in some industries, but this can produce its own problems. True comparability of data is hard to achieve, which, in turn, can lead to disappointing results and friction between the benchmarking partners. Other performance measures (which do not necessarily involve injury statistics) are the use of Key Performance Indicators within the health and safety management system, and the integration of health and safety management into a 'balanced scorecard' measuring system. Both of these techniques can be used advantageously by organisations with large numbers of departments, sectors or premises, and by bodies with autonomous subsidiaries.

ACCIDENT INVESTIGATION, RECORDING AND ANALYSIS

There are significant difficulties in using and comparing accident statistics, especially between different countries. This is because of underreporting to the authorities collecting the data (which can be as high as 70 per cent), differences between countries as to which accidents in working time count as recordable (eg UK road traffic accidents do not count at present), and differences in the formulae used to calculate rates.

In most countries there are no standard or formal requirements for the statistical formulae used for the analysis of accident data. Those most often encountered are:

Frequency rate:

$$\frac{\text{Number of injuries x 100,000}}{\text{Total number of hours worked}}$$

Incidence rate (helpful where the number of hours worked is either low or not available):

$$\frac{\text{Number of injuries x 1,000}}{\text{Average number employed during the period}}$$

Confusingly, the incidence rate most commonly used by the UK Government is:

$$\frac{\text{Number of fatal or major injuries x 100,000}}{\text{Number at risk in the particular industry sector}}$$

Severity rate shows the average number of days lost per time unit worked. Often, the time unit is expressed as 1,000 hours, but any suitable unit of measure can be used as long as it is stated clearly. For example:

$$\frac{\text{Total number of days lost x 1,000}}{\text{Total number of hours worked}}$$

A common experience for those new to health and safety management is to find that as the reporting and recording system is improved, the numbers of injuries and incidents reported rises. To the uninitiated this can be worrying, as it seems at first that there are more injuries following improvements in the control system than before the work started. What is usually happening in that case is that the system is simply capturing more information about the failures that are occurring.

REVISION

Eight features of the accident investigation process:
- Purpose
- Procedure
- Equipment
- Investigation
- Report
- Recording of results
- Analysis of results
- Presentation of results in meaningful format

TECHNIQUES OF INSPECTION

Introduction

Inspection for health and safety purposes often has a negative implication associated with fault-finding. A positive approach based on **fact-finding** will produce better results and co-operation from all those taking part in the process.

The objectives of inspections are:
- To identify hazardous conditions and start the corrective process
- To improve operations and conditions

There are a number of types of inspections:
- Statutory – for compliance with health and safety legislation
- External – by enforcement officials, insurers, consultants
- Executive – senior management tours
- Scheduled – planned at appropriate intervals, by supervisors
- Introductory – checks on new or reconditioned equipment
- Continuous – by employees, supervisors, which can be formal and preplanned, or informal

For any inspection, knowledge of the plant or facility is required, also knowledge of applicable regulations, standards and codes of practice. Some system must be followed to ensure that all relevant matters have been considered, and an adequate reporting system must be in place so that necessary remedial actions can be taken and the results of the inspection made available to management.

Some experts believe that 'assurance' is a better description of the activity – there is a need to assure that the system is working properly (safely). To be effective, inspection of this type needs measurement of how good or bad things are, which can then be compared with standards set either locally, corporately or nationally. Corrective action can then be taken.

Audits look at systems and the way they function in practice; **inspections** look at physical conditions. So, while inspections of a workplace could be done weekly, an audit of the inspection system throughout an organisation would examine whether the required inspections were being carried out, the way they were being recorded, action taken as a result, and so on. More information on audits can be found in Part 1 Section 2.

Safety tours are carried out in teams, led by a senior member of management. They are not inspections in the sense that they seek to find out and record all significant health and safety matters in the area under study, but rather they demonstrate the interest and involvement of senior management. Safety tours aim to find examples of both bad and good practice, perhaps to focus attention on current issues or topics under debate. They also offer opportunities for individual discussion between managers and all those directly involved in the work process.

Principles of inspection

Before any inspection, certain basic decisions must have been taken about aspects of it, and the quality of the decisions will be a major influence on the quality of the inspection and on whether it achieves its objectives. The decisions are reached by answering the following questions:

1. **What needs inspection?** Some form of checklist, specially developed for the inspection, will be helpful. This reminds those carrying out the inspection of important items to check; it also serves as a record. By including space for 'action by' dates, comments and signatures, the checklist can serve as a permanent record. Inspection requirements for work equipment are reviewed in Part 2 Section 2.

2. **What aspect of the items listed needs checking?** Parts likely to be hazards when unsafe – because of stress, wear, impact, vibration, heat, corrosion, chemical reaction or misuse – are all candidates for inspection, regardless of the nature of the plant, equipment or workplace.

3. **What conditions need inspection?** These should be specified, preferably on the

checklist. If there is no standard set for adequacy, then descriptive words give clues to what to look for – items which are exposed, broken, jagged, frayed, leaking, rusted, corroded, missing, loose, slipping, vibrating, etc.

4. **How often should the inspection be carried out?** In the absence of statutory requirements or guidance from standards and codes of practice, this will depend on the potential severity of the failure if the item fails in some way, and the potential for injury. It also depends on how quickly the item can become unsafe. A history of failures and their results may give assistance.

5. **Who carries out the inspection?** Every **worker** has a responsibility to carry out informal inspections of his or her part of the workplace. **Supervisors** should plan general inspections and take part in periodic inspections of aspects of the workplace considered significant under the above guideline. **Workers' representatives** may also have rights of inspection and their presence should be encouraged where possible. **Management** inspections should be made periodically; the formal compliance inspections should take place in their presence.

Techniques of inspection

The following observations have been of assistance in improving inspection skills:

1. Those carrying out inspections must be properly equipped to do so, having the necessary knowledge and experience, and knowledge of acceptable performance standards and statutory requirements. They must also comply fully with local site rules, including the wearing or use of personal protective equipment, as appropriate, so as to set an example.

2. Develop and use checklists, as above. They serve to focus attention and record results, but must be relevant to the inspection.

3. The memory should not be relied on. Interruptions will occur, and memory will fade, so notes must be taken and entered onto the checklist, even if a formal report is to be prepared later.

4. It is desirable to read the previous findings before starting a new inspection. This will enable checks to be made to ensure that previous comments have been actioned as required.

5. Questions should be asked and the inspection should not rely on visual information only. The 'what if?' question is the hardest to answer. Workers are often undervalued as a source of information about actual operating procedures and of opinions about possible corrections. Also, systems and procedures are difficult to inspect visually, and their inspection depends on those involved being asked the right questions.

6. Items found to be missing or defective should be followed up and questioned, not merely recorded on the form. Otherwise, there is a danger of inspecting a series of symptoms of a problem without ever querying the nature of the underlying disease.

7. All dangerous situations encountered should be corrected immediately, without waiting for the written report, if their existence constitutes a serious risk of personal injury or significant damage to plant and equipment.

8. Where appropriate, measurements should be taken of conditions. These will serve as baselines for subsequent inspections. What cannot be measured cannot be managed.

9. Any unsafe behaviour seen during the inspection should be noted and corrected, such as removal of machine guards, failure to use personal protective equipment as required, or smoking in unauthorised areas.

10. Risk assessments should be checked as part of the inspection process.

REVISION

Two objectives of inspections:
- Identification of hazards
- Improvement of operations/conditions

TECHNIQUES OF INSPECTION

Six types of inspection:

- Statutory
- External
- Executive
- Scheduled
- Introductory
- Continuous

Ten techniques of value:

- Have necessary experience and knowledge
- Use checklists
- Write things down
- Read previous reports first
- Ask questions
- Follow up on problems
- Correct dangerous conditions at once
- Measure and record where possible
- Correct unsafe behaviour seen
- Check risk assessments

INFORMATION SOURCES

Introduction

There is a great deal of information available on health and safety topics. The problem is that it is mostly unco-ordinated, in many places, and often written by specialists so that it cannot be easily understood by people who have to work with it. Information technology is moving towards the production of solutions to problems, by the combination of many of these sources.

Authoritative guides on particular topics are known as **primary sources**. The collected references to these guides are **secondary sources**, and include bibliographies, reading lists, abstracts and indexes. Most information sources specialise as primary or secondary sources, with a small amount of overlap – some sources have both facilities. Technical articles in journals have reading lists, data sheets refer to larger databases, and databases often do not carry complete texts. Systems for information provision designed since about 1980 recognise the need for 'one-stop' information shopping for answers to problems and avoid the temptation to cross-reference to a number of other sources.

Because of the numbers of sources, it is not possible to do more than provide a list of groups (see Table 1) with some well-known examples and a commentary on the material which is now available to carry the information.

Material

Most of our information is still provided on **paper** and this is not likely to change despite the introduction of new technologies. Some of these have problems associated with them – **photocopies** and **facsimile** transmission paper both suffer from ultraviolet light, so the image gradually disappears over time. Other photographic record systems for holding information such as **microfiche** are more permanent, but can still be damaged. They are inconvenient to read and copy, although they carry complete primary source material in a small space.

Computer files held at the workplace are widely

TABLE 1: Providers of information

Sources	
Company safety policy	Organisation and arrangements
In-company safety services	Company safety staff, library
Corporate safety services	Central group resource, database
Enforcement agencies	HSE and local authorities (EHOs) – advise and enforce
Government bodies and departments	HMSO
Manufacturers	Product literature, updates, MSDS
Trade associations	Handbooks, advice to members
Standards organisations	BSI, CEN, CENELEC, ISO
Subscription services	Magazines, journals, newsletters
Consultancies	External audits, information, advice
Voluntary safety bodies	RoSPA, British Safety Council
Professional bodies	IOSH, IChemE
International safety bodies	ILO
Educational institutions	University programmes, colleges

used as information storage, although new generations of computers are often unable to decipher material stored on older systems. **Computer networks**, set up between offices using telephone or fibre-optic lines, are able to share much information, which is often stored centrally on a mainframe. Access to such a system enables a large amount of information to be accessed at short notice at a local site. Disadvantages are the cost and the need to service the system regularly.

INFORMATION SOURCES

The expense of using computer data resources can be minimised by gaining access to someone else's information by using an electronic database through a modem connection, and there are now a number of computer resources which accept worldwide connections through the Internet. Most are secondary sources, although the ability to carry full text and graphics is spreading. NIOSHTIC and HSELINE are the best known English-language databases.

It is also possible to access versions of these and other databases at the workplace using a **CD-ROM** reader. Compact disc technology allows up to 280,000 pages of information to be stored on a single compact disc, which can be read by a personal computer. Recording onto CD-ROM and **DVD** is now achieved cheaply. The main advantage of doing so is having, close at hand, a huge volume of material which can be stored and quickly accessed. CD-ROM constructed databases are available for purchase through providers such as Technical Indexes, who also update and extend their products regularly. In recent times, the trend for these providers is to hold their information on Web servers that can be accessed by password (and subscription). This avoids the need for the user to hold very large quantities of data personally.

International data resources mostly store information on US requirements. A major supplier of chemical data sheets and other health and safety information on CD-ROM is the Canadian Centre for Occupational Health and Safety (CCINFO).

Information can also be stored in learning programmes and combined with video into an interactive system, available on the Web and on CD-ROM, and played through specially-adapted visual display screens. The use of multimedia, which combines still and moving images with sound and text information, has increased rapidly. It can be produced relatively easily and accessed through simple computer configurations.

The Internet

Searching the Internet for health and safety information can be extremely rewarding. There are now many thousands of 'home pages' on the World Wide Web giving access to safety, health and environmental information, but it is important to remember that not all of it can be relied on. Just as trade associations can be expected to publish information and views favourable to the members of the association, it should not be forgotten that many interest groups have websites and are anxious to promote a particular view in the guise of unbiased information. A list of websites which have been reviewed for their technical content and usefulness can be found through CCINFO.

Other tools on the Internet include **newsgroups**, which enable questions to be asked and answered in front of an international audience, and facilitate the exchange of software. The user should be aware that most postings to newsgroups will be picked up by search engines, and could result in a flood of unwanted e-mails. Mostly these will be 'spam' messages (the electronic equivalent of junk mail), but some may be hostile and contain viruses.

It is essential to use a virus checking program to screen incoming material from the Web. Also, unexpected e-mail attachments (files that accompany an e-mail) should never be opened directly from the Web until screened in this way. Failure to observe this basic principle can result in the entire computer system being scrambled, as well as the invading message being passed on automatically to anyone e-mailed previously from the infected system.

Unless a unique home page has been given as a reference, the searcher will have to use one of an estimated 1,550 available 'search engines' to track down a particular subject. Search engines are electronic directories which automatically scour the Web for new material and record its presence. Examples of search engines which are suitable for health and safety queries include Google, Lycos, HotBot and Excite. When the word being searched for is entered, the search engine will return a list of 'hits' – Web pages which contain the word.

Some refinement of the search is usually required to avoid being swamped by data not required or even relevant. Information on how to refine a search will be available from the 'Help' link on the search engine's home page. Translation systems can be viewed to provide instant interpretation of pages in unfamiliar languages.

The most important factor is not the number of hits but whether the material required can easily be found within the first few pages offered. The search engines attempt to place the most useful hits at the front, but it can still take significant time to find relevant material without a very precise set of significant keywords to search with. Much time can be saved by not viewing any Web page hit dated more than about three months back from the current date. This is because search engines do not distinguish between live and derelict pages.

Table 2 contains a selected list of websites that provide useful information on a wide variety of topics likely to be of interest to the general reader. Once the address has been typed in to a computer's Web browser, it can be saved to visit again by using the 'Favorites' menu. (This allows repeat visits to be made without having to type the full address of the page each time.) But it should be remembered that Web pages often change their addresses, and even disappear altogether, so the only guarantee that can be given is that all the selections in Table 2 were open to access in mid-2002.

NB: Not all Web browsers require the address to start with 'www'. If an address does not load, re-enter the address without the 'www'. Alternatively, type the main part of the address into a Google search and use the hyperlinks (underlined words) to get to the page you need. For example, if 'www.workcover.nsw.gov.au' does not appear to work, type 'Workcover' into Google.

INFORMATION SOURCES

TABLE 2: Web references

WEB ADDRESS	TOPIC AND COMMENTS
Search engines	
www.google.com	The best search engine
UK Government sites	
www.hse.gov.uk	HSE home page
www.hse.gov.uk/condocs	Download consultative documents from here
www.hse.gov.uk/hsestats.htm	HSE statistics
www.hse.gov.uk/pubns	Gateway to information on COSHH, noise and much more
www.legislation.hmso.gov.uk	The place to go for UK law texts as published
www.dti.gov.uk/er/work_time_regs/index	The Working Time Regulations explained
www.dti.gov.uk/strd/strdpubs.htm	Download PDF documents relating to product and electrical safety
www.homeoffice.gov.uk	The Home Office, direct link to their fire safety advice for employers
www.official-documents.co.uk/document/fire	*Fire Safety: An Employer's Guide* – covers risk assessment, means of escape and more
www.hawnhs.hea.gov.uk	NHS site dealing with health at work
European sites	
www.europe.osha.eu.int	European Agency for Health and Safety at Work
www.occuphealth.fi/e/eu/haste	European health (and safety) database
Organisations	
www.iosh.co.uk	Free best practice guidance and information, and a discussion forum for help from professionals
www.bohs.org	British Occupational Hygiene Society
www.who.int	World Health Organisation
www.ccohs.ca	CCINFO home page, huge database of links to other health and safety sites
www.rospa.co.uk	RoSPA home page, good for general interest especially for small organisations
www.eevla.ac.uk/vts/healthandsafety	Free training on Internet use for safety searches
www.blpc.bl.uk	British Library Public Catalogue
www.joule.pcl.ox.ac.uk/MSDS	The best place for pure chemicals data sheets
www.stress.org.uk	Information on stress
www.dstress.com	Stress Education Centre
www.asthma.org.uk	Asthma and general occupational health
www.bad.org.uk	Professional society for dermatology
Good foreign (non-EU) sites	
www.safetyline.wa.gov.au	Helpful Australian site of general use
www.workcover.nsw.gov.au	Good free downloads
www.dermnet.org.nz/index	Dermatitis and other skin conditions
www.innerbody.com	Learn anatomy here

HUMAN FACTORS AND CHANGE

Introduction

Health and safety at work are heavily influenced by change. Few things remain the same over time. In organisations, priorities and values change as do the people who put them into practice. The challenge is to maintain continuity of purpose and to seek continual improvement. Because of this, the health and safety professional is an agent of change; a facilitator, not just an expert. It follows that the skills of the professional need to include the ability to recognise the signs of change and influence it within the organisation. For successful health and safety management, input into the management process is required from a number of disciplines – engineering, human factors, industrial relations, occupational health as well as 'safety'. Just as accidents are described as the results of multiple causes, so is change the product of many influences.

Change

Achieving real, meaningful change within any organisation is very difficult. It requires recognition at the most senior level that change is both necessary and inevitable, and that the direction and extent of it can be influenced. Planned change needs a focus, and a directed and managed plan, complete with measured milestones on the way to the stated objectives, is essential.

In order to put in place the reforms that have been described elsewhere in this book, the most senior people must put their personal support behind the plan. Without this, the plan is sure to fail to achieve its objectives, as no-one will be persuaded that the proposed change has been fully sanctioned. Without getting the buy-in from all levels, it will fail.

Success can be and has been achieved where such a 'health and safety business plan' is presented to the board or 'most senior' level for approval. This should show the present costs to the organisation of failure to manage health and safety adequately, the proposed cost of actioning the plan, and the timescale for carrying it out. The cost of research and audit should be included, together with training for all levels. With acceptance of the plan, it should then be driven down to the next layer of management by insisting on their attendance at a workshop designed to show precisely what steps those attending are required to take. Change initiatives that fail usually have in common an inability to persuade the second tier of management that they can and must make a difference.

Change must be measured, so the plan should include details of parameters that will measure the extent of success. The use of Key Performance Indicators, in addition to the counting of injuries, will be useful. These can show the degree to which the plan is being followed in each unit of the business, by agreed measurement of key events required by the plan, and progress towards agreed targets.

Human factors

Human factors are those that affect performance, including obvious elements such as the social and inherited characteristics of work groups and their members, and the individual capabilities of workers. They include:

- Mental, physical and perceptual capability
- Interaction between people, their jobs, the environment and the employer
- System and equipment design influences
- Characteristics of organisations that affect safety-related behaviour
- Individual social and inherited characteristics

The cumulative effects of all of these can result in **human failure**. There are many ways of categorising behaviours that are significant for health and safety at work.

We can distinguish between **active failure**, when there is the potential for immediate unwanted consequence, and **latent failure**, as a result of which the stage is set for something to go wrong. For example, taking a chance in not isolating a machine before delving inside it is an active failure, and a manager ignoring persistent breaches of safe working practice shows a latent failure. Individual incorrect or inappropriate behaviour can also be grouped into **errors**, which are unintended deviations from safe practices,

HUMAN FACTORS AND CHANGE

and deliberate **violations**, where rule-breaking becomes standard practice.

Peer influence is a powerful motivator for behaviour, especially in small work groups. The inexperienced are likely to take their leads from the behaviour of others. Many other factors can influence concentration on the task, including age and the effects of drugs, including alcohol.

Knowledge of what constitutes safe behaviour does not guarantee that it will be forthcoming. It is a truism that 'to err is human', and we recognise this when we accept that one of the long-term objectives of health and safety management is to attempt progressively to reduce the opportunities for people to make mistakes. Recent legislative initiatives, particularly from the European Union, have incorporated the human factors approach.

Safety culture

Producing and maintaining a positive safety culture requires recognition of the significance of the above elements, and planning strategies to identify and resolve human factors issues. Key points are:

- Good communications between and with employees and management
- Ensuring a real and visible commitment to high standards by senior management
- Maintaining good training standards to achieve competence
- Achievement of good working conditions

Stress

Stress can be defined as the reaction people have to excessive pressures, traumatic experiences or any abnormal demand placed on them because of their life circumstances. Therefore, bereavement produces stress, as does overwork. Everyone has to deal with pressures and there is some evidence that pressure is necessary for maximum effectiveness to be achieved. However, response to pressure can be physically and mentally damaging if sustained over long periods.

Illness, including depression and heart disease, can result from excessive exposure to stress.

Surveys indicate that stress is a significant workplace issue. Nearly a fifth of UK managers surveyed in 1997 admitted to taking time off during the previous 12 months because of work-related stress. Stress poses a significant risk, but is certainly the least well controlled of all workplace risks.

Factors which contribute to stress include:

- The physical work environment, including noise and thermal effects
- 'Office politics' – relationships with work colleagues and with third parties encountered while at work
- Volume of work – too much or too little
- Worries about job security
- Lack of ability to control the pace and nature of work activities
- Changes in working practices – these can lead to alterations in the sense of self-worth and ability to cope
- Shift or other unusual work timetables
- Poor communication and lack of input into decision-making
- Non-work environment

Stress can cause sleeplessness. The importance of sleep to mental wellbeing is significant, as it affects memory, learning and physical condition. Studies at the Finnish Institute of Occupational Health have shown that sleep deprivation affects the body's immune system, metabolism and hormonal functions.

Attempts should be made by the employer to identify and manage workplace stress, which is thought to reduce the effectiveness of individuals, increase labour turnover and sickness absence, and increase the chance of injury.

Communicating safety

Various forms of propaganda selling the 'health and safety message' have been used for many years – posters, flags, stickers, beer mats and so on. They are now widely felt to be of little measurable value in changing behaviour and influencing attitudes to health and safety issues. Because of the long tradition of using safety propaganda as part of safety campaigns, however, there is a reluctance to abandon them. Possibly, this is because they are seen as constituting visible management concern while being both cheap and causing minimal disturbance to production. In contrast, much money is spent on advertising campaigns and measuring their effectiveness in selling products.

How can safety messages be effective?

Avoid negativity – Studies show that successful safety propaganda contains positive messages, not warnings of the unpleasant consequences of actions. Warnings may be ineffective because they fail to address the ways in which people make choices about their actions; these choices are often made subconsciously and are not necessarily 'rational' or logical. Studies also show that people make poor judgments about the risks involved in activities, and are unwilling to accept a perceived loss of comfort or money as a trade against protection from a large but unquantified loss – which may or may not happen at some point in the future.

'It won't happen here' – the non-relevance of the warning or negative propaganda needs to be combated. The short-term loss associated with some (but not all) safety precautions needs to be balanced by a positive short-term gain such as peace of mind, respect and peer admiration.

Safety propaganda can be seen as management's attempt to pass off the responsibility for safety to employees. Posters, banners and other visual aids used in isolation without the agreement and sanction provided by worker participation in safety campaigns can easily pass the wrong message. The hidden message can be perceived as: 'The management has done all it can or is willing to do. You know what the danger is, so it's up to you to be safe and don't blame us if you get hurt – we told you work is dangerous.'

Management can have high expectations of the ability of safety posters to communicate the safety message. This will only be justified if they are used as part of a designed strategy for communicating positive messages.

Expose correctly – The safety message must be perceived by the target audience. In practice, this means the message must be addressed to the right people, be placed at or near to the point of danger, and have a captive audience.

Use attention-getter techniques carefully – Messages must seize the attention of the audience and pass their contents quickly. However, propaganda exploiting this principle can too readily fail to give the message intended – sexual innuendo and horror are effective attention-getters, but as they may be more potent images, they may only be remembered for their potency. Other members of the audience may reject the message precisely because of the use of what is perceived as a stereotype, eg 'flattering' sexual imagery can easily be rejected by parts of the audience as sexist and exploitative.

Strangely, the attention-grabbing image may be too powerful to be effective. An example to consider is the 'model girl' calendar. If the pictures are not regarded as sexist and rejected, they may be remembered. But who remembers the name of the sender? This is, after all, the point of the advertising.

Comprehension must be maximised – For the most effect, safety messages have to explain problems either pictorially or verbally in captions or slogans. To be readily understood, they must be simple and specific, as well as positive. Use of too many words or more than one message inhibits communication. Use of humour can be ineffective; the audience can reject the message given because only stupid people would act as shown and this would have no relevance to themselves or their work conditions.

Messages must be believable – The audience's ability to believe in the message itself and its relevance to them is important. Endorsement or approval of the message by peers or those admired, such as

HUMAN FACTORS AND CHANGE

the famous, enhances acceptability. The 'belief factor' also depends on the perceived credibility of those presenting the message. If the general perception of management is that health and safety has a low priority, then safety messages are more likely to be dismissed because the management motivation behind them is questioned.

Action when motivated must be achievable – Safety propaganda has been shown to be most effective when it calls for a positive action, which can be achieved without perceived cost to the audience and which offers a tangible and realistic gain. Not all of this may be possible for any particular piece of propaganda, and the major factor to consider is the positive action. Exhortation simply to 'be safe' is not a motivator.

Does safety propaganda work?

There is little evidence for the effectiveness of health and safety propaganda. This is mainly because of the difficulty of measuring changes in attitudes and behaviour which can be traced to the use of propaganda. For poster campaigns, experience suggests that any change in behaviour patterns will be temporary, followed by a gradual reversion to previous patterns, unless other actions such as changes in work patterns and environment are made in conjunction with the propaganda.

Limited experimental observations by the author show that the effectiveness of safety posters, judged by the ability of an audience to recall a positive safety message, is good in the short term only. One week after exposure to a poster, 90 per cent of a sample audience could recall the poster's general details and 45 per cent could recall the actual message on it. Two weeks after exposure, none of the audience remembered the message, and only 20 per cent could recall the poster design. In both cases, the attention of the audience was not drawn specifically to the poster when originally exposed to it.

Safety propaganda can be useful in accident prevention, provided its use is carefully planned in relation to the audience, the message is positive and believable, and it is used in combination with other parts of a planned safety campaign. Safety posters which are not changed regularly become part of the scenery, and may even be counter-productive by giving a perceived bad image of management attitude ('All they do is stick up a few old posters!').

REVISION

Change:
■ Planned
■ Measured

Safety culture factors:
■ Communications
■ Commitment
■ Competence
■ Conditions

Human failures:
■ Active
■ Latent
■ Errors
■ Violations

Nine stress factors:
■ Physical work environment
■ Relationships
■ Volume of work
■ Job security concerns
■ Lack of ability to control work
■ Changes in working practices
■ Work timetables
■ Poor communication
■ Non-work environment

Six important elements in safety propaganda:
■ Positive message
■ Correct exposure
■ Attention-getting
■ Comprehension
■ Belief
■ Motivation

PART 2
Workplaces and work equipment

WORKPLACE HEALTH AND SAFETY ISSUES

Introduction

This Section covers hazards in the workplace that are independent of the work processes and equipment used. It is plainly not possible to review all of the many different kinds of workplace that will be encountered – from shops to airport baggage handling areas, from control rooms to assembly lines, from hospitals to hotels – in principle, these are simply workplaces, where people spend most if not all of their working time.

For the purpose of this Section, definitions of terms such as 'workplace' and 'work' take their everyday meaning, although precise definitions may be given in specific legislation. Also, some of the topics discussed below have more detailed or more specific requirements within detailed local or national regulations, which should be consulted.

Ventilation

The basic requirement for every enclosed workplace is for sufficient fresh or purified air. Human body wastes are liberated into the workplace atmosphere – carbon dioxide, heat, smells and water vapour – which rapidly become unpleasant unless the ventilation is adequate. Air pollution from the processes in the workplace can include traces of ozone and smoke particles, and raised humidity levels may be found. Pollution can also enter from the outside from processes there or exhausts from plant items.

Where opening windows does not give sufficient ventilation, mechanical systems should be considered. The fresh air supply rate should not fall below five litres per second per occupant, but this will depend on processes and equipment, the cubic capacity of the workplace and the level of physical activity carried out there.

Temperature

Generally, where people normally work for more than a short period, the temperature should be at least 16 degrees Celsius, and where much of the work involves severe physical effort, the temperature should be at least 13 degrees Celsius. Other factors may impinge on these, such as air circulation and relative humidity. Where it is not physically practicable to maintain these temperatures (eg rooms open to the external air or where food is kept in cold storage), the actual temperatures should be as close as practicable to these. Lower maximum temperatures may be required by law.

High temperatures in the workplace can be reached because of the action of sunlight on the building or structure which exceeds the building's designed ability to protect the occupants. Management action should be taken when discomfort becomes apparent to limit the exposure time to uncomfortable temperatures. A continuous temperature of 30 degrees Celsius is widely used as the point at which work should stop. Thermometers should be available so that temperatures can be monitored.

Lighting

The general need is for adequate and appropriate lighting, preferably by natural light. To achieve this, several topics need to be reviewed:

- Lighting design, including emergency lighting
- The type of work to be done
- Overall work environment
- Health issues and individual requirements
- Maintenance, replacement, disposal

Lighting design for **internal areas** needs to deliver illuminance that is reasonable for the requirements of the work environment and at uniform levels in each work area. It must minimise glare and the casting of shadows. **General** lighting does this for the entire work area, **localised** lighting aims to provide different levels in different parts of the same area, and **local** lighting combines background and a close local light source (luminaire) close to where the work is done to produce a high level of illuminance in a small area. The term 'luminaire' describes a lamp holder and its lamp. **External** lighting designs are also expected to deliver uniform levels of illuminance, as well as to minimise glare to users and third parties.

International Principles of Health and Safety at Work | Allan St John Holt

WORKPLACE HEALTH AND SAFETY ISSUES

Emergency lighting is either standby (so people can continue to work in safety) or escape (so people can leave in safety).

Light levels are measured directly in **lux**, using a simple meter. The 'average' illuminance across a work area can be deceptive because the figure may conceal low readings in some critical areas. It is, therefore, necessary to know the measured illuminance at critical points. Recommended values for light levels are shown in Table 1.

The **type of work** being done may require special local lighting to augment general lighting for specific tasks. Higher illuminance is required for fine detail.

Where colour perception is necessary, for example, provision of lighting that does not alter the natural appearance of colours will be required. The strobe effect of some lighting can make moving parts appear to be stationary.

Overall **work environment** considerations include the level of natural light. Most people prefer to work in daylight, which often needs to be supplemented. Glare is an important issue which can often be minimised by use of reflected light from walls and ceilings, eg by employing uplighters. The presence of dust or flammable material may call for use of special designs for luminaires.

Health aspects of lighting include the potential for symptoms of eyestrain and the use of unsuitable postures to get closer to the work. The human eye (and the rest of the body) accommodates to low light levels, so that sufferers may be unaware of the cause of their discomfort. Individual preferences and special needs must not be ignored. Lighting flicker can produce seizures in some epileptics.

Light output decreases over time, so regular planned **maintenance** should include a replacement policy as well as arrangements for:
- Cleaning of all lighting, including emergency lighting and control equipment
- Replacing damaged lighting
- Safe access
- Safe disposal of lamps and luminaires (some contain substances hazardous to health such as mercury and sodium)

Windows

In addition to their contribution to lighting the interior, windows make an important contribution to

TABLE 1: Task and area light levels

Work activity	Example locations and types of work	Average illuminance (lux)	Minimum measured illuminance
People, vehicle, machine movement	Lorry park, traffic route, corridor	20	5
Rough work, detail perception not necessary	Loading bays, construction site clearance	50	20
Work requiring limited perception of detail	Kitchens, assembly lines	100	50
Work requiring perception of detail	Offices, bookbinding	200	100
Where perception of fine detail is necessary	Drawing office, proofreading, assembly of electronic components	500	200

WORKPLACE HEALTH AND SAFETY ISSUES

ventilation and a general sense of wellbeing at work. Windows, and glazed openings in doors and partitions to improve visibility, need to be protected against breakage unless they are made of 'safety materials' where necessary for safety. This is important where glass is present below shoulder level, and every such case should be assessed.

'Safety materials' are either:

- Inherently robust, eg blocks of glass
- Glass which breaks safely if it breaks. 'Safety glass' is flat glass or plastic sheet that breaks so as not to leave large sharp pieces
- Ordinary annealed glass of adequate thickness in relation to its maximum size

Where necessary, glass should be marked to make it apparent. This marking is known as 'manifestation', which can take any form as long as it is conspicuous.

Windows, skylights and ventilators need a safe way of opening them, and must not expose anyone to risks when in the open position. They also need to be cleaned in a safe way if this cannot be done from the ground. Ways of achieving this include:

- Selecting pivoting windows that can be cleaned from inside
- Provision of access equipment, limiting the height of ladders used to 9m unless landing areas are provided
- Provision for the use of access equipment including ladder tie points/facilities
- Adequate anchor points for safety harnesses

Cleanliness

Standards of cleanliness that should be achieved depend on the activities in the workplace. A pharmaceutical 'clean-room' will be cleaner than a factory floor. All workplaces need to be kept clean, specifically to avoid accumulation of dirt or refuse on any surface. An appropriate minimum cleaning frequency for floors and traffic routes is once a week, but some environments such as food stores will need a much tighter regime to remove debris quickly. The surfaces

concerned will have been designed for easy cleaning, and must be free of holes and worn areas. Keeping to an appropriate cleaning regime is part of what is often called 'good housekeeping'; other parts include fostering safe and tidy stacking habits, clearing desks at night, and generally removing the small but important primary causes of most work injuries.

Working space

The minimum allowance should be 11 cubic metres for each person normally working in a workplace. In rooms with high ceilings, the approximate minimum floor area should be 3.7m^2. There should be enough height and space around objects in the workplace to allow access to work areas, and these figures should apply when the room is empty and not when full of furniture and equipment. Some rooms are necessarily small (eg ticket booths) but in these cases layout planning will be needed in order to meet the test of 'sufficient' space for those working there.

Seating

Most people at work will need to sit down at some point, if not all the time. Seating design for the workplace must relate to individual needs, what work is being done and the dimensions of the workplace. Special needs may include providing special seating for disabled employees where necessary, special backrests, and access for wheelchair users. A guide weight limit for users of gas lift chairs is 100kg. Risk assessments must include the issue of seating, usually a part of the work system.

Important considerations in seating include:

- Supportive upholstery – padded edges, and sharp points
- Adjustability – range, seat height and forward tilt for some users such as checkout staff, back rest height and tilt, forward movement
- Back rest – presence, adjustability for real support
- Footrests – should be provided where needed
- Armrests – as an option where requested

- Training provision – people need to know how to adjust their seating

Slips, trips and falls

Slips, trips or falls on the same level rival manual handling injuries as the most common cause of non-fatal major injuries to employees. Solutions are often inexpensive, easy to devise and put in place, and their benefits are considerable. They need to be part of a health and safety management system that includes regular inspection, maintenance and good housekeeping. When they occur, investigation will often expose failures in the system as well as primary causes of the incident. Table 2 gives a summary of the main hazards and control measures.

Traffic routes

The potential for slips, trips and falls has been outlined above, and the same general considerations for floors apply to 'traffic routes', a term which includes routes for vehicles as well as pedestrians.

Wherever practicable, separation of pedestrians from vehicles should be achieved by making the route wide enough, and traffic routes should be indicated by road or other marking as appropriate. On enclosed or constricted routes such as bridges, doorways and tunnels, there should be physical separation by a solid barrier or kerb. Doors, especially those that swing in both directions, should have a transparent section.

Welfare facilities

The key points for **toilet and washing facility** provision are:

- Privacy
- Ventilation and lighting
- Cleanliness
- Location
- Quantity

Toilets should be in separate closed areas, with doors

that can be secured from within. Windows should be obscured unless they cannot be looked through from outside. Urinals should not be visible when entrance or exit doors are open. Rooms with toilets should not communicate directly with a food preparation or consumption area. Walls and floor surfaces should be such that wet cleaning can be carried out, and a cleaning system should be in place.

Washing facilities must include soap or other means of cleaning, and towels or other means of drying. Running hot and cold or warm water should be provided to allow effective washing of the face, hands and forearms, although workers facing dirty or strenuous work, or work which contaminates the skin significantly, should be provided with showers or baths. Hot water supplies should be fitted with means of reducing the effective temperature so that inadvertent scalding cannot occur. A warning notice is a poor substitute for this control measure.

Welfare facilities should be located so as to be reasonably available to those who may use them. The numbers of washing facilities, toilets and urinals is often specified in regulations. Broadly, one of each should be provided for every 10 to 15 people at work, although the exact needs should be based on the use made of them so as to allow for congestion at times, and also where the general public may share them.

Drinking water must be readily accessible at suitable places and marked with a sign where necessary (to warn people which is drinkable water and which is not). Except where drinking fountains or jets are supplied, cups or beakers are required.

Clothing worn at work only and not taken home (eg hats worn for food hygiene reasons and uniforms) should be stored at work in suitable **accommodation**. There should be a storage area for personal clothing worn travelling to and from work, and a means of drying such clothing. The extent of these facilities will vary, but adequate personal clothing space and security is important. Changing rooms may be needed, especially to prevent contamination of personal clothing by work materials. Separate facilities for men and women may be necessary for reasons of propriety.

WORKPLACE HEALTH AND SAFETY ISSUES

TABLE 2: Guide to slip, trip and fall hazards and controls

	Examples	Common control measures following risk assessment	Aggravating factors
Slip hazards			• Inadequate design specifications
Inappropriate footwear	Platform-soled shoes, stiletto-heeled shoes	Footwear policy where necessary	• Poor or uneven lighting
Wet walking surfaces	After cleaning, walking inside from wet conditions	Spill clean-up procedures, signs, barriers, door mats	• Lack of premises maintenance
Highly-polished or other unsuitable walking surfaces	Over-waxing, accumulation of cleaning product(s)	Follow suppliers' instructions for cleaning procedures, change cleaning product, consider change of surface	• Lack of equipment maintenance
Insecure walking surfaces	Loose carpets, rugs	Securing strips	• Wrong or no cleaning procedure
Contaminated walking surfaces	Spillage of dry material from process	Clean-up and rubbish removal policy	• Effects of alcohol/drugs
Sudden gradient change	Unmarked change from flat to steep slope	Insert steps, add visible tread nosings	• Fatigue
Trip hazards			• Moving around too quickly
Loose floor surfaces	Loose, worn or frayed carpets	Replace floor covering	• Disability not taken into account, especially impaired vision or lack of sight
Loose materials on floor	Objects left in walk routes	Improve housekeeping, inspections	
Uneven surface	Raised paving slabs, surface cracks in car parks	Identify for maintenance, regular inspections	
Cables across routes	Trailing telephone leads	Remove leads or provide covers for cable runs	
Low fixtures	Door stops	Review design	
Low socket outlets	Floor socket boxes left open	Inspection, training on need to close boxes, consider repositioning	
Fall hazards			
Temporary access	Standing on chairs to reach high objects	Reposition commonly-used objects, provide steps or kick-stools	
Carrying objects down stairs	Missing footing while carrying delicate object	Training, review handrail provision	
Missing parts of floor surfaces	Floor raised by contractors	Regular inspection, preplanning, barriers, signs	
Unguarded edges	Unprotected return slopes	Review all changes of level for fall potential, handrails	

56

WORKPLACE HEALTH AND SAFETY ISSUES

The key points for **rest facilities** provision are:

- Required when contamination from the workplace is likely
- Rest rooms and areas require seats with back-rests and tables
- Must protect non-smokers from tobacco smoke
- Pregnant women and nursing mothers require convenient facilities, including a means of lying down
- Seats in work areas are not excluded as rest and eating areas provided they are clean and there is a suitable surface
- Means of heating water and food is required where hot food and drink cannot be bought in or near the workplace

Facilities for **smoking** are to be arranged so that non-smokers do not experience discomfort from smoke. Usually, this is done by banning smoking altogether in the workplace, or in rest rooms and other rest areas, or by providing a specially-ventilated room for smokers to use.

REVISION

Five considerations for workplaces:

- Design
- What work is to be done
- Work environment
- Health issues and individual requirements
- Maintenance

Five principles for welfare facilities:

- Privacy
- Ventilation and lighting
- Cleanliness
- Location
- Adequacy and quantity of provision

Allan St John Holt | International Principles of Health and Safety at Work

WORK EQUIPMENT

Introduction

Hazards from work equipment can arise in two physical ways. The first is possibly the easier to recognise – **equipment and machinery hazards**, including traps, impact, contact, entanglement or ejection of parts of and by the equipment, or failure of components. The second way is by **non-equipment hazards**, which can include electrical failure, exposure to chemical sources, pressure, temperature, noise, vibration and radiation. Hazards can also arise from the 'software element' – computer control, human intervention by the person carrying out the task using the equipment, and lack of maintenance. It is important to distinguish between continuing hazards associated with the normal working of the equipment, such as not having guards fitted where necessary to protect the operator, and those arising from the failure of components or safety mechanisms, such as breakdown of the guarding mechanism.

This Section mainly covers identification and control of work equipment and machinery hazards. Obviously, not all work equipment is machinery; the principles of guarding described below apply to all work equipment, but 'machine guarding' is the term normally used to describe the topic and this convention will be followed here. The principles apply to all work equipment. The amount of detailed consideration required in respect of individual pieces of equipment will be proportionate to the risks of use.

Work equipment safety

The definition of 'work equipment' is extremely wide. Almost any equipment used at work falls within the scope of the term, from hand tools to machinery and apparatus, even motor vehicles not owned privately. However, livestock, substances and structural items are not considered within the scope of this Section.

The principles for the safe use of work equipment of all kinds are:

1. It must be **suitable** for the purpose in the particular circumstances of the use. To establish this, a suitable and sufficient risk assessment is required. For example, electrical equipment is not suitable for use in flammable atmospheres unless specifically designed for that purpose. Risk assessments need to consider ergonomic factors associated with equipment use.

2. It must be **installed**, **located** and **used** so as to minimise risk to operators and others. This means the risk assessment has to take into account the physical circumstances of use. For example, there may not be adequate space between particular pieces of equipment and the environment (see below for a summary of layout considerations).

3. All forms of energy and all substances used or produced by the equipment must be capable of **safe supply and/or removal**.

4. It must be **maintained** in an efficient condition and working order (with respect to its safety, not its production capacity), and in good repair. In order to achieve this, the equipment needs to be **designed** and installed appropriately. High-risk equipment should have a detailed maintenance log.

5. It must be **inspected** by competent persons at suitable intervals and after safety-critical situations. This is to assure that the equipment can be operated, adjusted and maintained safely where there is a significant risk (of major injury) as a result of incorrect installation, deterioration or exceptional circumstances that could affect safe operation of the equipment. Some work equipment, including lifting equipment such as cranes and some ventilation installations, will need specific examinations under local or national legislation. Examples are given in Table 1.

6. There must be adequate **information**, **instruction** and **training** given to the operator or user and their supervisors, covering safe use, the risks and their control measures.

Pressurised equipment

Relevant pressurised systems are generally those at a pressure of more than 0.5 bar above atmospheric. Common examples of such equipment with high potential for injury are boilers and air receivers. In addition to

TABLE 1: Recommended inspection requirements

Type of work equipment	Inspection	More detailed thorough examination
All types, general requirement	At installation or reassembly in new location, before use (may be visual only)	As determined by manufacturer, insurer or local policy or law
Lifting equipment, general	Weekly – (from HSE guidance on adequacy, not statutory)	• Before first use, unless already supplied with a current thorough examination report or new with a declaration of conformity with local legal requirements • After installation or assembly where those conditions will determine safety • Every 12 months • When exceptional circumstances are liable to affect safety
Lifting equipment used for lifting persons	As above	Every 6 months and as above, or in accordance with an examination scheme prepared by a competent person
Work platforms and supports of all kinds, including scaffolding	• Before first use and thereafter at least every 7 days • After alteration or any event likely to affect strength or stability	No
Pressure systems	As specified in a written scheme of examination	In accordance with a written scheme of examination prepared by a competent person

the general matters mentioned in this Section, current legal practice is to require a competent person to draw up a new, or certify an existing, written scheme of examination. This practice has generally replaced former requirements to comply with national rules which were often either over-complicated and unnecessary, or not really relevant to the needs of a particular system.

- Condition-based – centred on monitoring safety-critical parts and maintaining them as necessary to avoid hazards
- Breakdown – fix when broken only, not appropriate if a failure presents an immediate risk without correction, and needs an effective fault-reporting system

Maintenance of work equipment

Maintenance can be:
- Planned preventive – adjusting or replacing at predetermined intervals

Risk assessment

The amount of risk depends on several factors. These include the type of equipment and what it is used for (its suitability), the need for approach to or contact with it, its age and condition, the ease of access, the

WORK EQUIPMENT

FIGURE 1: Work equipment safety verification checklist

WORK EQUIPMENT TYPE:	
MAKE AND MODEL: SUPPLIER/SOURCE:	

No	HEALTH AND SAFETY ELEMENTS			COMMENTS
1	**Suitability**			
a)				
b)				
c)				
2	**Installation or location**			
a)				
b)				
3	**Physical circumstances of use**			
a)				
b)				
c)				
4	**Safe use requirements**	YES	NO	
a)				
b)				
c)				
5	**Maintenance requirements**			
a)				
b)				
c)				
d)				
6	**Design sign-off**	YES	NO	**(name)**
a)	The design of the equipment has been reviewed and is considered appropriate for the equipment, its likely users and work location(s)			
7	**Inspection requirements**			**(name/agency)**
a)	Who will undertake statutory inspections?			
b)	Are the frequencies of all inspections, tests and thorough examinations required known and recorded?	YES	NO	
8	**Information, instruction and training requirements**			
a)				
b)				
c)				
9	**Legislation**			
	What are the relevant regulations?			
10	**Health issues identified**	YES	NO	
a)				
b)				
c)				
d)				
11	**Risk assessment carried out**	YES	NO	
	Date of risk assessment: Done by: Date of review required:			

The checklist has been completed in respect of the work equipment identified.

Signed: Position:

Date:

quality of supervision of the operator's behaviour, and the complexity of its operation. Risk levels also depend on the knowledge, skills and attitude of the person(s) present at a particular time, and the general awareness of any danger and the skills needed to avoid it. The identification of those at risk and when the risk occurs is important, and applies to management as well as to operators. The process of risk assessment is described in Part 1 Section 3.

Methods of preventing equipment accidents

Equipment hazards can be controlled by:
- Eliminating the cause of the danger ('intrinsic safety' – see below)
- Reducing or eliminating the need for people to approach any dangerous part(s) of the equipment
- Making access to the dangerous parts difficult (or providing guards or other safety devices so that access does not lead to injury)
- Appropriate maintenance and inspection regimes
- The provision of protective clothing or equipment

(These are listed in order of preference and effectiveness, and may be used in combination.)

The safety of operators and those nearby can be achieved by:
a) Training to improve people's ability to recognise danger
b) Redesigning to make dangers more obvious (or use warning signs)
c) Training to improve skills in avoiding injury
d) Improving motivation to take the necessary avoiding action

Safety by design

Intrinsic safety – A process by which the designer eliminates dangers at the design stage with consideration for the elimination of dangerous parts,

making parts inaccessible, reducing the need to handle workpieces in the danger areas, provision of automatic feed devices, and enclosure of moving parts.

Control selection – The design and provision of controls which:
- Are in the correct position
- Are of the correct type
- Remove the risk of accidental start-up
- Have a directional link (control movement matched to equipment movement)
- Are distinguished by direction of movement
- Possess distinguishing features (size, colour, feel, etc)

Failure to safety – Designers should ensure that mechanical and electrical equipment fails to safety and not to danger. Examples of this are clutches scotched to prevent operation, provision of arrestor devices to prevent unexpected strokes and movement, fitting of catches and fall-back devices, and fail-safe electrical limit switches.

Maintenance and isolation procedures – Designers should consider the safety of operatives during cleaning and maintenance operations. Routine adjustments, lubrication, etc, should be carried out without the removal of safeguards or dismantling of components. Where frequent access is required, as in the case of large fixed machinery, interlock guards can be used. Access equipment, where essential, should be provided, as long as access to dangerous parts is prevented. Self-lubrication of parts should be considered if access is difficult. Positive lock-off devices should be provided to prevent unintentional restarting of the equipment. Permit-to-work systems (see Part 1 Section 5) will be required in some circumstances, notably where a third party could energise a system without the knowledge of persons exposed to risks from the equipment or system when in operation.

Safety by position – Parts of machines and other work equipment which are out of reach and kept out of reach are called 'safe by position'. However, designers must consider the likelihood of dangerous parts normally out of reach becoming accessible in

WORK EQUIPMENT

some circumstances. An example of when this could happen is during painting of a factory machinery area from ladders.

Work equipment layout – The way in which equipment such as static machinery is arranged in the workplace can reduce accidents significantly. Safe layout will take account of:

- Spacing – to facilitate access for operation, supervision, maintenance, adjustment and cleaning
- Lighting – both general lighting to the workplace (natural or artificial but avoiding glare) and localised for specific operations
- Cables and pipes – should be placed to allow safe access and to avoid tripping, with sufficient headroom
- Safe access for maintenance

Machine guarding

Many serious accidents at work involve the use of machinery. In circumstances where intrinsic safety (see above) has not been achieved, machinery guarding will be the final option to eliminate the remaining risks. Whether a particular guard is effective or not will depend on its design and construction, and the way in which it relates to the operating procedures and what the machine is used for.

People can be injured directly by work equipment in five different ways. Some machines can injure in more than one way. These are:

Traps – The body or limb(s) become trapped between closing or passing motions of a machine. In some cases, the trap occurs when the limb(s) are drawn into a closing motion, eg in-running nips.

Impact – Injuries can result from being struck by moving parts of machinery, or the machine itself.

Contact – Injuries can result from contact of the operator with sharp or abrasive surfaces. Alternatively, contact with hot or electrically live components will cause injury.

Entanglement – Injuries resulting from the entanglement of hair, rings and items of clothing in moving (particularly rotating) parts of equipment.

Ejection – Injuries can result from elements of the workplace or components of the work equipment being thrown out during the operation of the equipment, eg sparks, swarf, chips, molten metal splashes and broken components.

Machinery guard material

The selection of the material from which the guards will be constructed is determined by four main considerations. These are:

- Strength, stiffness and durability
- Effects on reliability (eg a solid guard may cause the equipment to overheat)
- Visibility (there may be operational and safety reasons for needing a clear view of the danger area)
- The need for control of other hazards (eg limiting the amount of noise output by choice of special materials)

Ergonomics and the design of machinery guards

Guards should be designed with people in mind. The study of the relationship between man and work equipment is called **ergonomics**, and the study of the relationship between differing body shapes and the requirements for reaching and vision in the safe operation of a machine is called **anthropometry**. For an outline of the topic, see Part 3 Section 9.

Stress and fatigue contribute significantly to the causes of accidents, and designers should aim to reduce this to a minimum by considering a range of layout issues and facilities:

- The correct placing of controls
- The positioning of operating stations and height of work tables
- The provision of seating
- Suitable access to the workstation

International Principles of Health and Safety at Work | Allan St John Holt

Similar thought will be needed to ensure that guards are fully functional and are seen by equipment operators and users as aids rather than obstructions.

Types of guard

Fixed guard – A fixed guard should be fitted wherever practicable and should, by design, prevent access to dangerous parts of work equipment. It should be robust to withstand the process and environmental conditions. Its effectiveness will be determined by the method of fixing and the size of any openings, allowing for an adequate distance between the opening and the danger point. This may be determined by national standards or regulations. The guard should only be removable with the use of a special tool, such as a spanner or wrench.

Interlocked guard – The essential principles of an interlocked guard are that the machine cannot operate until the guard is closed, and the guard cannot be opened until the dangerous parts of the machine have come fully to rest. Interlocked guards can be mechanical, electrical, hydraulic, pneumatic or a combination of these. Interlocked guards and their components have to be designed so that any failure of them does not expose people to danger.

Control guard – If the motion of the machine can be stopped quickly, control guards can be used. The principle of control guarding is that the machine must not be able to operate until the guard is closed. When the guard is closed by the operator, the machine's operating sequence is started. If the guard is opened, the machine's motion is stopped or reversed, so the machine must be able to come to rest or reverse its motion quickly for this technique to be effective. Generally, the guard in a control system is not locked closed during the operation of the machine.

Automatic guard – An automatic guard operates by physically removing from the danger area any part of the body exposed to danger. It can only be used where there is adequate time to do this without causing injury, which limits its use to slow-moving work equipment.

Distance guard – A distance guard prevents any part of the body from reaching a danger area. It could take the form of a fixed barrier or fence designed to prevent access.

Adjustable guard – Where it is impracticable to prevent access to dangerous parts (eg they may be unavoidably exposed during use), adjustable guards (fixed guards with adjustable elements) can be used. The amount of protection given by these guards relies heavily on close supervision of the operative, and on correct adjustment of the guard and its adequate maintenance.

Self-adjusting guard – This guard is automatically opened by the movement of the workpiece and returns to its closed position when the operation is completed.

Trip devices – These automatically stop or reverse the machine before the operative reaches the danger point. They rely on sensitive trip mechanisms and on the machine being able to stop quickly (the stopping action may be assisted by a brake). Examples include trip wires and mats containing switches which stop the machine when they are trodden on.

Two-hand control devices – These devices force the operator to use both hands to operate the machine controls. However, they only provide protection for the operator and not for anyone else who may be near the danger point. Guards should be arranged to protect all persons. Where these devices are provided, the controls should be spaced well apart and/or shrouded, the machine should only operate when both controls are activated together, and the control system should require resetting between each cycle of the machine.

Which guard?

Fixed guards provide the highest standard of protection and should be used (where practicable) when access to the danger area is not required during normal operation.

The following gives guidance on the selection of

WORK EQUIPMENT

safeguards (in order of merit):

a) Where access to the danger area is not required during normal operation:
   1. Fixed guard, where practicable
   2. Distance guard
   3. Trip device

b) Where access to the danger area is required during normal operation:
   1. Interlocking guard
   2. Automatic guard
   3. Trip device
   4. Adjustable guard
   5. Self-adjusting guard
   6. Two-hand control

Supply of machinery

In addition to the special duties of the employer, manufacturers and others in the supply chain have duties to comply with the specific safety requirements set out in minimum safety standards for equipment manufactured, designed, imported and supplied in the European Union (EU).

Most machinery supplied must satisfy a broad range of health and safety requirements covering moving parts as well as other issues, and carry 'CE' marking and other information. In some cases, the machinery must have undergone type-examination by an approved body. The maker or the importer must also have records of relevant technical information related to the machine. Machines which do not comply cannot be supplied legally within the Member States of the EU.

It should be noted that these rules apply throughout the European Economic Area – the present 15 Member States of the EC plus Norway, Iceland and Liechtenstein. There are many types of work machinery which are excluded from their coverage. They include means of transport, seagoing vessels, steam boilers, fairground equipment and agricultural tractors.

REVISION

Danger can arise from work equipment hazards – such as traps and entanglement, and non-work equipment hazards – the operator, noise.

Safety can be achieved by design in the following **six** ways:

- Intrinsic safety
- Control selection
- Failure to safety
- Maintenance and isolation procedures
- Safety by position
- Machine layout

Three kinds of maintenance:

- Planned preventive
- Condition
- Breakdown

Five dangers associated with work equipment:

- Traps
- Impact
- Contact
- Entanglement
- Ejection

Six principles for work equipment:

- Suitability for purpose
- Design, installation, location and use
- Inputs and outputs evaluated
- Efficient condition maintained
- Inspection
- Information, instruction and training

Nine types of guard:

- Fixed
- Interlocked
- Control
- Automatic
- Distance
- Adjustable
- Self-adjusting
- Trip
- Two-hand control

MECHANICAL HANDLING

Introduction

Mechanical handling techniques have improved efficiency and safety, but have introduced other sources of potential injury into the workplace. Cranes, powered industrial trucks and fork-lifts, and conveyors are the primary means for mechanical handling. In all circumstances, the safety of the equipment can be affected by the safety of operating conditions, workplace hazards and the operator.

Cranes

Basic safety principles for all mechanical equipment apply to cranes. More details are given in the previous Section, but in summary the principles are that the equipment should be of good construction, made from sound material, of adequate strength and free from obvious faults. All equipment should be tested and regularly examined to ensure its integrity. The equipment should always be properly used.

What can go wrong

Overturning can be caused by weak support, operating outside the machine's capabilities and by striking obstructions.

Overloading by exceeding the operating capacity or operating radii, or by failure of safety devices.

Collision with other cranes, overhead cables or structures.

Failure of support – due to placing over cellars or drains, outriggers not being extended, or made-up or not solid ground – or of **structural components** of the crane itself.

Operator errors from impaired/restricted visibility, poor eyesight or inadequate training.

Loss of load from failure of lifting equipment, lifting accessories or slinging procedure.

Hazard elimination

Matters which require attention to ensure the safe operation of a crane include:

Identification and testing – Every crane should be tested and a certificate should be issued by the seller and following each test. Each should be identified for reference purposes, and the safe working load clearly marked. This should never be exceeded, except under test conditions.

Maintenance – Cranes should be inspected regularly, with any faults repaired immediately. Records of checks and inspections should be kept.

Safety measures – A number of safety measures should be incorporated for the safe operation of the crane.

These include:
a) Load indicators – of two types:
   – load/radius indicator
   – automatic safe load indicator, providing audible and visual warning
b) Controls – should be clearly identified and of the 'dead-man' type
c) Overtravel switches – limit switches to prevent the hook or sheave block being wound up to the cable drum
d) Access – safe access should be provided for the operator and for use during inspection/maintenance and emergencies
e) Operating position – should provide clear visibility of both hook and load, with the controls easily reached. Communication through a banksman by signal or radio is a potential weak link as messages may not be received or properly understood
f) Passengers – should not be carried without authorisation, and never on lifting tackle
g) Lifting tackle – chains, slings, wire ropes, eyebolts and shackles should be tested/examined, be free from damage and knots as appropriate, and be clearly marked for identification and safe working load, and be properly used (no use at or near sharp edges, or at incorrect sling angles)

MECHANICAL HANDLING

Operating area – All nearby hazards, including overhead cables and bared power supply conductors, should be identified, and removed or covered by safe working procedures such as locking-off and permit systems. Solid support should be available and on new installations the dimensions and strength of support required should be specified. The possibility of striking other cranes or structures should be examined.

Operator training – Crane operators and slingers should be fit and strong enough for the work. Training should be provided for the safe operation of the particular equipment.

Powered industrial trucks

Trucks should be of good construction, free from defects and suitable for the purpose in terms of capacity, size and type. The type of power supply to be used should be checked, because the nature of the work area may require one kind of power source rather than another. For example, in unventilated confined spaces, internal combustion engines will not be acceptable because of the toxic gases they produce.

Trucks should be maintained so as to prevent failure of vital parts, including brakes, steering and lifting components. Special facilities may be required for some tasks, such as mast replacement. Specific risk assessments should be made, which will take into account local conditions and availability of appropriate equipment. Any damage should be reported and corrected immediately. Overhead protective guards should be fitted for the protection of the operator. Powered industrial trucks and their attachments should only be operated in accordance with the manufacturer's instructions.

What can go wrong

Overturning from manoeuvring with load elevated, driving too fast, sudden braking, striking obstructions, use of forward tilt with load elevated, driving down a ramp with the load in front of the truck, turning on or crossing ramps at an angle, shifting loads, or unsuitable road or support conditions.

Overloading by exceeding the maximum lifting capacity of the truck.

Collision with structural elements, pipes, stacks or with other vehicles.

Floor failure because of uneven or unsound floors, or by exceeding the load capacity of the floor. The capacity of floors other than the ground level should always be checked before using trucks on them.

Loss of load can occur if devices are not fitted to stop loads slipping from forks.

Explosions and fire may arise from electrical shorting, leaking fuel pipes, dust accumulation (spontaneous combustion) and from hydrogen generation during battery charging. The truck itself can be the source of ignition if operated in flammable atmospheres.

Passengers should not be carried unless seats and other facilities are provided for them.

Hazard elimination

Matters which require attention for the safe operation of powered industrial trucks include:

Operating area – The floor should be of suitable construction for the use of trucks. It should be flat and unobstructed where movement of machines is expected, with gullies and openings covered. Storage and stacking areas should be properly laid out, with removal of blind corners. Passing places need to be provided where trucks and people are likely to pass each other in restricted spaces, and traffic routes need to be clearly defined with adequate visibility. Pedestrians should be excluded from operating areas; alternatively, clearly-defined gangways should be provided – with trucks given priority. Suitable warning signs will be required to indicate priorities.

FIGURE 1: Sample basic checklist – Common lifting appliances

PREMISES ADDRESS:	
COMPLETION BY:	
DATE:	

No		YES	NO	COMMENTS
	Public protection and information			
1.	Are the work areas fenced off, or is there other protection for the public against being struck by moving equipment or loads?			
2.	Is access to the work areas restricted to authorised visitors?			
3.	When work finishes, are the lifting appliances immobilised effectively?			
	Cranes and lifting appliances			
4.	Are crane erection and dismantling method statements available for all cranes and lifting appliances?			
5.	Are the safe working loads and other constraints known to operators?			
6.	Are all operators trained and competent?			
7.	Where appropriate, do all operators possess the appropriate certification or authority to operate equipment?			
8.	Are safe load indicators fitted where appropriate to all lifting appliances?			
9.	Have slingers or banksmen been appointed and identified to operators as the only persons entitled to give signals?			
10.	Have all slingers or banksmen been adequately trained in signalling and slinging?			
11.	Have all slingers or banksmen been specifically instructed in the identification of weight and centre of gravity before lifting a load?			
12.	Are all lifting appliances inspected at least weekly by a competent person, with the inspection results recorded?			
13.	Do all lifting appliances have appropriate in-date test certificates issued by a competent authority?			
14.	Are drivers of visiting mobile cranes and lifting appliances required to produce inspection documents and evidence of competence?			
15.	Are all mobile lifting appliances required to operate outriggers only with additional timber placed beneath to spread the load?			
16.	Is all plant and equipment in good repair?			
17.	Is a maintenance log maintained to record any defects and the date of their repair as well as preventive maintenance?			
	Hoists and lifts			
18.	Are all hoists and lifts inspected visually at least weekly by a competent person and the results recorded?			
19.	Do all hoists have appropriate in-date test certificates issued by a competent person?			
20.	Are effective gates and barriers in place at all landings, incl. ground level?			
21.	Are the gates kept shut other than when the platform or cage is at the landing?			
22.	Are the controls arranged so that operation is from one position only?			
23.	Are all operators trained and competent?			
24.	Are materials hoists and goods-only lifts marked to prevent people riding on them?			
25.	Is the safe working load clearly marked on all lifting appliances?			
26.	Are all hoists protected to prevent anyone being struck by any moving part, or materials falling down the hoistways?			
27.	Are the arrangements for maintenance appropriate?			
28.	Are arrangements for the release of trapped passengers appropriate and in place?			

MECHANICAL HANDLING

Lighting should be adequate to facilitate access and stacking operations. Loading bays should be appropriately designed and stable with chocks provided to place behind or beneath wheels. Ramps and slopes should not exceed 1:10 unless the manufacturer specifies that use on steeper gradients under load is acceptable. Battery charging areas should be separate, well ventilated and well lit, with no smoking or naked lights permitted. Battery-lifting facilities should be provided. Where possible, reversing lights and/or sound warnings should be fitted, especially where pedestrians may share floor space with trucks.

Training should be provided for operators in the safe operation of their equipment, followed by certification.

Conveyors

The most common types of conveyor are belt, roller and screw conveyors.

What can go wrong

Trapping – limbs can be drawn into in-running nips.

Contact with moving parts such as drive elements or screw conveyors.

Entanglement with rollers or drive mechanisms.

Striking – materials falling from heights or incorrectly handled.

Hazard elimination

Belt conveyors – require guards or enclosures at the drums, which are the main hazard because of the presence of trapping points between belt and drum. These are also required where additional trapping points or nips occur as the belt changes direction or at guide plates or feed points. Guards may be required along the length of a conveyor in the form

of enclosures or trip wires to cut off supply. Safe access at appropriate intervals should be provided over long conveyor runs.

Roller conveyors – where rollers may be either power-driven or free-running, guards at power drives are required. Other hazards can be present, which also require guarding – these include areas where in-running nips are created, where intermediate rollers are power-driven or when a belt is fitted. Walkways should be provided if access is required over the conveyor mechanism.

Screw conveyors – should be guarded to prevent access at all times. Repairs and maintenance should only be undertaken when the drive is locked off.

REVISION

Cranes fail through:
- Overturning
- Overloading
- Collision
- Foundation failure
- Structural failure
- Loss of load
- Operator error
- Lack of maintenance

Powered lift trucks fail through:
- Overturning
- Overloading
- Collision
- Floor failure
- Loss of load
- Operator error
- Presence of unauthorised passengers

Conveyor hazards:
- Trapping
- Contact
- Entanglement
- Non-machinery hazards, including noise, vibration
- Striking by objects

International Principles of Health and Safety at Work | Allan St John Holt

Introduction

It has long been recognised that the manual handling of loads at work contributes significantly to the number of workplace injuries with approximately a quarter of all reported accidents attributed to these activities. The majority of these injuries result in significant absence from work, almost half of the total being sprains or strains, often of the lower back, with other types of injury including cuts, bruises, fractures and amputations. Many of the injuries are of a cumulative nature rather than being attributable to any single handling incident.

Until recently, the training of employees to lift had concentrated on methods which would allow them to minimise the risks from moving and lifting the heavy loads expected of them. Films and videos explained how these techniques would help them to do the work without injury. Now, however, the aim is to reduce the opportunities for injury by reducing the amount of lifting and moving that the human body is required to do in the work environment. We should be asking not 'How do I lift this safely?' but 'Do I really need to lift this at all?' In the same way, people who ask 'What is the maximum weight people are allowed to lift?' are missing the point, because weight is only one of many factors contributing to the risks inherent in manual handling.

The casualties of the old approach are all around us – about 80 per cent of the working population will suffer some form of back injury requiring them to take time off work at some point in their lives. Those who are injured are three times as likely to be injured again in the same way as those without a back injury. This situation needs to be addressed by informed employers and employees, seeking to identify and remove hazardous lifting and to find new ways of doing work that has traditionally involved human effort to move loads.

Injuries resulting from manual handling

Some of the more common types of injury resulting from manual handling are considered here. It is important to remember that the spine is undergoing a process of 'ageing' which will affect the integrity of the spine. For example, loss of 'spinal architecture' (ie the natural curvature of the spine) produces excessive pressure on the edges of the discs, wearing them out faster. These effects are not considered here.

Disc injuries – An estimated 90 per cent of back troubles are attributable to **disc lesions**. The discs lie between the vertebrae, acting as shock absorbers and facilitating movement. They do not 'slip' in the conventional sense, as they are permanently fixed to the bone above and below. Roughly circular, the discs are made up of an outer rim of elastic fibres with an inner core containing a jelly-like fluid. When stood upright, forces are exerted directly through the whole length of the spine and in this position it can withstand considerable stress. However, when the spine is bent, most of the stress is exerted on only one part (usually at the part where the bending occurs). Also, due to the bending of the spine in one place, all the stress is exerted on one side of the intervertebral disc, thus 'pinching' it between the vertebrae. This 'pinching effect' may scar and wear the outer surface of the disc so that at some time it becomes weak and eventually, under pressure, it ruptures. Many authorities believe that all disc lesions are progressive, rather than sudden. It is also important to remember that the disc cores dry out with age, making them less flexible and functional, and more prone to injury. The disc contents are highly irritating to the surrounding parts of the body, causing an inflammatory response when they leak out.

Ligament/tendon injuries – Ligaments and tendons are connective tissues, and hold the back together. Ligaments are the gristly straps that bind the bones together while tendons attach muscles to other body parts, usually bones. Repetitive motion of the tendons may cause inflammation. Both can be pulled and torn, resulting in sprains. Any factor, such as the effects of age and cold weather, that produces tightness in ligaments and tendons predisposes the back to sprains. Two main ligaments run all the way down the spine to support the vertebrae.

Muscular/nerve injuries – The muscles in the back

MANUAL HANDLING

form long, thick bands that run down each side of the spine. They are very strong and active, but tiring of these muscles can result in aches and pains, and can create stress on the discs. Postural deformities can result from damage to the muscles. Fibrositis (rheumatic pain) can also result. Nerves can be become trapped between the elements of the spine causing severe pain and injury.

Hernias – A hernia is a protrusion of an internal organ through a gap in a wall of the cavity in which it is contained. For example, any compression of the abdominal contents towards the naturally weak areas may result in a loop of intestine being forced into one of the gaps or weak areas formed during the development of the body. When the body is bent forward, possibly during a lift, the abdominal cavity decreases in size causing a compression of internal components and increasing the risk of hernias.

Fractures, abrasions and cuts – These can result from dropping the objects that are being handled (possibly because of muscular fatigue), falling while carrying objects (perhaps as a result of poor housekeeping), from other inadequacies in the working environment such as poor lighting, or from the contents of the load.

Injury during manual handling

The injuries highlighted above can result from lifting, pushing, pulling or carrying an object during manual handling.

Lifting – Compressive forces on the spine, its ligaments and tendons can result in some of the injuries identified above. High compressive forces in the spine can result from lifting too much, poor posture and incorrect lifting technique. Prolonged compressive stress causes what is known as 'creep-effect' on the spine, squeezing and stiffening it. If the spine is twisted or bent sideways when lifting, the added tension in the ligaments and muscles when the spine is rotated considerably increases the total stress on the spine to a dangerous extent. The elastic disc fibres are also

put under tension during repetitive twisting and individual fibres are damaged.

Pushing and pulling – Stresses are generally higher for pushing than pulling. Because the abdominal muscles are active as well as the back muscles, the reactive compressive force on the spine can be even higher than when lifting. Pushing also loads the shoulders and the ribcage is stiffened, making breathing more difficult.

Carrying – Carrying involves some static muscular work which can be tiring for the muscles, the back, shoulders, arms and hands depending on how the load is supported. A weight held in front of the body induces more spinal stress than one carried on the back. Likewise, a given weight held in one hand is more likely to cause fatigue than if it was divided into equal amounts in each hand. As with pushing, carrying objects in front of the body or on the shoulders may restrict the ribcage. Thus, the way in which a load is carried makes a great difference to the fatiguing effects. This is why getting a good grip is important, as well as keeping the load close to the body – which places it closer to the body's centre of gravity. The 'power grip', where the load is taken deep into the hand by holding the fingers straight and essentially at right angles to the palm, involves less strain on tendons and joints than where the fingers alone are used to support the object's full weight. The potential for back injury is higher for the obese and pregnant, because the extent to which the centre of gravity of the load can approach the centre of gravity of the body is necessarily limited.

Manual handling assessments

The European Directive 90/269/EEC covering the manual handling of loads established a general requirement to avoid the need for manual handling of loads by workers, especially by the use of mechanical aids. It also requires risk to be reduced where manual handling cannot be avoided, and this is to be done by assessment of the work and the loads so as to take appropriate measures to reduce the risks. The annexes to the Directive draw attention to 'reference factors' to be taken into account when making these assessments.

The first principle, to avoid the need for manual handling, must be addressed in connection with a task under review. This can be done by posing three questions aimed at reducing the risks by eliminating manual handling. Only when the answers show that this is not possible does it become necessary to carry out an assessment and consideration of the factors identified in Annex 1 and Annex 2.

Is there a risk of injury? – An understanding of the types of potential injury will be supplemented with the past experiences of the employer, including accident/ill health information relating to manual handling and the general numerical guidelines contained in official guidance.

Is it necessary to move the load manually? – This question will be useful in establishing 'authorised' manual handling tasks within a certain workplace or department. Some work is dependent on the manual handling of loads and cannot be avoided (as, for example, in refuse collection). If moving the load can be avoided, then the initial exercise is complete and further review will only be required if conditions change.

Is it possible to automate or mechanise the operation? – It must be remembered that the introduction of these measures can create different risks (eg introduction of fork-lifts creates a series of new risks) which require consideration.

The aim of the **full assessment** is to evaluate the risk associated with a particular task and identify control measures which can be implemented to remove or reduce the risk (possibly mechanisation and/or training).

For varied work (such as done in the course of maintenance, construction or agriculture), it will not be possible to assess every single instance of manual handling. In these circumstances, each type or category of manual handling operation should be identified and the associated risk assessed. Assessment

should also extend to cover those employees who carry out manual handling operations away from the employer's premises (such as delivery drivers).

The assessment must be kept up to date. It needs reviewing whenever it may become invalid, such as when the working conditions or the personnel carrying out those operations have changed. Review will also be required if there is a significant change in the manual handling operation, which may, for example, affect the nature of the task or the load (eg changing to different bulk sizes).

Before beginning an assessment, the views of staff and employees can be of particular use in identifying manual handling problems. Involvement in the assessment process should be encouraged, particularly in reporting problems associated with particular tasks.

Records of accidents and ill health are also valuable indicators of risk, as are absentee records, poor productivity and morale, and excessive product damage. Individual industries and sectors have also produced information identifying risks associated with manual handling operations.

Annex 1 of the Directive specifies four interrelated factors which the assessment should take into account. The answers to the questions specified about the factors form the basis of an appropriate assessment. These are:

The tasks
Do they involve:
- Holding or manipulating loads at a distance from the trunk?
- Unsatisfactory bodily movement or posture, especially
  - twisting the trunk?
  - stooping?
  - reaching upwards?
- Excessive movement of loads, especially
  - excessive lifting or lowering distances?
  - excessive carrying distances?
  - excessive pushing or pulling of loads?
- Risk of sudden movement of loads?

MANUAL HANDLING

- Frequent or prolonged physical effort?
- Insufficient rest or recovery periods?
- A rate of work imposed by a process?

The loads

Are they:

- Heavy?
- Bulky or unwieldy?
- Difficult to grasp?
- Unstable, or with contents likely to shift?
- Sharp, hot, or otherwise potentially damaging?

The working environment

Are there:

- Space constraints preventing good posture?
- Uneven, slippery or unstable floors?
- Variations in levels of floors or work surfaces?
- Extremes of temperature or humidity?
- Conditions causing ventilation problems or gusts of wind?
- Poor lighting conditions?

Individual capability

Does the job:

- Require unusual strength, height, etc?
- Create a hazard to those who might reasonably be considered to be pregnant or to have a health problem?
- Require special information or training for its safe performance?

Other factors

- Is movement or posture hindered by PPE or clothing?

Reducing the risk of injury

In considering the most appropriate controls, an ergonomic approach to designing the manual handling operation will optimise health and safety as well as productivity levels associated with the task. The task, the load, the working environment, individual capability and the interrelationship between these factors are all important elements in deciding optimum controls designed to fit the operation to the individual rather than the other way around. Techniques of risk reduction include:

Mechanical assistance – This involves the use of handling aids, of which there are many examples. One could be the use of a lever, which would reduce the force required to move a load. A hoist can support the weight of a load while a trolley can reduce the effort needed to move a load horizontally. Chutes are a convenient means of using gravity to move loads from one place to another.

Improvements in the task – Changes in the layout of the task can reduce the risk of injury by, for example, improving the flow of materials or products. Improvements which will permit the body to be used more efficiently, especially if they permit the load to be held closer to the body, will also reduce the risk of injury. Improving the work routine by reducing the frequency or duration of handling tasks will also have a beneficial effect. Using teams of people and, where appropriate, personal protective equipment (PPE), such as gloves, can also contribute to a reduced risk of injury. All equipment supplied for use during handling operations (eg handling aids and PPE) should be maintained and there should be a defect reporting and correction system.

Reducing the risk of injury from the load – The load may be made lighter by using smaller packages/containers or specifying lower packaging weights. Additionally, the load may be made smaller, easier to manage, easier to grasp (eg by the provision of handles), more stable and less damaging to hold (clean, free from sharp edges, etc). On the other hand, the introduction of smaller and lighter loads may carry a penalty in the form of further bending and other repetitive movements to handle the load than were necessary before. This could result in no change in the overall risk.

Improvements in the working environment – This can be done by removing space constraints, improving the condition and nature of floors, reducing work to a single level, avoiding extremes in temperature and excessive humidity, and ensuring that adequate lighting is provided.

Individual selection – Clearly, the health, fitness and strength of an individual can affect his/her ability to perform manual handling tasks. Health screening is an important selection tool. Knowledge and training have important roles to play in reducing the number of injuries resulting from manual handling operations. There is little point in enquiring about any previous back injuries on a job application form if no attempt is made to ensure that those who do admit to previous problems are not given work which is foreseeably likely to produce them.

Back belts – These are claimed to offer protection against injury. As a sole solution, they are not likely to satisfy legal requirements. Their actual effectiveness is controversial; some authorities believe that for certain individuals a back belt may render them more likely to suffer an injury. Designs and functions vary widely, some preventing or limiting movement. Abdominal and back support belts provide protection, if at all, to individuals and not the group involved. They are, therefore, less desirable than controls which reduce the risks to all, using techniques described above.

Manual handling training

A training programme should include mention of:
- Dangers of careless and unskilled handling methods
- Principles of levers and the laws of motion
- Functions of the spine and muscular system
- Effects of lifting, pushing, pulling and carrying, with emphasis on harmful posture
- Use of mechanical handling aids
- Selection of suitable clothing for lifting and necessary protective equipment
- Techniques of:
  a) identifying slip/trip hazards
  b) assessing weight of loads and how much can be handled by the individual without assistance
  c) bending the knees, keeping the load close to the body when lifting (but avoiding tension and knee-bending at too sharp an angle)
  d) breathing, and avoiding twisting and sideways bending during exertion

e) using the legs to get close to the load, making best use of body and load weight
f) using the 'power grip'

There are several guiding principles for the safe lifting of loads. These are:
- Secure grip
- Proper foot position
- Bent knees and comfortably straight back
- Keep arms close to the body
- Keep the chin tucked in
- Body weight used to advantage

(All attending the training should have an opportunity to practise under supervision.)

Other factors which should be discussed with trainees include:
- Personal limitations (age, strength, fitness, girth)
- Nature of loads likely to be lifted (weight, size, rigidity)
- Position of loads
- Working conditions to minimise physical strain

REVISION

Five types of injury:
- Disc injuries
- Ligament/tendon injuries
- Muscular/nerve injuries
- Hernias
- Fractures, abrasion, cuts

Training programmes should include:
- The dangers of bad lifting technique
- The principles of leverage
- The functions of the body in lifting
- Demonstration of good technique
- Use of mechanical aids
- Opportunity to practise
- Requirements of regulations and risk assessments

Eight points for safe lifting:
- Check load characteristics – weight, size, position, destination

MANUAL HANDLING

- Be aware of personal limitations, ask for assistance if necessary
- Take secure grip
- Keep back straight and knees bent
- Keep arms close to body
- Keep the chin tucked
- Be aware of body weight and how to use it to advantage
- Co-ordinate two or more persons handling an object

Four main factors in assessment:
- Task
- Load
- Working environment
- Individual capability

74

Introduction

Many home and work injuries involve falls from heights. The human body is not designed to resist impacts well, and the resulting injuries are unpredictable in their extent.

This is where luck has a place in safety – the outcome of fall injuries is mostly dictated by chance. People have failed to survive a fall from as little as a metre; others have survived unbroken falls from 10 metres. Because the outcome in any individual case cannot be known in advance, the only course to follow must be one of prevention.

Fall prevention and fall protection

An understanding of the difference between these two concepts is essential. **Fall prevention** aims to remove the need for people to work exposed to falls. This is done by design and planning work. **Fall protection** is the use of techniques to protect those who are necessarily exposed to fall hazards so as to minimise the risks.

Changing luminaires in very high ceilings can be done from access equipment, but a safer solution is to design a fixed way of access above the ceiling space. Programming the early erection of fixed and final stairways during a building's construction removes the need for temporary access up ladders and also the need to protect an open stairwell. These solutions need to be considered before other access choices. The **safety precedence sequence**, mentioned in Part 1, shows why this is so (Table 1). Several of these controls may be used in combination to increase effectiveness.

For temporary access to heights, as in construction work, the principle is to provide protected access for every person likely to be at risk in preference to provision of personal protection. Thus, the use of a working platform with edge protection is always preferred to methods which do not prevent falls but provide protection when falls occur.

Access equipment

Each task should be assessed and a suitable means of access chosen based on an evaluation of the work to be done, the duration of the task, the working environment (and its constraints), and the capability of the person or people carrying out the task.

There are many different types of access equipment. This Section covers general principles, and the following:
- Ladders, stepladders and trestles
- General access scaffolds
- Scaffold towers
- Suspended cradles
- Mast-elevated work platforms
- Power-operated work platforms
- Personal suspension equipment (abseiling equipment and chairs)

Other, highly specialised equipment is available and the general principles will apply to their use. Usually, they have been specially designed for particular tasks and manufacturers' information should be used in operator training.

General principles

Accidents using access equipment occur because one or more of the following common problems have not been controlled in advance, or was thought to be an acceptable risk under the circumstances:
- Faulty design of the access structure itself
- Inappropriate selection where safer alternatives could have been used
- Subsidence or failure of base support
- Structural failure of suspension system
- Structural failure of components
- Structural failure through overloading
- Structural failure through poor erection/inspection/maintenance
- Structural failure through overbalancing
- Instability through misuse or misunderstanding
- Overreaching and overbalancing
- Climbing while carrying loads

WORKING AT HEIGHT

TABLE 1: Safety precedence sequence applied to working at height

Safety precedence ranking (the relative effectiveness of the control method)	Control principle	Application of the principle to working at height
1	Hazard elimination	Design improvements, eg design the erection sequence to remove need to bolt up at height
2	Substitution options	Use of access equipment, eg replace ladder access to steelwork with mobile elevated work platforms
3	Use of barriers	Supply suitable guardrails to open edges where people approach
4	Isolation	Supply barriers to walkways well back from exposed edges
5	Segregation	Lock access doors to areas where falls could occur, with limited keyholders, eg access to roof and liftshafts
6	Use of procedures	Introduce safe systems of work, procedures such as equipment maintenance and inspection
7	Use of warning systems	Fix signs, give instructions not to approach edges
8	Use of personal protective equipment	Must be used as a sole measure only when all other options have been exhausted, eg safety harnesses

- Slippery footing – wrong footwear, failure to clean
- Falls from working platforms and in transit
- Unauthorised alterations and use
- Contact with obstructions/structural elements
- Electrical and hydraulic equipment failures
- Trapping by moving parts

Ladders, stepladders and trestles

The key points to be observed when selecting and using this equipment are:

Ladders

1. See whether an alternative means of access is more suitable. Take into account the nature of the work and its duration, the height to be worked at, what reaching movements may be required, what equipment and materials may be required at height, the angle of placement and the foot room behind rungs, and the construction and type of ladder.

2. Check visually whether the ladder is in good condition and free from slippery substances.

3. Check facilities available for securing against slipping – tied at top, secured at bottom, or

footed by a second person if no more than 3m height access is required.

4. Ensure the rung at the step-off point is level with the working platform or other access point, and that the ladder rises a sufficient height above this point (at least 1.05m or five rungs is recommended), unless there is a separate handhold.

5. A landing point for rest purposes is required every 9m.

6. The correct angle of rest is approximately 75 degrees (corresponds to a ratio of one unit horizontally at the foot for every four units vertically).

7. Stiles (upright sections) should be evenly and adequately supported.

8. Ladders should be maintained free of defects and should be inspected regularly.

9. Ladders not capable of repair should be destroyed.

10. Metal ladders (and wooden ladders when wet) are conductors of electricity and should not be placed near or carried beneath low power lines.

11. It is important to ensure that ladders are positioned the correct way up. Timber pole ladders often have stiles thicker at the base than at the top and should have metal tie rods underneath the rungs. Metal ladders often have rungs with both flat and curved surfaces – the flat surface is the one on which the user's feet should rest.

Stepladders

1. Stepladders are not designed to accept side loading.

2. Chains or ropes to prevent overspreading are required, or other fittings designed to achieve the same result. Parts should be fully extended.

3. Stepladders should be levelled for stability on a firm base.

4. Work should not be carried out from the top step.

5. Overreaching should be avoided by moving the stepladder – if this is not possible, another method of access should be considered.

6. Equipment should be maintained free from defects. Regular inspection is required.

7. No more than one person should use a stepladder at one time.

Working platforms and trestles

1. Trestles are suitable only as board supports.

2. They should be free from defects and inspected regularly.

3. Trestles should be levelled for stability on a firm base.

4. Platforms based on trestles should be fully boarded, adequately supported and provided with edge protection where appropriate.

5. Safe means of access should be provided to trestle platforms, usually by a stepladder.

6. Working platforms in construction work may have minimum widths specified in local or national laws, and this requirement will usually apply to trestle-based platforms as well as traditional scaffolding platforms. As a guide, they should be no less than 600mm in width. Many older trestles may not be suitable to support such platforms as they will be too narrow.

General access scaffolds

There are three main types of access scaffold, commonly constructed from steel tubing or available in commercial patented sections. These are:

1. Independent tied scaffolds, which are temporary structures independent of the structure to which access is required but tied to it for stability.

2. Putlog scaffolds, which rely on the building (usually under construction) to provide structural support to the temporary scaffold structure through an arrangement of putlog tubes (with special flattened ends) placed into the wall.

3. Birdcage scaffolds, which are independent

WORKING AT HEIGHT

structures normally erected for interior work which have a large area and normally only a single working platform.

The key points to be observed when specifying, erecting and using scaffolds are:

1. Select the correct design with adequate load-bearing capacity.
2. Ensure adequate foundations are available for the loads to be imposed.
3. The structural elements of the scaffold should be provided and maintained in good condition.
4. Structures should be erected by competent persons or under the close supervision of a competent person, in accordance with any design provided and applicable local or national regulations and codes.
5. All working platforms should be fully boarded, with adequate edge protection, including handrails or other means of fall protection, nets, brickguards and/or toeboards to prevent materials or people falling from the platforms.
6. All materials resting on platforms should be safely stacked, with no overloading.
7. Adequate and safe means of access should be provided to working platforms.
8. Unauthorised alterations of the completed structure should be prohibited.
9. Inspections of the structure are required, prior to first use and then at appropriate intervals afterwards, usually weekly. Details of the results should be recorded on an inspection form.
10. Attention is needed in the erection and use of some commercial support sections, such as 'J-frames', because they may not be able to provide adequate platform support or sustain required platform widths and protective measures.

Scaffold towers

Scaffold towers are available commercially in forms comparatively easy to construct. They may also be erected from traditional steel tubing and couplers. In either form, competent and trained personnel are required to ensure that all necessary components are present and in the right place. Many accidents have occurred because of poor erection standards; a further common cause is overturning.

The key points to be observed in the safe use of scaffold towers are:

1. Erection should be in accordance with the manufacturer's or supplier's recommendations.
2. Erection, alteration and dismantling should be carried out by experienced, competent persons.
3. Towers should be stood on a firm level base, with wheel castors locked if present.
4. Scaffold equipment should be in good condition, free from patent defects including bent or twisted sections, and properly maintained.
5. The structure should be braced in all planes to distribute loads correctly and prevent twisting and collapse.
6. The ratio of the minimum base dimension to the height of the working platform should not exceed 1:3 in external use, and 1:3.5 in internal use, unless the tower is secured to another permanent structure at all times. Base ratios can be increased by the use of outriggers, but these should be fully extended and capable of taking loads imposed at all times.
7. Free-standing towers should not be used above 9.75m unless tied. The maximum height to the upper working platform when tied should not exceed 12m.
8. A safe means of access should be provided on the narrowest side of the tower. This can be by vertical ladder attached internally, by internal stairways, or by ladder sections designed to form part of the frame members. It is not acceptable to climb frame members not designed for the purpose.
9. Trapdoors should be provided in working platforms where internal access is provided.
10. Platforms should be properly supported and fully boarded.
11. Guardrails, toeboards and other appropriate means should be provided to prevent falls of workers and/or materials.

12. Mobile scaffold towers should never be moved while people are still on the platform. This is a significant cause of accidents.

13. Ladders or stepladders should not be placed on the tower platform to gain extra height for working.

Suspended access (cradles)

A **suspended access system** includes a working platform or cradle, equipped with the means of raising or lowering when suspended from a roof rig.

The key points to be observed in the safe installation and use of this equipment are:

1. It should be capable of taking the loads likely to be imposed on it.
2. Experienced erectors only should be used for the installation.
3. Supervisors and operators should be trained in the safe use of the equipment, and in emergency procedures.
4. Inspections and maintenance are to be carried out regularly.
5. Suspension arrangements should be installed as designed and calculated.
6. All safety equipment, including brakes and stops, should be operational.
7. The marked safe working load must not be exceeded and wind effects should also be considered.
8. Platforms should be free from obstruction and fitted with edge protection.
9. The electrical supply is not to be capable of inadvertent isolation and should be properly maintained.
10. Adverse weather conditions should be defined so that supervisors and operators know what is not considered acceptable.
11. All defects noted are to be reported and rectified before further use of the equipment.
12. Safe access is required for the operators and unauthorised access is to be prevented.
13. Necessary protective measures for those working below as well as the public should be in place before work begins.

Personal suspension equipment (chairs and abseiling equipment)

A **chair** is a seating arrangement provided with a means of raising or lowering with a suspension system. This should only be used for very short duration work, or in positions where access by other means is impossible.

Abseiling equipment is used by specialists to gain access where the duration of work is likely to be very short indeed and the nature of the work lends itself to this approach.

The key points to be observed in using personal suspension equipment are:

1. The equipment must be suitable and of sufficient strength for the purpose it is to be used for, and for the loads which are anticipated. A specific risk assessment should be made in every case.
2. The equipment must be securely attached to plant or a structure strong and stable enough for the circumstances.
3. Suitable and sufficient steps must be taken to prevent falls or slips from the equipment.
4. The equipment must be so installed or attached as to prevent uncontrolled movement.
5. A back-up safety line should always be used, in case the main suspension line or attachments fail.

Mast-elevated work platforms

Generally, this equipment consists of three elements:
- Mast(s) or tower(s) which support(s) a platform or cage
- A platform capable of supporting persons and/or equipment
- A chassis supporting the tower or mast

The key points to be observed in the erection and use of this equipment are:
1. Only trained personnel should erect, operate or dismantle the equipment.

WORKING AT HEIGHT

2. The manufacturer's instructions on inspection, maintenance and servicing should be followed.

3. Firm, level surfaces should be provided, and outriggers are to be extended before use or testing, if provided.

4. Repairs and adjustments should only be carried out by qualified people.

5. The safe working load of the equipment should be clearly marked on it, be readily visible to the operator, and never be exceeded.

6. Raising and lowering sequences should only be initiated if adequate clearance is available.

7. The platform should be protected with edge guardrails and toeboards, and provided with adequate means of access.

8. Emergency systems should only be used for that purpose and not for operational reasons.

9. Unauthorised access into the work area should be prevented using ground barriers.

10. Contact with overhead power cables should be prevented by preliminary site inspection and by not approaching closer than a given distance. Where necessary, this distance can be obtained from the power supply company concerned.

Power-operated mobile work platforms

A wide variety of equipment falls into this category, ranging from small, mobile tower structures with self-elevating facilities to large, vehicle-mounted, hydraulically-operated platforms.

The key points to be observed in their use are:

1. Operator controls should be at the platform level, with override at ground level for emergencies.

2. There should be a levelling device fitted to the chassis to ensure verticality in use.

3. Supervision should prevent use of the equipment during adverse weather conditions.

4. Outriggers, where provided for increased stability, should be fully extended and locked into position before the equipment is used/raised, in accordance with the manufacturer's instructions. The wheels may also require locking.

5. Materials and/or persons should not be transferred to and from the platform while in the raised position.

6. Training is required for operators before they are allowed to use the equipment in field conditions unsupervised.

7. Operators and others on the platform should wear safety harnesses secured to the inside of the platform cage.

8. When fitted, scissor mechanisms require the provision of adequate fixed guards, so as to prevent trapping of the operator or others during raising or lowering. (In some models, sensors are installed to limit operation of the mechanism should trapping occur.)

9. The equipment requires regular inspection, servicing, maintenance and testing in accordance with the manufacturer's instructions.

REVISION

Access equipment should be selected after consideration of:

- The work to be done
- The duration of the work
- The location of the work
- Means of access to the work area
- The environment
- The people who will do the work
- The people who will erect the access equipment
- Available technical specifications and information
- Loading requirements

Ten common causes of accidents using access equipment:

- Design fault
- Not using safer alternative
- Unsound base support
- Structural failure
- Instability

International Principles of Health and Safety at Work | Allan St John Holt

- Overreaching
- Contact with obstructions and energy sources
- Untrained personnel
- Poor maintenance
- Incorrect erection and/or use

TRANSPORT SAFETY

Introduction

For the purposes of this Section, any piece of mobile equipment that moves within the workplace is classed as a 'vehicle', including cars, trucks and self-propelled machinery. The safe operation of vehicles results from planning and activity, not chance. In the majority of vehicle accidents, the principal factors are driver failure and vehicle failure, both of which can be controlled. A relatively small proportion of these accidents is due to vehicle mechanical failure. A high proportion of them occurs to those who have no direct control of vehicles, chiefly pedestrians.

Causes of transport accidents

Transport accidents occur because of:
- Contact – with structures or services
- Overturning – through incorrect loading, speeding or surface conditions
- Collision – with other vehicles or pedestrians
- Impact – materials falling or the vehicle overturning onto the operator
- Entanglement – in dangerous parts of machinery or controls
- Explosion – when charging batteries or inflating tyres
- Operator/supervisor error – through inadequate training or experience

Preventing transport accidents

These accidents are preventable by good management, involving the use of a planned approach:
- Traffic control in the workplace – includes making decisions on needs, priorities, rights of way, and the separation of pedestrian and motor traffic
- Maintenance procedures – safety, economy and efficiency all benefit from periodic vehicle checks and inspections, in addition to local or national requirements of regulations or codes
- Driver selection, training, certification and supervision – the use of vehicles by unauthorised persons must be prevented. Authorisation should depend on the individual's progress through a training programme on the specific type(s) of vehicle to be driven and selection of the individual for the task
- Control of visiting drivers – any local rules must be communicated to visiting drivers, either in writing, as a contract condition, or by the provision of suitable traffic safety signs or markers
- Accident investigation – including reporting system, subsequent analysis of reports and corrective action follow-up

Traffic control in the workplace

The key to traffic control lies in planning safe routes, wide enough for necessary movements. Adequate clearance should be provided for safe movement of vehicles, identifying overhead or floor-level obstructions. Traffic should be kept away from vulnerable structures such as tanks and pipes. Vehicles and pedestrians should be separated where practicable, with warning lights and/or signs displayed. Signs will also be needed where there are unavoidable height limitations.

The basic principle is to keep pedestrians away from vehicles by providing separate routes where practicable. Barriers at building entrances and exits, and corners of buildings, should be considered. Safe pedestrian crossing places should be clearly marked and fitted with mirrors to improve visibility into blind areas. Indoor routes should be clearly marked on the floor to alert pedestrians.

Vehicle speeds should be controlled with speed limits, backed where necessary with speed ramps. Movements should be properly supervised when reversing or where access is difficult or blind, using recognised signals. Access routes and parking areas should be lit where practicable, especially where pedestrians and vehicles share routes.

Loading and unloading of vehicles should take place

82

in designated areas without obstruction to other traffic. Vehicles not in use or broken down should be left where obstruction is minimised. Vehicle loads must be both stable and secure. Drivers should be adequately protected against falling objects or rollover. Keys should be removed from vehicles when not in use, to immobilise and guard against theft or misuse. Parking areas should be located in safe places so that drivers leaving vehicles are not put at risk of crossing dangerous work areas.

The vehicles should be checked to ensure that dangerous parts of machinery are guarded, and that there is safe means of access and egress to driving positions. Reminders of the correct means of access, and the need to wear appropriate clothing, should be part of the training of drivers and maintenance staff.

Maintenance procedures

Maintenance of the workplace itself is an important aspect of transport safety. Spilled or dropped loads and other loose items should be removed from traffic routes as soon as possible. The road surface must be kept in good condition, with worn markings renewed and pot-holes removed. Signs and lighting also need maintenance.

Planned maintenance procedures for vehicles prevent accidents and delays due to mechanical failures, minimise repair downtime, and prevent excessive wear and breakdown. Drivers and operators are usually the first to notice when defects develop, and should check their vehicles against a basic checklist before work starts. Vehicle checklists should cover the following items:

- Brakes
- Headlights
- Stoplights and indicators
- Tyres
- Screens and wipers
- Steering wheel
- Glass
- Horn
- Mirrors
- Instruments

- Exhaust system
- Emergency equipment
- Ignition problems
- Connecting cables

In addition to other health and safety considerations, **vehicle repair** requires attention to the following:

Brakes must be applied and wheels chocked, especially before entry under vehicle bodies. Raised bodies must be propped unless fitted with proprietary devices for stability in the raised position. Axle stands must be used in conjunction with jacks; hydraulic jacks should not be relied on alone. When charging batteries, the risk of explosion or burns should be eliminated. Precautions are also required to prevent explosion risks when draining, repairing or carrying out hot work near fuel tanks. Tyre cages should be provided for inflating vehicle tyres. Steps must be taken to eliminate exposure to dangerous dusts and fumes, eg from operating internal combustion engines in confined areas. Only trained personnel should carry out maintenance work.

Driver selection, training and supervision

Selection will require an evaluation of age, experience, driving record, maturity and attitude. People who drive safely also have other qualities such as a courteous manner and the ability to get on well with others. These can be used to pick potential safe drivers. Local or national driver qualification requirements must also be observed; a usual requirement for heavy good vehicles is that drivers must be aged 21 or over.

Training of drivers may be for remedial, refresher or special reasons in addition to basic instruction for drivers unfamiliar with the vehicle to be driven. Generally, driver training courses should cover applicable local and national driving rules, company driving rules, what to do in the event of an accident to comply with local, national and company requirements, and defensive driving techniques. The risk assessment should give guidance on the amount and level of training that will be needed. Drivers'

TRANSPORT SAFETY

experience and training should be checked and verified so that training can supplement and fill any gaps. Refresher training should be planned. A standard training package for new employees should include:

- Job information, including route layout and how to report faults or incidents
- Information specific to the vehicle, speed limits and loading areas, and dangers of unsafe working practices
- Information on the management structure and supervision given, including penalties likely to be imposed for failure to comply with safe working practices

Supervision must ensure that all vehicle drivers engage in safe practices. They should be aware of their drivers' safety performance and how this compares with other company areas and equivalent industry figures. They will also be responsible for the investigation and recording of accidents.

Control of visiting drivers

For any workplace, visitors are unlikely to be familiar with work practices, layout and local rules, and will require to have this information presented to them in an appropriate way. This can be done by publication of written material, or by positioning appropriate signs. Control of visitors must be exercised, since if the breaking of local rules is condoned, this will have a negative effect on attitudes of those who observe them being broken.

Transport accident investigation

In addition to the requirements of local or national laws and codes concerning reporting and recording of accidents, feedback of information gained from investigations is very useful. Information of this kind will have consequences for the driver training programme, trigger discussions with the persons involved, add to company experience and records, and provide a means of assessing each driver.

Each driver should be required to complete a standard report form for each accident involving a vehicle. Personal investigation by supervisory staff should also be made, where possible, to verify the driver's data and obtain any necessary extra information.

A record should be maintained for each driver, as well as for each vehicle. Driver records can form the basis for awards, and reviews of them will identify repetitions of inappropriate behaviour which may be rectified by further training.

Carrying hazardous loads

Manufacturers of hazardous substances should have final responsibility for safety, in the sense that they are likely to have most knowledge of the specific properties of the substances they make, and to be best able to recommend safe handling and emergency procedures. This information should be provided in data sheets (at least) and be made available to all concerned, including drivers and dispatch points.

There are many codes and regulations covering this subject. They contain specific, detailed requirements about containers and packaging, and their marking. They also have requirements on identifying substances by their properties, including flammability, and ways in which information has to be given to those handling and carrying the loads, and to the public. This is done in a number of ways, including by the display of special signs on the packaging and on the vehicle. Requirements differ slightly between countries, and there are also international standards; reference to these and to national codes and regulations is essential if loads are carried between countries.

The instruction and training of drivers is also covered extensively by codes and regulations. The provisions usually include the need to alert emergency services in the event of accidents, use of any emergency equipment required to be carried on the vehicle, and the steps which can be taken safely following an accident to minimise the consequences before the arrival of emergency services. The driver should also be able to give these services the information they need to

FIGURE 1: Sample basic summary checklist – Transport safety

PREMISES ADDRESS:	
COMPLETION BY:	
DATE:	

No		YES	NO	COMMENTS
	Workplace			
1.	Are vehicle traffic routes suitable for the traffic that uses them? (Surfaces well maintained? Wide enough? One-way system?)			
2.	Are the traffic routes appropriate to keep pedestrians and vehicles apart? (Crossing points, barriers in place? Are people using them?)			
3.	Are all necessary safety features in place? (Mirrors, road markings, signs?)			
	Vehicles			
4.	Are the vehicles safe and suitable for their intended use? (Lights, horns, guards, rollover protection, good cab access/egress?)			
5.	Is a preventive maintenance programme in place for each vehicle? (Vehicle log, driver's pre-use checks?)			
	Drivers			
6.	Is there a procedure for selection of new drivers? (Experience check, test?)			
7.	Is there an active training programme for drivers, containing specific information on job hazards and the workplace?			
8.	Is there a refresher training programme for drivers?			
9.	Is there adequate supervision of drivers during their work? (Speeding, stress, safe practices observed?)			
	High risk transport tasks			
10.	Has attention been given to reversing as an issue in the premises? (Scope for improvement? All vehicles left braked and secured?)			
11.	Are parking facilities appropriate for work and private vehicles? (Location, condition, lighting, and are they actually used?)			
12.	Are vehicles ever loaded beyond their capacity? (System in place for checks on this?)			
13.	Are loading and unloading operations carried out safely, with loads secured as necessary?			
14.	Are tipping operations carried out safely? (Checks on this? Power lines, pipework, people put at risk?)			
15.	Are sheeting and unsheeting operations carried out safely? (Risk assessment, checks on this?)			
16.	Is there a system in place which avoids the need for anyone to climb on a vehicle or load?			

TRANSPORT SAFETY

know about the load, including methods of treating spillages and/or fire. Special attention is required to the selection of mature drivers for hazardous loads, with appropriate skills and abilities.

REVISION

Transport accidents occur through:

- Contact
- Overturning
- Collision
- Impact
- Entanglement
- Explosion
- Operator/supervisor error
- Poor maintenance

The **five** main elements of transport safety are:

- Driver selection, instruction and supervision
- Control of visiting drivers
- Workplace traffic control and its general condition
- Accident investigation
- Preventive maintenance and vehicle repair

CLASSIFICATION OF DANGEROUS SUBSTANCES

Introduction

Dangerous substances can be categorised in many ways. When discussing or describing them in health and safety terms, they are categorised according to the type of harm they can cause. Many can fall into more than one category. Some can cause harm after a single exposure or incident, others may have only long-term effects on the body following repeated exposure.

Classification

Generally, substances can be placed into one or more of the following broad categories:

Explosive or flammable – dangerous because of their potential to release energy rapidly, or because the product(s) of the explosion or combustion are harmful in other ways. Examples of these are organic solvents.

Harmful – substances which, if inhaled, ingested or enter the body through the skin, present a limited risk to health.

Irritants – adversely affect the skin or respiratory tract, eg acrylates. Some people overreact to irritants like isocyanates, which are sensitisers and can cause allergic reactions.

Corrosives – substances which will attack chemically either materials or people, eg strong acids and bases.

Toxics – substances which prevent or interfere with bodily functions in a variety of ways. They may overload organs such as the liver or kidneys. Examples are chlorinated solvents and heavy metals (such as lead).

Carcinogens, mutagens and teratogens – prevent the correct development and growth of body cells. Carcinogens cause or promote the development of unwanted cells as cancer. Teratogens cause abnormal development of the human embryo, leading to stillbirth or birth defects. Mutagens alter cell development and cause changes in future generations.

Agents of annoxia – vapours or gases which reduce the oxygen available in the air, or prevent the body using it effectively. Carbon dioxide, carbon monoxide and hydrogen cyanide are examples.

Narcotics – produce dependency, and act as depressors of brain functions. Organic solvents are common narcotics.

Oxidising – a substance which gives rise to an exothermic reaction (gives off heat) when in contact with other substances, particularly flammable ones.

Labelling

In most jurisdictions, substances with potential for harm are required to be safely packaged and labelled according to various codes of practice and regulations. These involve the use of descriptive labels showing the hazard in the form of pictograms, accompanied by required descriptive phrases which convey necessary information in a shortened form. The labels also carry the details of the manufacturer. In all cases, management should not be content to rely on the packaging to provide sufficient information to make decisions about safe storage, use, handling, transportation and disposal of the substance. The data sheet widely required to be supplied with the substance will provide the necessary information for these purposes.

REVISION

Substances are categorised according to the type of harm they can cause.

Nine classifications:
- Explosive/flammable
- Harmful
- Irritant
- Corrosive
- Toxic
- Carcinogens/mutagens/teratogens
- Agents of anoxia
- Narcotic
- Oxidising

CHEMICAL AND BIOLOGICAL SAFETY

Introduction

Chemical and biological incidents at work can affect many people including operators, nearby workers, others on site and members of the public. Systems for the control and safe use of chemicals, substances and biological agents are crucial to the safe operation of any workplace which handles, uses, stores, transports or disposes of them, regardless of the quantity involved. Planning for safety requires the setting out of broad principles which can then be translated into specific detail at the workplace.

Planning for chemical safety

The way in which we plan for chemical safety is based on the principles for the control of all types of risk, which will be familiar to you by the time you complete working through this book. Section 3 of Part 1 discusses the principles of risk assessment, which are applicable to chemical safety. The stages of control include risk assessment as the basis for control measures. For ease of reference, the six stages of control are summarised here:

- Identification of the hazard to be controlled
- Assessment of the risk
- Control of the risk
- Training of staff
- Monitoring the effectiveness of the strategy
- Necessary record-keeping

Identification of the hazard – In the present case, we already know the hazard, as 'chemical safety' is the objective. '**Hazard**' means the inherent property or ability of something to cause harm – it is not the same as '**risk**', which is the likelihood of the harm occurring in given circumstances. The extent of the hazard posed by a chemical or substance can be established by the use of information – from the supplier, the manufacturer, from records, historical knowledge and other sources of information. Some substances are labelled on their containers; others, such as reaction products, are not brought into the workplace from outside, have no containers, and must be identified and checked against reference material.

Assessment of the risks – The risks presented by a chemical or substance will not be dependent only on its physical and chemical properties, but will also be a function of the way it is used, where it is used, and how it may be misused or mishandled. Assessment of these factors is essential in determining local risk at a particular location.

Controlling the risks – This can be achieved by elimination of the hazardous substance entirely, by its substitution with a less hazardous alternative, mechanical/remote handling, total enclosure, exhaust ventilation, special techniques such as wet methods or use of personal protective equipment. These control techniques may be used in combination, but they are set in order of effectiveness and desirability. There is also the possibility of reducing exposure time and numbers of personnel at risk.

Training of operators – Instruction in the nature of the hazards they face and the degree of risk, associated with the procedures devised to eliminate hazards where possible, and the effective control of the remaining risks, is necessary. Especially, this will ensure that operators do not use their own solutions to problems. In-house procedures involving chemicals are often written down for all to see and understand; where this is done, it is important that the procedures are publicised, available and readable. Language difficulties with minority groups should be resolved and translations provided where necessary.

Monitoring effectiveness – Regular monitoring of the effectiveness of control measures is needed to ensure that change – in work conditions, quality, information and systems – is taken into account and anticipated in procedures. This can include regular monitoring of work practices, sampling of air/process quality and purchasing procedures. Except for workplaces where little change is expected, monitoring and appropriate measuring should take place at regular intervals specified in the procedures. This is especially important where personal protective equipment is relied on as a major method of controlling risks.

Record-keeping – Keeping records helps to ensure

the regular maintenance of plant at prescribed intervals and enhances awareness of change. Medical surveillance of operators may be required by local or national codes and regulations.

Risk control issues

The following topics should be considered and adopted as appropriate to reduce exposure:

Plant design – Chemical processes can be controlled by introducing containment and process control (the safe design of plant processes and the use of automated and/or computer-controlled systems). Plant should not be altered without specific authority and review.

Safe systems of work – These include the use of detailed operating and emergency instructions, permit-to-work systems (especially for maintenance operations), and the installation, use and maintenance of protective equipment.

Transport – Controlled movement of chemicals in containers or vehicles intended for that purpose reduces the likelihood of exposure to operators and third parties. Adequate emergency procedures will be required.

Storage – Chemicals should not be affected by adjacent processes or chemical storage. External storage of chemicals should be the method of choice, as this gives quick dispersion, minimises sources of ignition, and provides secure storage which reduces the risk of damage to containers. Features of storage facilities should include a hard standing, bund retention, adequate separation, adequate access for mechanical handling, contents gauges for fixed tanks, relief valves if required, security of stacking, firefighting facilities, and warning signs in accordance with applicable codes and regulations.

Waste disposal – Adequate steps must be taken to ensure the correct disposal of waste, preventing harm to members of the public and damage to the environment, in accordance with legislative requirements.

Emergency procedures – These must be drawn up for production and storage areas, and for the site as a whole. Emergency services and operatives alike should be briefed on the procedures to be followed, and adequate time must be given for training and rehearsal at regular intervals.

The relative importance of each of these topics will depend on the assessed degree of risk at the workplace.

Biological safety

Pathogenic micro-organisms that could affect health are known as **biological agents**. They can affect people who work with them directly, as in a laboratory environment, or indirectly, as a result of exposure to them during the course of normal work. An example of the latter means of exposure is infection of people who work with animals by micro-organisms that cross the 'species gap'. The diseases that these produce are known as **zoonoses**. They include Weil's disease (leptospirosis), which is caused by bacteria passed from rats via urine, and psittacosis, which is acquired by contact with affected birds. Most infections are relatively mild, but evidence is growing that some long-term health effects may result from them.

Some biological agents produced, liberated or encouraged by work processes can affect the public as well as employees. Examples include legionellosis and hospital-acquired infections (HAI). Legionella bacteria are found in natural water sources, but can become trapped and will multiply rapidly within water systems such as wet cooling towers and hot water systems in buildings. They can cause a number of diseases which resemble pneumonia in their symptoms, including legionnaire's disease.

REVISION

There are **six** stages of control:
- Hazard identification
- Risk assessment
- Risk control

CHEMICAL AND BIOLOGICAL SAFETY

- Staff training
- Monitoring
- Record-keeping

Hazard – the inherent ability to cause harm

Risk – likelihood of harm in particular circumstances

There are **six** topics for control of chemical risk:
- Plant design
- Systems of work
- Transport
- Storage
- Disposal
- Emergencies

Recognised **zoonoses** include:
- Anthrax
- Bovine tuberculosis
- Leptospirosis
- Psittacosis
- Lyme disease
- Rabies

ELECTRICITY AND ELECTRICAL EQUIPMENT

Introduction

The ratio of fatalities to injuries is higher for electrical accidents than for most other categories of injury – if an electrical accident occurs, the chances of a fatality are about one in 30 to 40. Despite the beliefs of some, including some electricians, the human body does not develop tolerance to electric shock.

The consequences of contact with electricity are: electric shock, where the injury results from the flow of electricity through the body's nerves, muscles and organs and causes abnormal function to occur (eg the heart stops); electrical burns resulting from the heating effect of the current which burns body tissue; and electrical fires caused by overheating or arcing apparatus in contact with a fuel (see the next Section).

Causes of electrical failures

Failures and interruption of electrical supply are most commonly caused by:

- Damaged insulation
- Inadequate systems of work
- Inadequate overcurrent protection (fuses, circuit breakers)
- Inadequate earthing/grounding
- Carelessness and complacency
- Overheated apparatus
- Earth leakage current
- Loose contacts and connectors
- Inadequate ratings of circuit components
- Unprotected connectors
- Poor maintenance and testing

Preventing electrical failures

These failures can be prevented by regular attention to the following points:

Earthing/grounding – providing a suitable electrode connection to earth through metal enclosure, conduit, frame, etc. Regular inspections and tests of systems should be carried out by a competent person.

System of work – when working with electrical circuits and apparatus, and when switching and locking off the supply. Then, the supply and any apparatus should be checked personally by the worker to verify that it is 'dead'; permit-to-work systems should be used in high-risk situations previously identified. Working on live circuits and apparatus should only be permitted under circumstances which are strictly controlled and justified in each case. Rubber or other non-conducting protective equipment may be required. Barriers and warning notices should be used to ensure that persons not directly involved in the work do not expose themselves to risk. The use of insulated tools and equipment will always be necessary.

Insulation – where work is required near uninsulated parts of circuits. In all circumstances, making the apparatus 'dead' must be considered as a primary aim, and rejected only if the demands of the work make this impracticable. A variety of permanent or temporary insulators may be used, such as cable sheathing and rubber mats.

Fuses – these are strips of metal placed in circuits which melt as a result of overheating in the circuit, effectively cutting off the supply. Different fuses 'melt' at predetermined current flows. A factor in the selection of fuses is that there is a variable and appreciable delay in their action, which may expose those at risk to uninterrupted current for unacceptable periods.

Circuit breakers – detect electromagnetically and automatically any excess current flow and cut off the supply to the circuit.

Residual current devices – detect earth faults and cut off the supply to the circuit.

Competency – only properly trained and suitably experienced people should be employed to install, maintain, test and examine electrical circuits and apparatus.

Static electricity

Electrical charging can occur during the movement of powders and liquids, which can cause sparking, and

ELECTRICITY AND ELECTRICAL EQUIPMENT

this may ignite a dust cloud or a flammable vapour. Less critically, static electricity in other working environments may be a cause of annoyance to workers, and can be a factor in other types of accident where attention has been distracted by static discharge.

Protection against static electricity can be achieved by earthing and not using or installing equipment which can become statically charged (see the next Section). Operators in critical environments should also wear anti-static shoes.

Electrical equipment

Electrical tools used should be selected and operated bearing in mind the following considerations:

Substitution – electrical tools and equipment may be replaced with pneumatic equipment – which have their own dangers.

Switching off circuits and apparatus – this must be readily and safely achievable.

Reducing the voltage – use of the lowest practicable voltage should be practised in every circuit.

Cable and socket protection – should be provided to protect against physical and environmental effects, such as rain, which could have adverse consequences on the integrity of circuits and apparatus.

Plugs and sockets – must be of the correct type and specification, and meet local and national regulations and codes of practice.

Explosive atmospheres – require the careful consideration and selection of equipment for service in dusty or flammable environments. The type of equipment to be used is commonly specified by law.

Maintenance and testing – should be carried out at regular and prescribed intervals by competent and experienced personnel. Fixed equipment and installations should be maintained at regular intervals following the advice of the supplier, manufacturer or designer.

For portable and transportable equipment (operating at more than 50 volts AC or 120 volts DC) a planned maintenance regime appropriate to the risk should be followed. This is because fixed equipment is usually better able to withstand damage, and portable equipment is more likely to receive damage and operate in unfavourable conditions.

There are three levels of preventive maintenance for this equipment:

Visual checks by the user – for visual evidence of damage or faulty repair to connectors, leads and equipment.

Visual checks by an authorised third party – more detailed, including removal of connector covers and checks on fuses. Done at regular set intervals, these should detect misuse, abuse and incorrect selection of equipment.

Inspection and testing by a third party – periodic thorough visual examination by someone other than the normal user of the equipment, includes use of portable appliance tester (PAT) equipment. Appropriate competency is required, wider than for visual-only checks.

Recording of the results and values measured will provide a baseline figure for assessing any subsequent deterioration in performance or quality, and for monitoring the effectiveness of the maintenance programme. Labelling equipment passed as safe with a date for the next test is good practice.

Frequency of maintenance checks depends on a range of factors, including the likelihood and type of potential damage. Frequency can be altered following experience of the maintenance programme. Different pieces of equipment may require different schemes.

The treatment of electric shock

NB: *Advice given in this Section is not intended as a*

ELECTRICITY AND ELECTRICAL EQUIPMENT

substitute for, or an alternative to, attending a recognised first-aid course.

Recognising a casualty

Apart from proximity to a source of electrical energy, casualties may show symptoms of asphyxia and have no discernible pulse. Violent muscular contraction caused by contact with high voltage supplies can throw casualties some way from the original point of contact. In cases of electric shock, breathing and heartbeat can stop together, accounting for the pallid blue tinge to the skin sometimes seen. There may also be burns visible which can indicate contact with electricity.

Breaking the contact

Low voltage supplies, commonly at or below 240 volts, can be switched off at the mains or meter if readily accessible. If not, or if it cannot be found quickly, the supply can be turned off at the plug point or by pulling out the plug. The important point to remember when removing the casualty from the source is not to become a casualty in turn. Dry insulating material such as newspaper or wood can be used to push or pull the casualty clear by wrapping around or pushing at arms and legs near the source. Do not touch the casualty directly.

Higher voltage supplies, such as those found in overhead or underground power lines, produce deep burns and are frequently fatal on contact. It is important not to approach a casualty touching or lying close to one of these lines, until the line has been isolated by the supply authority. Close approach can lead on occasions to electrical arcing. At higher voltage levels, insulating material requires special properties not possessed by anything likely to be close to hand.

Treatment

The order of priority for treatment is:
1. Resuscitation if required.

2. Place in the Recovery Position (see below) if casualty is still unconscious but breathing normally.
3. Treat any burns.
4. Treat for shock.
5. Remove to hospital in all cases where resuscitation was required, or where casualty was unconscious, received burns or developed symptoms of shock; pass to hospital any information on duration of electrical contact.

Resuscitation

Mouth-to-mouth ventilation should be used where a casualty is not breathing and ventilation of the lungs is required to restart breathing reflexes.

Cardiopulmonary resuscitation (CPR) will be needed if the heart has stopped in addition to breathing. Both these techniques require practice; descriptions of them are beyond the scope of this Section but they are taught on first-aid courses and details can also be found in first-aid manuals.

Recovery position

A casualty in this position maintains an open airway and stability of the body is improved. Placing of the casualty into the Recovery Position is not difficult, but a description of the method is beyond the scope of this Section. The position to be achieved is one where the casualty lies on the front and side, with the head supported for comfort and slightly flexed backwards to maintain a clear airway. The uppermost hand is near the face with the arm bent at the elbow to give support, and the uppermost leg is bent at the hip and knee forming a right angle at the knee with the thigh well forward.

Burns treatment

For severe burns likely to be associated with electric shock, it is important to immobilise the burned part, and to cover the burned area with a dry, sterile,

ELECTRICITY AND ELECTRICAL EQUIPMENT

unmedicated dressing or anything similar, and secure with a bandage if available.

The important things **not to do** are:

1. Do not allow clothing to restrict any swelling of the burned part.
2. Do not apply anything to the burn.
3. Do not break blisters or attempt to treat or touch the injured area.
4. Do not remove anything sticking to the burned part.

Giving sips of cold water will help the casualty to replace lost fluid, but give no medication.

Shock treatment

Traumatic shock can prove fatal even when other injuries have been treated. It is a consequence of a reduction in volume of body fluids. The casualty feels faint, sick and possibly thirsty, and has shallow breathing or yawning. The pulse rate may increase but may also become weak and irregular. The skin is pale and cold.

Treatment involves keeping the casualty warm, loosening tight clothing and elevating the legs if possible. Do not give anything by mouth, or apply external heat, or allow the casualty to smoke. Do not move the casualty unless this cannot be avoided.

REVISION

Three results of electrical failure:

- Electric shock
- Electrical burns
- Electrical fires

Ten preventive measures:

- Earthing
- Safe system of work
- Insulation
- Fuses
- Circuit breakers
- Residual current devices
- Competency
- Reduced voltage
- Maintenance
- Isolation

Introduction

The control of the start and spread of fire is an important feature of the prevention of accidents and damage. Fire needs fuel, oxygen and a source of energy to ignite it; these are known as the 'fire elements'. Examples of these are wood, air and heat in the right combination. The ratio of fuel to oxygen is crucial; too much or too little of either will not permit a fire to start. Also, the source of ignition must be above a certain energy level.

There are five main hazards produced by fire: oxygen depletion, flame/heat, smoke, gaseous combustion products and structural failure of buildings.

Classification of fire

There are four main categories of fire, which are based on the fuel and the means of extinction. These are:

Class A – Fires which involve solid materials, predominantly of an organic kind, forming glowing embers. Examples are wood, paper and coal. The extinguishing mode is by cooling and is achieved by the use of water.

Class B – Fires which involve liquids or liquefiable solids; they are further subdivided into:

> **Class B1** – which involve liquids soluble in water, eg methanol. They can be extinguished by carbon dioxide, dry powder, water spray, light water and vaporising liquids.

> **Class B2** – which involve liquids not soluble in water, such as petrol and oil. They can be extinguished by foam, carbon dioxide, dry powder, light water and vaporising liquids.

Class C – Fires which involve gases or liquefied gases (eg methane or butane) resulting from leaks or spillage. Extinguishment can be achieved by using foam or dry powder in conjunction with water to cool any leaking container involved.

Class D – Fires which involve metals such as aluminium or magnesium. Special dry powder extinguishers,

which may contain powdered graphite or talc, are required to fight these. No other extinguisher type should be used.

Electrical fires, which involve the electricity supply to live equipment, can be dealt with by extinguishing mediums such as carbon dioxide, dry powder or vaporising liquids, but not water. Electricity is a cause of fire, not a category of fire. Electrical fires have been removed from the traditional 'categories' of fire for this reason.

Knowledge of the correct type of extinguisher to use, or install, in areas at particular risk is essential. Halon-based extinguishers should be phased out because of their potential for damage to the environment.

Fire protection

There are three strategies for protecting against and dealing with fire:

Structural design precautions – providing protection through insulation, integrity and stability permitting people to escape, eg compartmentalisation, smoke control, unobstructed means of escape.

Fire detectors and alarms – activated by sensing heat, flame, smoke or flammable gas, eg heat detectors, radiation detectors, smoke detectors.

Firefighting – with portable extinguishers or fixed firefighting equipment (manually or automatically operated).

Structural and design precautions

Controlling the likelihood of fire occurring can be achieved by the removal of one of the fire elements by:

a) **Removing sources of ignition** – Heat is the most common source of ignition, and can result from:

> ● friction – parts of a machine, which require proper lubrication

FIRE

- hot surfaces – machine panels, which can be cooled by design, insulation or maintenance
- electricity – arcing or heat transfer, removed by selection or design of appropriate electrical protection
- static electricity – through relative motion and/or separation of two different materials, prevented by providing an earth path, humid atmosphere, high voltage device or ion exchange
- smoking – spent smoking materials, prevented by restricting the activity or confining it to defined areas

Heat transfer can be by radiation, conduction or convection.

b) **Controlling the fuel** – Supply of materials should be kept to a minimum during work or in storage areas. The main fuel sources are:

- waste, debris and spillage
- gases and vaporising liquids
- flammable liquids
- flammable compressed gases and liquefied gases
- liquid sprays
- dusts

Means of fire detection and alarms

Fire, or flammable atmospheres, can be detected in the following ways:

Heat detection – sensors operate by the melting of a metal (fusion detectors) or expansion of a solid, liquid or gas (thermal expansion detectors).

Radiation detection – photoelectric cells detect the emission of infrared/ultraviolet radiation from the fire.

Smoke detection – using ionising radiations, light scatter (smoke scatters a beam of light), or obscuration (smoke entering a detector prevents light from reaching a photoelectric cell).

Flammable gas detection – measures the amount of flammable gas in the atmosphere and compares the value with a reference value.

Fire alarms must make a distinctive sound, audible in all parts of the workplace. The meaning of the alarm sound must be understood by all. They may be manually or automatically operated.

Firefighting

Fires can be extinguished by suppression or removal of one of the three fire elements. This can be done by fuel starvation, by preventing fuel flow or removing its source, and by containment. For example, covering a fire will prevent oxygen from reaching fuel, and cooling with water removes a primary source of ignition. Interference with the combustion process can also be done as a chemical process. Selection of the appropriate type of extinguishing agent depends on knowledge of the likely source and composition of the fire.

A fire plan should be available and practised regularly in even the smallest premises. Such a plan will be of value to professional firefighters who need to know the location of flammable and hazardous material in premises. The associated evacuation procedure should also be practised at intervals.

Fire extinguishers

The selection of appropriate extinguishing media has been discussed above. All portable fire extinguishers and hose reels should be inspected regularly for signs of damage or obstruction which might affect their operation, and also to make sure that extinguishers have not been discharged or operated. Their useful life is about 20 years. They should receive an annual service, and extended service every five years.

Signs and training

Signs should be provided to identify courses of action to be taken, means of escape and location of firefighting equipment. Training should be given in the use of systems and equipment provided, and to minimise undesirable or apparently illogical behaviour.

Means of escape in case of fire

The purpose of a means of escape is to enable people confronted by fire to proceed in the opposite direction to an exit away from the fire, through a storey exit, a protected staircase and/or a final exit to ground level in open air away from the building. Any means of escape must not rely on rescue facilities from the fire service.

Means of escape in buildings other than those with only a ground floor generally consist of three distinct areas. These are:

- Any point on a floor to a staircase
- The route down a staircase
- The route from the foot of the staircase to the open air, clear of the building

Essentially, there are two physical areas associated with means of escape:

- The area in which people escaping from a fire are at some risk (the unprotected zone)
- Areas where risk is reduced to an acceptable minimum (protected zones). Protected zones at an exit must be fully protected, using walls or partitions which have a fire-resisting capability

Emergency escape lighting may be needed in areas without daylight or which are used at night. It should:

- Indicate the escape route clearly
- Provide illumination along escape routes
- Ensure that fire alarm call points and firefighting equipment can be located

Determining the means of escape

Types of means of escape will be determined by:

- Occupancy characteristics – numbers, physical capability of users

- Building uses – residential, commercial, manufacturing, entertainment, etc
- Construction characteristics of the building
- Evacuation times
- Occupant movements

Travel distance

This is a technical term used in fire safety, and is the greatest allowable distance which has to be travelled from the fire to reach the beginning of a protected zone of a means of escape or final exit. This distance must be limited, although it will vary according to the fire risk.

Protected lobbies and staircases

As parts of the protected zone, these must be of fire-resisting capability. Doors must be self-closing. The objective is to ensure that people entering lobbies and staircases on any floor are to be able to remain within their safe confines until reaching the ground. Such protection serves the purposes of preventing smoke and heat from obstructing the staircase so making it unsuitable for escape purposes, and of preventing a fire from spreading into a staircase from one storey and passing to another.

Staircases should be protected, usually by a ventilated lobby. Staircases should:

- Be continuous
- Have risers and treads of dimensions specified in standards
- Be ventilated
- Have any internal glazing and spaces underneath able to resist fire
- Be fitted with handrails on both sides

Lifts and escalators

Lifts and escalators must be disregarded as potential means of escape. Lifts have limited capacity, may be delayed in arriving and have potential for mechanical failure. Escalators have restricted width, and the stair

FIRE

pitch when not in operation may lead to possible injury, congestion and undesirable behaviour. Both normally require an electrical supply which may terminate at any time.

Width and capacity of escape routes

There should be no risk of overcrowding, delay or formation of 'bottlenecks' in the event of mass evacuation. Escape routes should be at least 1m wide, and 1.2m if wheelchair access is required. Protected zones must not contain stores, electrical equipment, portable heaters or other items that could compromise protection.

Fire doors

These have the main functions of preserving the safe means of escape by retarding the passage of fire (so they must be fire-resistant) and retarding the spread of smoke and hot gases in the initial stages of a fire.

Final exit doors

General principles of design and function apply to all means of escape final exit doors, which may be modified in particular cases. The operating principles are that these doors must:

a) Open in the direction of escape
b) Preferably not open onto steps
c) Not be revolving doors
d) Be capable of being opened at any time while the building is occupied, preferably without using keys
e) Be protected from fires in the basement or in adjacent buildings
f) Be of adequate width
g) Be provided with adequate dispersal space

Other means of exit

Means of escape via roof – this is generally unacceptable, but if it must be used, then it must be protected from smoke, fire and falls. A safe means of access must be provided to the ground.

High level access – across roof or other areas at height to protected means of escape. If required to be a means of escape, it must be protected against fire, be clearly defined and protected against falls.

Ramps – ramps may be used if they have a non-slip surface, a uniform pitch, do not exceed a slope of 1:10 and are provided with handrails.

External fire escapes – these are not desirable, as they are subject to weather conditions, such as ice and snow, which make them potentially dangerous. However, they are sometimes necessary. They must be protected against fire, and windows adjacent to them must be fire-resistant and not open outwards so as to obstruct passage down the fire escape. It is obviously important that they can be reached easily, and not sited behind or beyond significant obstructions to passage.

Action to be taken in the event of fire

In the presence of fire, the urge to get away is a natural reaction. Information about the action to take, and practice in that action (where possible), is essential to ensure the optimum response in the event of fire. This should be contained in an emergency plan for the premises.

Notices to employees and others

Copies of notices giving simple guidance on what to do in the event of fire should be displayed in all workplaces and premises where persons could be at risk from fire. The details of each notice, which may be written as a safety sign, will vary and depend on the layout, fire risk and circumstances likely to be encountered. For this reason, they should be specially written. Diagrams of layouts showing the means of escape in each case will be helpful, especially where people are likely to be unfamiliar with the layout of the structure.

In drafting notices, attention should be paid to the needs of those who are infrequent visitors to the premises and who may have had no need or opportunity to practise any fire drill there. Instructions in the notice should, therefore, be straightforward and simple to understand. They may need to be given in translated form if speakers of a number of languages are likely to be present in the building. This will be the case in hotels, for example.

Notices should explain simply what to do if a fire is discovered, or if the fire alarm is sounded. In the latter case, the actual sound made by the fire alarm should be explained if there is any possibility of confusion.

Notice contents

The displayed notices should cover the following points:
1. Identification of fire alarm sound.
2. What to do when the alarm is sounded (eg close windows, switch off appropriate equipment, leave the room, close doors behind, follow signs, report to assembly point at specified location, do not re-enter building until advised).
3. What do if a fire is discovered (eg how to raise the alarm, what fires may be tackled by staff, evacuation procedure previously described).

Fire risk assessment

A fire risk assessment should be carried out for every workplace, regardless of the existence of any approval or certification which may have been given. It is a practical exercise, requiring a tour to verify its completeness and accuracy. The purposes of the assessment are:

- To identify the extent of the fire risk
- To assess the likelihood of a fire occurring
- To identify any additional precautions that

may be needed, or control systems that do not function adequately

The approach to risk assessment discussed in Part 1 can be used as an assessment format:
1. Identify potential fire hazards.
2. Decide who might be harmed or at significant risk in the event of a fire, and identify their location.
3. Evaluate the levels of risk from each hazard, and decide whether existing precautions are adequate – or whether the hazard can be removed or controlled more effectively.
4. Record the findings and advise employees of the results, and prepare or revise emergency plan.
5. Review the assessment as necessary, as conditions change and at regular intervals in any case.

There are also checklists and formats available commercially. The reader's attention is drawn particularly to the UK Home Office booklet *Fire Safety: An Employer's Guide* (ISBN 0 11 341229 0), which is a mine of information. This publication was used to derive the assessment format and checklists which follow this Section.

The use of a simple code can be convenient to describe the extent of compliance, the condition or the degree of control. The following gives an easily-understood picture:

CODE	DEFINITION
A Fully satisfactory	Meets all requirements, does not require improvement
B Adequate	Some improvement possible
C Less than adequate	Significant improvement required, action must be taken
D Poor	Action is required urgently to improve the condition
N/A Not applicable	Condition or circumstances not present or applicable

FIRE

REVISION

Three fire elements:
- Fuel
- Oxygen
- Ignition

Four classes of fire:
- Class A – wood, paper
- Class B – liquid
- Class C – gases
- Class D – metals
  (but **not** electrical fires, extinguishable by all mediums except water)

Three protection strategies:
- Structural design precautions
- Fire detectors and alarms
- Firefighting

Five fire hazards:
- Oxygen depletion
- Flame/heat
- Smoke
- Gaseous combustion products
- Structural failure

TABLE 1: Reducing sources of ignition

POTENTIAL PROBLEMS	POSSIBLE CORRECTIVE ACTIONS
Unnecessary sources of heat in the workplace	Remove Replace with safer alternative
Build-up of static electricity	Earthing, electrician to survey and advise Increase numbers of broad-leafed plants, spray for carpets
Fuses and circuit breakers not suitable or of incorrect rating	Electrician to advise on appropriate protection for the system
Faulty or overloaded electrical or mechanical equipment	PAT testing system required Maintenance system required
Machinery or equipment with risk of fire or explosion	Remove Replace with better design to minimise risk
Naked flame or radiant heaters in use	Remove Replace with fixed convector heaters or central heating system
Ducts and flues not cleaned, especially kitchen areas	Maintenance system needs review
Metal/metal impact	Consider spark-free tools containing beryllium compounds
Arson, vandalism	Seek advice from police, fire authority Protection of stored materials Prompt and efficient waste disposal Ban on burning of rubbish
Equipment not left in a safe condition after use	Identify relevant equipment, provide training to users and inspection at end of work
Maintenance workers and others carrying out 'hot' work – eg welding and flame-cutting	Permit-to-work system required
Smoking on the premises	Safe smoking policy in designated areas, prohibiting it elsewhere
Matches and lighters allowed in high-risk areas	Enforce prohibition
Smouldering material	Check work areas before leaving

Allan St John Holt | International Principles of Health and Safety at Work

FIRE

TABLE 2: Reducing potential fuel sources

POTENTIAL PROBLEMS	POSSIBLE CORRECTIVE ACTIONS
Accumulated waste materials	Store flammable wastes and rubbish safely Improve housekeeping standards
Presence of flammable materials and substances	Remove, or reduce quantities to the minimum requirement for the business Replace with less flammable alternatives Review arrangements for use, handling, storage, transport
Storage of flammables	Ensure adequate separation distances Store in fire-resisting stores Minimum work-room quantities
Flammable wall and ceiling linings	Remove, cover or treat to reduce rate of flame spread
Furniture with damaged upholstery	Replace or repair where the foam lining is exposed
Workplace construction and materials	Improve fire resistance of the structure
Arson and vandalism	Make storage areas secure

TABLE 3: Reducing sources of oxygen

POTENTIAL PROBLEMS	POSSIBLE CORRECTIVE ACTIONS
Oxidising materials	Store away from heat sources and flammable materials Mark clearly
Oxygen cylinders	Control their use and storage, arranging for regular leakage checks Check that adequate ventilation is provided, measure and benchmark
Doors, openings and windows	Keep closed all those not required for ventilation, especially outside working hours
Ventilation systems	Shut down non-essential systems

TABLE 4: Detecting and warning about fire

POTENTIAL PROBLEMS	POSSIBLE CORRECTIVE ACTIONS
Means of giving warning cannot be heard throughout premises when initiated from a single point	Review means of giving warning Regular maintenance
Means of detection not quick enough to allow all occupants to escape?	Review type of detection and equipment
Emergency plan	Fire detection and warning arrangements should be detailed in the emergency plan for the premises
Lack of knowledge of how the fire warning system works	Instruct employees – how to operate it, respond to it Put instructions in writing
Power supply for detection and warning system	Back-up supply should be provided for electrical systems

TABLE 5: Safe means of escape

POTENTIAL PROBLEMS	POSSIBLE CORRECTIVE ACTIONS
Arrangements not included in the emergency plan (Recently approved – Building Regulations, licence or fire certificate)	Review the emergency plan (Existing arrangements will be deemed to be satisfactory unless circumstances have changed since inspected)
Length of time taken for all occupants to escape to a place of safety following detection of a fire	Everyone should reach a place of relative safety within the time available for an escape, including their reaction time Carry out practice drill to confirm times
Exits – Not enough, not in the right place Exits – type and size not suitable, eg wheelchair width Fire could affect all available exits	750mm doorway is suitable for up to 40 people per minute; 1000mm doorway for up to 80 people per minute Assume largest exit doorway may not be available for use; remaining should be enough for expected evacuation use
Escape routes not easily identifiable, free from obstruction, adequately illuminated	Review safety signs and markings Review escape routes for presence of prohibited items Doors must open in the direction of travel where near foot of a stairway or where more than 50 people may have to use them Any securing device needs explanatory notice Review emergency lighting
Employees not trained in using the means of escape	Review safety training arrangements
No instructions for employees about the means of escape	Review need for training and drill Consider preparing a diagram to show the routes of escape

FIRE

TABLE 6: Means of putting out a fire

POTENTIAL PROBLEMS	POSSIBLE CORRECTIVE ACTIONS
Extinguishers (including hose reels) not big enough or wrong type for the foreseen fire risk	Review provision of extinguishers
Not enough extinguishers	Increase number of extinguishers
Extinguishers not accessible, not close to the fire	Relocate or increase numbers of extinguishers
Locations of extinguishers are not obvious	Indicate their position using correct signs
Those likely to use extinguishers have not been trained to do so	Provide adequate instruction and training
Use of firefighting equipment not covered in emergency plan	Revise emergency plan

TABLE 7: Maintenance and testing of fire equipment

POTENTIAL PROBLEMS	POSSIBLE CORRECTIVE ACTIONS
All fire doors not regularly checked All firefighting equipment not regularly checked Fire detection/alarm equipment not regularly checked Other means of escape equipment not regularly checked	Give instructions to employees to make checks and make or arrange for tests as required
Employees testing or maintaining equipment not trained to do so	Arrange for necessary training, or outsource tasks

TABLE 8: Maintenance requirements for fire precautions

EQUIPMENT	PERIOD	ACTION REQUIRED
Fire detection and warning systems, including smoke alarms and manual devices	Weekly	Check for operation and state of repair Test operation Repair or replace items as necessary
	Annually	Full check and test by competent service engineer Change batteries in alarms and detectors, where battery-powered
All types of emergency lighting equipment	Weekly	Operate torches, check batteries Repair or replace items as necessary
	Monthly	Check all systems for state of repair and apparent working order
	Annually	Full check and test by competent service engineer
All types of firefighting equipment including hose reels	Weekly	Check all items for correct installation and apparent working order
	Annually	Full check and test by competent service engineer

TABLE 9: Daily fire safety checks

1.	Control panel – system is operating normally	YES	NO	N/A
2.	Emergency lighting systems that include signs are lit	YES	NO	N/A
3.	All defects in the above have been recorded and dealt with	YES	NO	N/A
4.	All escape routes are clear, free from obstruction, free from slipping and tripping hazards, and available for use when the premises are occupied	YES	NO	N/A
5.	All door fastenings along escape routes operate freely	YES	NO	N/A
6.	All self-closing devices and automatic door closers work correctly	YES	NO	N/A
7.	Each door on the escape route closes correctly, including any fitted flexible edge seals	YES	NO	N/A
8.	All exit and directional signs are correctly positioned, unobstructed and can be seen clearly at all times	YES	NO	N/A
9.	All fire extinguishers are in position and ready for service	YES	NO	N/A

TABLE 10: Weekly fire safety checks

1.	Manually-operated fire alarms are tested to ensure they can be heard throughout the workplace	YES	NO	N/A
2.	Electrical detection and warning systems are tested weekly for function and audibility	YES	NO	N/A
3.	Domestic-type smoke alarms are tested weekly	YES	NO	N/A
4.	Portable fire extinguishers are inspected weekly (Checking the safety clip and indicator devices and checking for external corrosion, dents or other damage)	YES	NO	N/A
5.	Hose reels are checked for any damage or obstruction	YES	NO	N/A

TABLE 11: Checklists for emergency plan and training

1.	There is an emergency plan for the premises	YES	NO	N/A
2.	The emergency plan takes account of all reasonably foreseeable circumstances	YES	NO	N/A
3.	Employees are familiar with the emergency plan, and have been trained in its use	YES	NO	N/A
4.	Drills are held regularly to demonstrate the use of the emergency plan	YES	NO	N/A
5.	The emergency plan is made available to all who need to be aware of it	YES	NO	N/A
6.	The procedures to be followed are clearly shown throughout the premises	YES	NO	N/A
7.	The emergency plan takes account of all those likely to be present in the premises and those who may be affected by a fire emergency in the premises	YES	NO	N/A

PART 2 SECTION 10

FIRE

CHECKLIST – The emergency plan contents

			YES	NO	N/A
1.	What employees must do if they discover a fire		YES	NO	N/A
2.	How people will be warned if there is a fire		YES	NO	N/A
3.	How the evacuation should be carried out		YES	NO	N/A
4.	Where people should assemble after leaving the premises		YES	NO	N/A
5.	How the premises will be checked to ensure they have been vacated		YES	NO	N/A
6.	Identification of key escape routes and how to access them		YES	NO	N/A
7.	Details of the firefighting equipment supplied		YES	NO	N/A
8.	Names and duties of employees given specific responsibilities in case of fire		YES	NO	N/A
9.	Arrangements for the safe evacuation of people identified as especially at risk, including the handicapped and all visitors		YES	NO	N/A
10.	Any processes, machines or power supplies that must be shut down		YES	NO	N/A
11.	Specific arrangements for any high-risk areas		YES	NO	N/A
12.	The means of calling the emergency services and who is responsible for doing so		YES	NO	N/A
13.	Procedures for liaison with the emergency services on arrival and notifying them of any special risks such as flammable material stores		YES	NO	N/A
14.	What training employees need and the arrangements for providing it		YES	NO	N/A

SPECIMEN FIRE RISK ASSESSMENT
STEP 1 – INFORMATION GATHERING

ORGANISATION:	
OFFICE ADDRESS:	
PERSON IN CHARGE:	
ASSESSMENT DATE:	

No	ITEM	CODE	COMMENTS
	IDENTIFICATION OF FIRE HAZARDS		
	(hazards that could ignite fuel)		
1.	**SOURCES OF IGNITION**		
	Workplace sources (specify):		
	Work equipment sources:		
	Electrical equipment		
	Static electricity		
	Friction		
	Fixed or portable space heaters		
	Boilers, kitchen equipment, cooking		
	Metal/metal impacts		
	Arson, vandalism		
	Hot work processes		
	Poor, obstructed ventilation		
	People sources:		
	Smokers (cigarettes, pipes, matches)		
	Other (specify):		
2.	**SOURCES OF FUEL**		
	(anything that burns enough to fuel a fire)		
	Flammable substances:		
	Gases (eg LPG, acetylene)		
	Liquids (eg all solvents)		
	Solids (eg wood, paper, rubber, plastics, foam)		
	Flammable parts of structure, fittings:		
	Shelving		
	Upholstered items, textiles		
	Stored materials:		
	Files, archives		
	Paper stocks and packaging		
	Supplies		
	Process stores inward		
	Finished goods		
	Waste, especially finely-divided material including shredder waste		
3.	**SOURCES OF OXYGEN**		
	Ventilation system		
	Oxidising substances		
	Oxygen sources (eg cylinders and piped supplies)		

FIRE

STEP 2 – CATEGORISE THE FIRE RISK LEVEL FOR THE PREMISES

Based on the foregoing hazards identified and the guidance in *Fire Safety – An Employer's Guide* (HSE Books, ISBN 00 11 341229 0), these premises are classed as:	COMMENTS TO AID DEFINITIONS:
HIGH RISK	Where: Flammables are stored in quantity, there are unsatisfactory structural features Permanent or temporary work has the potential to cause fires There is significant risk to life in case of fire
NORMAL RISK	Where: Fire is likely to remain confined or only spread slowly so as to allow people to escape The number present is small and layout is simple Premises have effective automatic warning and suppression systems
LOW RISK	Where: There is minimal risk to people's lives *and* The risk of fires starting is low *or* The potential for fire, heat and smoke spreading is negligible

STEP 3 – IDENTIFY THOSE AT RISK

CATEGORY	NUMBERS	LOCATION
Employees (NOTE: A diagram or floor plan may be of assistance)		
Visitors to the premises		
Contractors		
Others		

STEP 4 – EVALUATE THE RISKS*

1.	What is the chance of a fire occurring?	HIGH MEDIUM LOW INSIGNIFICANT		
2.	Can the sources of ignition be reduced?	YES	NO	
3.	Can the potential fuel for a fire be reduced?	YES	NO	
4.	Can the sources of oxygen be reduced?	YES	NO	
5.	Are the means of detecting a fire adequate?	YES	NO	
6.	Can everyone be warned in case of a fire?	YES	NO	
7.	Are the means of escape safe?	YES	NO	
8.	Are the means available to put out a fire adequate (if it is safe for people to do so)?	YES	NO	
9.	Are maintenance and testing arrangements adequate?	YES	NO	
10.	Are regular fire safety checks held and adequately detailed?	YES	NO	
11.	Are fire procedures and training adequate for the needs of the premises?	YES	NO	
12.	**Are existing precautions adequate for the remaining risks?**	YES	NO	

* These questions can be answered using the checklists within this Section

STEP 5 – RECORDING OF FINDINGS AND ACTIONS REQUIRED

Significant hazards	Those who are at risk from the hazards	List all existing controls	What more needs to be done	Action required by: (Name and agreed date)	Action completed (Signed and dated)

FIRE RISK ASSESSMENT CARRIED OUT BY:

DATE:

DATE OF NEXT REVIEW:

CONSTRUCTION SAFETY

Introduction

Over the last 150 years, the construction industry has had an unenviable safety record. In Great Britain, the Victorians instituted a massive programme of building and civil engineering with little thought for the safety of the huge workforce – as a result thousands were killed. We live now in more enlightened times, where the taking of risks at work and the exposure of non-employees to risk are seen as less acceptable than before. Even so, the European Union construction sector employs about seven per cent of the total workforce, yet accounts for 15 per cent of all occupational accidents and 30 per cent of all fatalities in the industrial sector. Significant organisational changes in the industry itself have had consequences for accident prevention, the effects of which have probably balanced out improved attitudes.

A variety of management systems – including project management by intermediaries, a lack of acceptance of responsibility for control, and the increasing complexity of design, materials and equipment – have all contributed to the industry's poor accident record.

For the most part, the hazards and technical solutions for hazard prevention and risk reduction are well known. A possible exception is the general lack of awareness (and data) on the occupational health record of the industry's workers, who are potentially exposed to the elements as well as a wide variety of hazardous substances. It seems that industry workers are aware of the dangers they face. In a 1991 survey, about half of those questioned thought that their work posed a risk to their personal health and safety.

Statistics show that the injuries which happen today are largely the same as those of yesterday, and even of 50 years ago, and are happening for much the same reasons.

The reader is referred to Part 1 for information on control techniques, which are as applicable to the construction industry as elsewhere. This Section will examine other aspects of the control of construction health and safety, after reviewing the available statistical evidence on causation.

The accident record

The most recent studies by the UK's Health and Safety Executive using the Labour Force Surveys (which send questionnaires to households) indicate that only 52 per cent (1999/2000) of all non-fatal reportable injuries in construction are actually reported as required by law. The experience of the author in other countries is that this is not a phenomenon confined to the UK. For this reason, the only reliable source of statistical information about construction injuries in any country is the number of fatalities recorded. Deaths are less easy to ignore, although even these may be underreported because of poor diagnosis of ill health exposures, for example, and also where a significant time may elapse between the injury and the consequent death.

The need for care when relying on the more plentiful statistics for construction injuries is best illustrated by a quotation from the report presented annually by the UK Health and Safety Commission. *Statistics 2000/01* states on page 9, paragraph 1.27: "These figures [for all-industry non-fatal injuries] suggest that employers reported around 44 per cent of the injuries that should have been reported in 1999/2000."

Broadly, in the UK two workers are killed in the industry every week, and one member of the public is killed every six weeks by construction activities. Over the last decade, there have been an average of 87 fatalities a year to workers in the construction industry. The number in 2000/01* was 106, 31 per cent higher than in the previous year and the highest for 10 years.

TABLE 1: Fatalities to employees in the construction industry, sample years between 1961 and 2000/01 inclusive

YEAR	TOTAL
1961	272
1966	292
1971	156
1981	105
1990/91	96
1995/96	62
1998/99	47
1999/2000	61
2000/01	72

TABLE 2: Percentage of UK construction fatal injuries by kind of accident, all workers

	1996/97	1997/98	1998/99	1999/2000	2000/01
All falls from a height	56%	58%	60%	52%	44%
Struck by moving vehicle	11%	6%	12%	6%	17%
Struck by moving or falling object	12%	15%	12%	21%	8%
Trapped by something collapsing or overturning	7%	5%	5%	2%	17%
Other	14%	16%	11%	19%	14%
TOTAL FATALITIES	**90**	**80**	**65**	**81**	**106**

Until the 'blip' in 2000/01, the annual fatality rate had remained roughly the same since the early 1990s.

Types of injury

In most countries, at least 40 per cent of all construction fatalities have been falls from a height. The figures for falls as a percentage of total fatalities and major injuries has been remarkably constant over past years in the UK (see Tables 2 and 3), justifying the attention given to fall protection in its own right in the UK Construction Regulations. The information presented shows that the most serious construction injuries cluster into relatively few causal groups.

Accident causes

Canadian studies have shown that active involvement in safety management by the most senior levels in a construction company is directly correlated with reductions in numbers of accidents and injuries.

Knowledge of causation patterns provides a starting point for focusing preventive measures. Case studies and descriptions of accidents can be used to give information about prevention techniques. In a sample studied, 90 per cent of fatalities were found to be preventable, and positive management action could have saved lives in 70 per cent of cases. The three worst task areas found by the study (75 per cent of all deaths) were maintenance (42 per cent), transport and mobile plant (20 per cent), and demolition/dismantling (13 per cent) – each receives detailed treatment in this book.

Table 2 shows the distribution of causes of fatalities over the last five years, considering all workers in the industry. Some activities, of course, are frequent sources of injury, but rarely result in a fatality – manual handling, for example. Others occur relatively

TABLE 3: Percentage of UK construction major injuries by causation, employees only

	1996/97	1997/98	1998/99	1999/2000	2000/01
All falls from a height	35%	37%	37%	36%	37%
Slip, trip or fall on same level	19%	19%	20%	21%	21%
Struck by moving vehicle	3%	2%	3%	2%	2%
Struck by moving or falling object	21%	20%	18%	18%	18%
Injured while handling, lifting or carrying	8%	9%	9%	10%	8%
Other	14%	13%	13%	13%	14%
TOTAL MAJOR INJURIES	**3,227**	**3,860**	**4,289**	**4,386**	**4,268**

CONSTRUCTION SAFETY

TABLE 4: Fatalities to employees in UK construction by causation, 1999/2000 and 2000/01

CATEGORIES OF ACCIDENT CAUSATION	TOTAL 1999/2000	% OF TOTAL	TOTAL 2000/01	% OF TOTAL
Falls – >2m	24	39.35	27	37.50
– <2m	2	3.28	–	–
– unknown height	3	4.92	–	–
Total falls	29	47.54	27	37.50
Contact with moving machinery	–	–	2	2.78
Struck by moving or falling object	17	27.87	7	9.73
Struck against fixed or stationary object	–	–	–	–
Struck by moving vehicle	5	8.20	16	22.23
Manual handling	–	–	–	–
Slip, trip or fall on same level	–	–	–	–
Trapped by collapse	2	3.28	11	15.28
Asphyxiation or drowning	–	–	2	2.78
Exposure to harmful substances	–	–	–	–
Explosion	–	–	–	–
Exposure to fire	1	1.64	2	2.78
Electrocution	6	9.84	4	5.56
Other	1	1.64	1	1.39
TOTAL	**61**	**100.01**	**72**	**100.03**

infrequently, but when they do, there is a higher than usual chance of not surviving them – becoming trapped by collapse or overturning and electrocution are examples of this.

We need this information in order to estimate risk, which is a measure combining the chances of something happening with the potential outcome in terms of injury. For this reason, Table 5 includes statistical information about all reportable types of injury, but too much reliance should not be placed on the data because of the underreporting factor mentioned above.

The definition of 'major injury' is contained within UK law, and is related to the seriousness of the injury rather than the length of absence from work. It requires there to have been hospital treatment for the injury as a minimum.

Occupations most at risk

Sample information on the occupations of those killed is shown in Table 6. While no data is available on the percentage distribution of occupations across the workforce, it can be seen that a) some groups of workers in particular occupations are more at risk than others, and b) some are at high risk relative to their assumed numbers (and may well be unaware of it). Most construction managers are surprised at the numbers of their colleagues killed and seriously injured each year.

Occupational health and hygiene

Traditionally, the construction industry's high level of injury-causing accidents has received the attention of

TABLE 5: Reported injuries to UK employees in construction by causation, 1999/2000 and 2000/01

CATEGORIES OF ACCIDENT CAUSATION	1999/2000		2000/01	
	FATALITIES	MAJOR INJURIES	FATALITIES	MAJOR INJURIES
Falls – >2m	24	740	27	687
– <2m	2	774	–	795
– unknown height	3	80	–	78
Total falls	29	1,594	27	1,560
Contact with moving machinery	–	136	2	146
Struck by moving or falling object	17	788	7	778
Struck against fixed or stationary object	–	126	–	129
Struck by moving vehicle	5	102	16	90
Manual handling	–	429	–	345
Slip, trip or fall on same level	–	908	–	907
Trapped by collapse	2	57	11	57
Asphyxiation or drowning	–	7	2	10
Exposure to harmful substances	–	53	–	63
Explosion	–	6	–	8
Exposure to fire	1	11	2	20
Electrocution/electric shock	6	96	4	71
Animal injury	–	1	–	3
Acts of violence	–	10	–	15
Other and unclassified	1	62	1	66
TOTAL	**61**	**4,386**	**72**	**4,268**

PART 2 SECTION 11

enforcement, media publicity and management action. Arguably, the size of that problem has led to a neglect of the less tangible consequences of occupational hygiene and health problems, apart from well-publicised topics such as asbestos. Reports worldwide suggest that construction workers age prematurely due to hypothermia caused by working in the cold and wet. Respiratory diseases such as bronchitis and asthma are also thought to occur at above average levels in construction workers, who also commonly suffer from dermatitis.

Experience shows that there is little industry

CONSTRUCTION SAFETY

TABLE 6: Numbers of employees reported as killed in construction work over a 10-year period, in selected occupations

OCCUPATION	YEAR										
	90/91	91/92	92/93	93/94	94/95	95/96	96/97	97/98	98/99	99/00	TOTAL
Bricklayer	4	4	1	5	2	–	1	2	2	1	22
Carpenter/joiner	2	1	1	1	2	3	3	–	1	2	16
Demolition worker	4	3	4	2	–	1	2	7	2	2	27
Electrician fitter	1	1	3	–	–	1	1	–	1	5	13
Labourer	31	21	11	20	10	17	6	13	7	6	142
Painter	5	4	2	4	–	2	2	1	–	2	22
Driver	7	9	5	5	4	2	4	6	1	2	45
Management/ professional	9	6	7	8	2	5	–	1	1	2	41
Plumber/glazier	3	1	1	2	1	–	2	1	2	–	13
Steel erector	3	5	3	2	–	–	–	4	3	1	21
Scaffolder	5	4	6	2	2	4	5	3	1	1	33
Roofer	4	8	4	10	7	4	8	9	7	6	67

awareness of the principles of assessment, or significant appreciation of the risks to workers from substances brought onto the site – and especially from those created there.

Controlling construction accidents

The successful control of hazards and limitation of the risks in the construction industry depends on exactly the same principles as in other industries. Specific organisational problems do exist, and need to be addressed, chiefly by recognising the need to appreciate health and safety matters at the very earliest stages – design, specification of materials, their delivery quantities and batch sizes, work planning and interaction between contractors, and between contractors and the public.

World best practice now calls for specific control and planning to be done prior to and during the construction phase of projects, which require health and safety plans to be drawn up before work starts, on which tenders will have been based.

The plan will be passed to the selected competent principal or general contractor, who has well-defined responsibilities for control of the safety of work on site, including the activities of other contractors. The plan will be revised and augmented by the general contractor, in particular to incorporate the risk assessments provided by all contractors. Thus, it becomes a working document throughout the duration of the project. Also, a completion document or health and safety file contains the detail of how the construction was done, for use of the client and future modifiers or demolishers of the structure concerned.

Method statements covering high-risk operations should be required in advance from those doing the work. Each should contain the acknowledgement that, if operational conditions force any deviation from the method statement, this must be agreed by site supervision and accepted by them in writing. Tasks where method statements should always be

International Principles of Health and Safety at Work | Allan St John Holt

used include demolition, the use of explosives, erection of steel and structural frames, deep excavations and tunnelling, lifting with more than one appliance, use of suspended access equipment, and falsework. They should also be considered for roofwork, especially if fragile roofs are identified. Roofwork method statements should detail access methods, work procedure and fall protection systems. All method statements are plans for work which are based on risk assessments (see Part 1 Section 3).

Training in techniques and skills for workers should include a strong health and safety element. Management training is especially important; it fosters that positive commitment to health and safety and the positive safety culture within the organisation which is necessary before the construction process can be successfully managed.

Safety in excavations

Death in excavations is not uncommon. A cubic metre of earth weighs a tonne, and even those only partly buried can die because of pressure from below and the sides which results in suffocation. Next at risk are the rescuers.

A short review of excavation safety, just one of the many topics in construction work, gives the opportunity to show how organisation and planning is a key factor in ensuring health and safety of construction workers. The control of every hazard discussed below will be inadequate if there is little or no preplanning.

Lack of personal awareness and supervisory knowledge can only be combated with the training programmes and certification that the industry is beginning to push out beyond the major contractors.

The main hazards are:
- Falls into the excavation
- Falls of materials from the top of the excavation
- Falls of the sides into the excavation
- Getting in and out

- Unanticipated undermining of adjacent structures
- Unanticipated discovery of underground services
- Lack of oxygen or presence of fumes
- Occupational health exposures

Falls into excavations should be prevented by solid guardrails where a fall exceeding 2m can occur. Points of public access should be protected in this way, regardless of the potential depth of fall. Preplanning must anticipate the demand for materials to achieve this.

Falls of materials can be prevented by insisting that spoil and materials are kept back from the edges and a gap 1m wide is left clear. Traffic routes must be planned to keep vehicles away from the edges, and anchored blocks are required to prevent delivery vehicles falling in as well as their materials.

Falls of the sides will occur sooner or later unless either the soil is verified by a geological survey as sound and without need of support, or the sides are sloped back at an appropriate angle (usually shallower than 60 degrees), or supporting material is provided under the supervision of a competent person. The work also needs inspection at regular intervals. It will be seen that in all cases preplanning is needed for each control – to provide the survey, the space or the equipment. Nobody exposed to the potential of collapse should be working unprotected at any time.

Safe access and egress is needed at least every 25m by means of a fixed ladder with a good handhold at the top.

Undermining is easily done, and can affect nearby foundations and traffic routes. Scaffolding that has been undermined will need special bracing support to retain load-bearing ability.

Underground services must be looked for on plans before excavation work begins. But plans are relatively unreliable and cable detectors should always be used to supplement their information. Where the

CONSTRUCTION SAFETY

presence of a cable or other service is known, digging by hand in the immediate vicinity should be required rather than by machine.

Lack of oxygen is always a possibility in an excavation – it is a potential 'confined space'. Fumes and unwanted gases can also accumulate, so tests with a meter may be required. This should be noted in the risk assessment and method statement.

Occupational health exposures for workers in excavations include Weil's disease and tetanus, as well as contaminated soil as a result of previous industrial activities. Good protective clothing and washing facilities are essential, plus an awareness of the need for a high standard of personal hygiene.

Acknowledgement: *The assistance of the UK Health and Safety Executive's Strategy and Analytical Support Division in supplying statistics for use in this Section is gratefully acknowledged.*

*Figures for 2000/2001 were provisional at the time of writing.

Introduction

Research studies show that accidents during demolition work are more likely to be fatal than those in many other areas of construction work. Causes of accidents which have high potential for serious injury are premature collapse of buildings and structures, and falls from working places and access routes. A common feature of demolition accidents is that investigation shows that there is usually a failure to plan the work sufficiently at an appropriate stage, which leaves operatives on site to devise their own methods of doing the work without knowledge and information about the dangers that confront them. Failure to plan is, of course, not confined to demolition or even the construction industry, but it is difficult to think of many other situations where the consequences are visited so rapidly on the employees.

'Demolition' is defined here as the taking down of load-bearing structures and/or the production of a substantial quantity of demolished material – about five tonnes as a minimum. This rule attempts a practical definition based on the level of risk attached to the work.

Planning for safety

As much information should be obtained about the work to be done, at the earliest possible time. Who provides the information? The extent to which the client is willing or able to provide structural information will partly depend on whether it is actually available to him. However, it should not be up to the contractor to discover a particular hazard of the structure or building to be demolished, although it is entirely possible that hazards may reveal themselves during work which could not reasonably have been anticipated. All parties to demolition work must remain alert to this possibility. An experienced structural engineer or surveyor should be employed if the owner cannot provide structural details, building drawings or surveyors' reports, to obtain the necessary information.

Information on storage and use of chemicals on a site

due for demolition can usually be obtained from the owner, but the services of a competent analyst may be needed in cases where:

- The site has been vacant for some time
- Previous ownership is unclear, *or*
- Environmental contamination by a previous occupier could have occurred

Architectural or archaeological items for retention must be defined before the preferred method of demolition is determined.

Demolition is normally carried out by specialist contractors with experience. Control of the actual work is required to be progressed under the supervision of a competent person – by people experienced in demolition – and this may not be achieved by a general contractor. Clients and owners should ensure that work of this type done on their behalf is carried out by contractors who are competent to recognise at an early stage any features likely to cause complications or require further investigation.

Demolition surveys

Using information supplied, prospective contractors should carry out a survey in sufficient detail to identify structural problems, and risks associated with flammable substances or substances hazardous to health. The precautions required to protect employees and members of the public from these risks, together with the preferred demolition procedure, should be set out in a **method statement** (see below).

The survey should:

- Take account of the whole site; access should be permitted for the completion of surveys and information made available in order to plan the intended method of demolition
- Identify adjoining properties which may be affected by the work – structurally, physically or chemically; premises which may be sensitive to the work, other than domestic premises, include hospitals, telephone exchanges and industrial premises with machines vulnerable to dust, noise or vibration

DEMOLITION

- Identify the need for any shoring work to adjacent properties or elements within the property to be demolished; weatherproofing requirements for the work will also be noted
- Identify the structural condition, as deterioration may impose restrictions on the demolition method

Preferably, the survey should be divided into structural and chemical aspects, the latter noting any residual contamination. Structural aspects of the survey should note variations in the type of construction within individual buildings and among buildings forming a complex due for demolition. The person carrying out the survey should be competent. An assessment of the original construction method including any temporary works required can be very helpful.

Preferred method of work

The basic ideal principle is that structures should be demolished in the reverse order to their erection. The method chosen should gradually reduce the height of the structure or building, or arrange its deliberate controlled collapse so that work can be completed at ground level.

Structural information obtained by the survey should be used to ensure that the intended method of work retains the stability of the parts of the structure or building which have not yet been demolished. The aim should be to adopt methods which make it unnecessary for work to be done at height. If this cannot be achieved, then systems which limit the danger of such exposure should be employed. The use of balling machines, heavy duty grabs or pusher arms may avoid the need to work at heights. If these methods are possible, the contractor must be satisfied that sufficient space is available for the safe use of the equipment, and that the equipment is adequate for the job.

When work cannot be carried out safely from part of a permanent structure or building, working platforms can be used. These include scaffolds, towers and power-operated mobile work platforms. Where these measures are not practicable, safety nets or harnesses (properly anchored) may be used.

Causing the structure or building to collapse by the use of wire ropes or explosives may reduce the need for working at heights, but suitable access and working platforms may still be needed during the initial stages.

Knowledge of structural engineering principles is necessary to avoid premature collapse, especially an understanding of the effect of preweakening by the removal, cutting or partial cutting of structural members.

Method statements

The production of a method statement is widely recognised as necessary for all demolition work. Because of the special demolition needs of each structure, an individual written statement about how the work will be done, and the sequence and timescale to be followed, should be made by the employer undertaking the work. Investigation of demolition failures – including collapses, unidentified problems, lack of safe access for workers – shows that reliance on experience alone is never sufficient to guarantee safety. Production and possession of a written method statement demonstrates competence, and the document can also be used for training.

The detailed method statement should be drawn up before work starts, and communicated to all involved as part of the health and safety plan. It should identify the work procedure, associated problems and their solutions, and should form a reference for site supervision.

Method statements should be easy to understand, agreed by and known to all levels of management and supervision, including those of subcontracting specialists.

The method statement should include:
1. The sequence of events and method of

demolition or dismantling (including drawings/diagrams) of the structure or building.

2. Details of personnel access, working platforms and machinery requirements.

3. Specific details of any preweakening of structures which are to be pulled down, or demolished using explosives.

4. Arrangements for the protection of personnel and public, and the exclusion of unauthorised people from the work area; details of areas outside the site boundaries which may need control during critical aspects of the work must be included.

5. Details of the removal or isolation of electrical, gas and other services, including drains.

6. Details of temporary services required.

7. Arrangements for the disposal of waste.

8. Necessary action required for environmental considerations (noise, dust, pollution of water, disposal of contaminated ground).

9. Details of controls covering substances hazardous to health and flammable substances.

10. Arrangements for the control of site transport.

11. Training requirements.

12. Welfare arrangements appropriate to the work and conditions expected.

13. Identification of people with special responsibilities for the co-ordination and control of safety arrangements.

Demolition techniques

Piecemeal demolition is done by hand, using hand-held tools, sometimes as a preliminary to other methods. Considerations include provision of a safe place of work and safe access/egress, and debris disposal. It can be completed or begun by machines such as balling machines, impact hammers or hydraulic pusher arms. Considerations for these include safe operation of the machines, clearances, capability of the equipment and protection of the operator.

Deliberate controlled collapse involves preweakening the structure or building as a preliminary, and completion by use of explosives or overturning with wire rope pulling. Considerations for the use of explosives include competence, storage, blast protection, firing programmes and misfire drill. Wire rope pulling requires a similar level of expertise, as well as selection of materials and clear areas for rope runs.

REVISION

Six elements in planning for safety in demolition:

- Information
- Demolition surveys
- Preferred method of work
- Method statements
- Consultation
- Training

Two main demolition techniques:

- Piecemeal – by hand or machine
- Deliberate controlled collapse, including preweakening, using explosives or overturning

INTRODUCTION TO OCCUPATIONAL HEALTH AND HYGIENE

PART 3
Occupational health and hygiene

INTRODUCTION TO OCCUPATIONAL HEALTH AND HYGIENE

Occupational health anticipates and prevents health problems which are caused by the work which people do. In some circumstances, the work may aggravate a pre-existing medical condition, and stopping this is also the role of occupational health. Health hazards often reveal their effects on the body only after the passage of time; many have cumulative effects, and in some cases, the way this happens is still not fully understood. Because the effects are often not immediately apparent, it can be difficult to understand and persuade others that there is a need for caution and control. Good occupational hygiene practice encompasses the following ideas:

- **Recognition** of the hazards or potential hazards
- **Quantification** of the extent of the hazard – usually by measuring physical/chemical factors and their duration, and relating them to known or required standards
- **Assessment** of risk in the actual conditions of use, storage, transport and disposal
- **Control** of exposure to the hazard, through design, engineering, working systems, the use of personal protective equipment and biological monitoring
- **Monitoring change** in the hazard by means of audits or other measurement techniques, including periodic re-evaluation of work conditions and systems

Historical development

There is evidence that the Greeks and Romans were aware of the hazards and risks to health, not to mention safety, in work activity, especially in the mining and extraction processes. Major milestones in the history of occupational health up to the beginning of the 20th century are as follows:

1526 Georg Bauer (in Latin texts Georgius Agricola) was appointed as physician to the miners of Joachimsthal. He recommended mine ventilation, and the use of veils over faces to protect the miners from harmful dust. His treatise on mining of metals, including health aspects, *De Re Metallica*, was published in 1556.

1567 Von Hohenheim (in Latin texts Paracelsus) had a monograph published after his death on the lung diseases of miners and smelters.

1700 The Italian physician Bernardino Ramazzini wrote the first comprehensive document on occupational health, *De Morbis Artificium Diatriba*, a history of occupational diseases. Working in Padua, he was the first to suggest that physicians should ask their patients about their work when diagnosing illness.

1802 The Health and Morals of Apprentices Act passed in Great Britain, the world's first occupational health and safety legislation.

1831 Dr Charles Thackrah, early UK occupational health pioneer, published *The Effects of Principal Arts, Trades and Professions... on Health and Longevity*.

1898 Thomas Legge (knighted for his work in 1925) appointed as first Medical Inspector of Factories.

Health hazards

Health hazards can be divided into four broad categories: physical, chemical, biological and ergonomic. Examples of the categories are:

- **Physical** – air pressure, heat, dampness, noise, radiant energy, electric shock
- **Chemical** – exposure to toxic materials such as dusts, fumes and gases
- **Biological** – infection, eg tetanus, hepatitis and legionnaire's disease
- **Ergonomic** – work conditions, stress, man-machine interaction

Toxicity of substances

Toxicity is the ability of a substance to produce injury once it reaches a site in or on the body. The degree of harmful effect which a substance can have depends not only on its inherent harmful properties but also on the **route** and the **speed** of entry into the body. Substances may cause health hazards from a single exposure, even for a short time (**acute effect**), or after prolonged or repeated exposure (**chronic effect**). The substance may affect the body at the point of contact, when it is known as a **local agent**, or at some other point, when it is described as a **systemic agent**.

Absorption is said to occur only when a material has gained access to the bloodstream and may consequently be carried to all parts of the body.

What makes substances toxic?

The effect a substance will have on the body cannot always be predicted with accuracy, or explained solely on the basis of physical and chemical laws. The influence of the following factors combine to produce the **effective dose** (see Section 2):

- **Quantity** or **concentration** of the substance
- The duration of **exposure**
- The **physical state** of the material, eg particle size
- Its **affinity** for human tissue
- Its **solubility** in human tissue fluids
- The **sensitivity** to attack of human tissue or organs

Long- and short-term exposure

Substances which are toxic can have a toxic effect on the body after only one single, short exposure. In other circumstances, repeated exposure to small concentrations may give rise to an effect. A toxic effect related to an immediate response after a single exposure is called an **acute effect**. Effects which result after prolonged exposure (hours or days or much longer) are known as **chronic effects**. 'Chronic' implies repeated doses or exposures at low levels; they generally have delayed effects and are often due to unrecognised conditions which are, therefore, permitted to persist.

Body response

The body's response against the invasion of

substances likely to cause damage can be divided into external or **superficial** defences and internal or **cellular** defences. These defence mechanisms interrelate, in the sense that the defence is conducted on a number of levels at once, and not in a stage-by-stage pattern.

Superficial mechanisms of defence

The superficial mechanisms work by the action of cell structures, such as organs and functioning systems.

The body's largest organ, the **skin**, provides a useful barrier against many foreign organisms and chemicals (but not against all of them). Its effect is, of course, limited by its physical characteristics. Openings in the skin, including sweat pores, hair follicles and cuts, can allow entry, and the skin itself may be permeable to some chemicals such as toluene. The skin can withstand limited physical damage because of its elasticity and toughness, but its adaptation to cope with modern substances is usually viewed by its owner as unhelpful – dermatitis, with thickening and inflammation, is painful and prominent.

Defences against **inhalation** of substances harmful to the body begin in the **respiratory tract**, where a series of reflexes activate the coughing and sneezing mechanisms to expel forcibly the triggering substance. Many substances and micro-organisms are successfully trapped by nasal hairs and the mucus lining the passages of the respiratory system. The passages are also well supplied with fine hairs which sweep rhythmically towards the outside and pass along larger particles. These hairs form the **ciliary escalator**. The respiratory system narrows as it enters the lungs, where the ciliary escalator assumes more and more importance as the effective defence. In the deep lung areas, only small particles are able to enter the alveoli (where gas exchange with the red blood cells takes place), and cellular defence predominates there.

For **ingestion** of substances entering the mouth and **gastrointestinal tract**, saliva in the mouth and acid in the stomach provide useful defences to substances

INTRODUCTION TO OCCUPATIONAL HEALTH AND HYGIENE

which are not excessively acid or alkaline, or present in great quantity. The wall of the gut presents an effective barrier against many insoluble materials. Vomiting and diarrhoea are additional reflex mechanisms which act to remove substances or quantities which the body is not equipped to deal with without damage to itself. Thus, there are a number of primitive defences, useful at an earlier evolutionary stage to prevent man unwittingly damaging himself, which are now available to protect against a newer range of problems as well as the old.

Eyes and **ears** are potential entry routes for substances and micro-organisms. The eyes prevent entry of harmful material by way of the eyelids, eye lashes, conjunctiva (the thin specialised outer skin coating of the eyeball), and by bacteria-destroying tears. The ears are protected by the outer shell or pinna, and the ear drum is a physical barrier at the entrance to the sensitive mechanical parts and the organ of hearing. Waxy secretions protect the ear drum and trap larger particles.

Other orifices may be invaded by micro-organisms. Generally acid environments, such as in the urethra, do not promote their growth. Sexual contact is the main source of exposure.

Cellular mechanisms of defence

The cells of the body possess their own defence systems.

Prevention of excessive blood loss from the circulation through blood clotting and coagulation prevents excessive bleeding and slows or prevents the entry of germs into the blood system.

Phagocytosis is the scavenging action of a defensive body cell (white blood cell) against an invading particle. A variety of actions can be used, including chemical, ingestion, enzyme attack and absorption.

Secretion of defensive substances is done by some specialised cells. Histamine release and heparin,

which promotes the availability of blood sugar, are examples.

Inflammatory response can isolate infected areas, remove harmful substances by an increased blood flow to the area, and promote the repair of damaged tissue.

Repair of damaged tissue is a necessary defence mechanism, which includes the removal of dead cells, increased availability of defender cells, and replacement of tissue strength and soundness by means of temporary and permanent repairs, eg scar tissue.

Immune response is the ability to resist almost all organisms or toxins that tend to damage tissues. Some immunity is **innate**, such as the phagocytosis of organisms and their destruction by acid in the gut. In addition, the human body has the ability to develop extremely powerful specific immunity against invading agents. This is **acquired** immunity, also known as **adapting** immunity. Acquired immunity is highly specific, the resistance developing days or weeks after exposure to the invading agent.

Routes of entry

Substances harmful to the body may enter it by three main routes. These are:

Absorption – through the skin, including entry through cuts and abrasions, and the conjunctiva of the eye. Organic solvents are able to penetrate the skin, as a result of accidental exposure to them or by washing. Tetraethyl lead and toluene are examples.

Ingestion – through the mouth, which is generally considered to be a rare method of contracting industrial disease. However, the action of the main defence mechanisms protecting the lungs rejects particles and pushes them towards the mouth, and an estimated 50 per cent of the particles deposited in the upper respiratory tract and 12.5 per cent from the lower passages are eventually swallowed.

Inhalation – the most important route of entry,

which can allow direct attacks against lung tissue which bypass other defences such as those of the liver. The lungs are very efficient in transferring substances into the body from the outside environment, and this is the way inside for 90 per cent of industrial poisons.

Results of entry

Having gained entry into the body, substances can have the following effects:

Cause diseases of the skin such as:

Non-infective dermatitis – an inflammation of the skin especially on hands, wrists and forearms. This can be prevented by health screening, good personal hygiene, use of barrier creams and/or protective clothing.

Scrotal cancer – produced by workers' clothing, impregnated with a carcinogen such as mineral oil, rubbing against the scrotum. This can be prevented by substitution of the original substance, by use of splash guards, and by the provision of clean clothing and washing facilities for soiled work clothing.

Cause diseases of the respiratory system such as:

Pneumoconioses – resulting from exposure to dust which deposits on the lung, such as metal dust and man-made mineral fibre. Other examples of these fibroses of the lungs are **silicosis** due to the inhalation of free silica, and **asbestosis** from exposure to asbestos fibres.

Humidifier fever – giving influenza-like symptoms and resulting from contaminated humidifying systems.

Legionnaire's disease – from exposure to legionella bacteria.

Cause cancer and birth defects – by encouraging cells to undergo fundamental changes by altering the genetic material within the cell. Substances which can do this are **carcinogens**, which cause or promote the development of unwanted cells as cancer.

Examples are asbestos, mineral oil, hardwood dusts and arsenic. **Teratogens** cause birth defects by altering genetic material in cells in the reproductive organs, and cause abnormal development of the embryo. Examples are organic mercury and lead compounds. **Mutagens** trigger changes affecting future generations.

Cause asphyxiation – by excluding oxygen or by direct toxic action. Carbon monoxide does this by competing successfully with oxygen for transport in the red cells in the blood.

Cause central nervous system disorders – by acting on brain tissue or other organs, as in the case of alcohol eventually causing blindness.

Cause damage to specific organs – such as kidneys and liver. An example is vinyl chloride monomer (VCM).

Cause blood poisoning – and producing abnormalities in the blood, as in benzene poisoning, where anaemia or leukaemia is the result.

REVISION

Four main health hazards:
- Physical
- Chemical
- Biological
- Ergonomic

Six factors determine toxicity:
- Concentration
- Duration
- Physical state
- Affinity
- Solubility
- Sensitivity

Acute effects are immediate responses to single short-term exposures

Chronic effects are long-term responses to prolonged exposures

INTRODUCTION TO OCCUPATIONAL HEALTH AND HYGIENE

The body's response to potentially harmful substances
and micro-organisms can be:

Superficial:

■ Respiratory tract

■ Mouth and gut

■ Skin

■ Eyes and ears

■ Other orifices

or

Cellular:

■ Prevention of blood loss

■ Phagocytosis

■ Secretion of defensive substances

■ Inflammatory response

■ Repair of damaged tissue

■ Immune response

Three main routes of entry:

■ Absorption

■ Ingestion

■ Inhalation

OCCUPATIONAL EXPOSURE LIMITS

Introduction

An important part of an occupational hygiene programme is the measurement of the extent of the hazard. This is generally done by measuring physical and/or chemical factors, including exposure duration, and relating them to occupational hygiene standards. Authorities in several countries publish recommended standards for airborne gases, vapours, dusts, fibres and fumes. The two primary (English language) sources are:

The **Health and Safety Executive (HSE)** in the United Kingdom, which publishes Occupational Exposure Limits annually and as necessary. The UK standard is essentially in two parts, specifying Maximum Exposure Limits (MELs) and Occupational Exposure Standards (OESs).

The **American Conference of Governmental Industrial Hygienists (ACGIH)**, which publishes a list of Threshold Limit Values (TLVs) annually. The **Occupational Safety and Health Administration (OSHA)** publishes national standards based on recommendations from the National Institute of Occupational Safety and Health (NIOSH).

MELs and OESs (for the UK)

Maximum Exposure Limit (MEL) is the maximum concentration of an airborne substance, averaged over a reference period (eg eight-hour long-term) to which employees may be exposed by inhalation under any circumstances. Some substances have been assigned short-term MELs (eg 15-minute reference period). These substances give rise to acute effects and, therefore, these limits should never be exceeded.

Occupational Exposure Standard (OES) is the concentration of an airborne substance, averaged over a reference period, at which there is no current evidence that repeated (day after day) exposure by inhalation will be injurious to the health of employees. OESs should not be exceeded, but where this occurs effective steps should be taken as soon as practicable to reduce the exposure. These values are given in units of parts per million (ppm) and milligrams per cubic metre (mgm^{-3}). They are given for two periods: long-term exposure (eight-hour time-weighted average (TWA)) and short-term exposure (15-minute TWA). Some substances are designated 'SK' which indicates that they can be absorbed through the skin.

Health and Safety Executive Guidance Note EH40 is published annually, reproducing the current statutory list of Maximum Exposure Limits (MELs) and approved Occupational Exposure Standards (OESs). It is obviously important to see that the current document is the one consulted. This is identified by a suffix to the number EH40, showing the year of currency. EH40 also contains an up-to-date list of references (Part 5) and a list of substances defined as carcinogens for the purposes of the relevant UK regulations.

Threshold Limit Values

The **Threshold Limit Value (TLV)** is the concentration of an airborne substance and represents conditions under which it is believed that nearly all workers may be repeatedly exposed day after day without adverse health effects. There are different types of TLV:

Time Weighted Average TLV (TLV-TWA) – limits for indefinitely continued exposure eight hours a day, five days a week.

Short-Term Exposure Level TLV (TLV-STEL) – maximum concentrations of contaminant in air, beyond which the worker should not be exposed for more than a continuous exposure time period of 15 minutes.

Ceiling TLV (TLV-C) – this converts the TLV-TWA into a value not to be exceeded at any time.

All values quoted are for inhalation, and the units are milligrams per cubic metre (mgm^{-3}) or parts per million (ppm). Skin absorption is also denoted with 'SK'. For most practical purposes, there is no difference between TLVs and OESs.

OCCUPATIONAL EXPOSURE LIMITS

It should be remembered that all occupational exposure limits refer to healthy adults working at normal rates over normal shift durations and patterns. In practice, it is advisable to work well below the standards set, and to bear in mind the desirable goal of progressive risk reduction over time.

REVISION

UK standards:
- OESs
- MELs

USA standards:
- TLV-TWA
- TLV-STEL
- TLV-C

ENVIRONMENTAL MONITORING

Introduction

The key to preventing exposure to substances which could be hazardous to health depends on the first two steps mentioned in Section 1 – recognition of the hazard or potential hazard, and evaluation of the extent of the hazard. People in the workplace may encounter hazards from several sources. An important means of evaluation is measurement to determine the extent of the threat.

Some useful definitions

Dusts are solid particles suspended in air, which will settle under gravity. They are generated usually by mechanical handling processes including crushing and grinding. They can be of organic or inorganic origin. Particle size lies between 0.5 and 10 microns.

Fumes are solid particles formed by condensation from the gaseous state, eg metal oxides from volatilised metals. They can flocculate and coalesce. Their particle size is between 0.1 and 1 micron.

Mists are suspended liquid droplets formed by condensation from the gaseous state or by break-up of liquids in air. They can be formed by splashing, foaming or atomising – their particle size lies between 5 and 100 microns. Fogs are fine mists comprised of suspended liquid droplets at the lower end of the particle size range.

Vapours are the gaseous forms of substances which are normally in the solid or liquid state, eg sodium vapour in luminaires. They are generated by decrease from normal pressure or temperature increase.

Gases are any substances in the physical condition of having no definite volume or shape, but tending to expand to fill any container into which they are introduced.

Aerosol is a term used to describe airborne particles which are small enough to float in air. These can be liquids or solids.

Smoke contains incomplete combustion products of organic origin, the particle sizes of which range between 0.01 and 0.3 microns.

NB: A **micron** is a unit of length corresponding to one millionth of a metre. The equivalent SI unit is micrometre (μm).

Measurement – Which technique?

As discussed in Part 3 Section 1, the health effects of exposure to toxic substances can be acute or chronic. It will, therefore, be necessary to distinguish appropriate types of measurement:

1. Long-term measurements which assess the average exposure of a person over a given time period.
2. Continuous measurements capable of detecting short-term exposure to high concentrations of contaminants which cause an acute exposure.
3. Spot readings can be used to measure acute hazards if the exact point of time of exposure is known and the measurement is taken at that time; chronic hazards may be assessed if a statistically significant number of measurements are made.

Measurement techniques

The more common air quality measuring techniques are:

Grab sampling – Stain detectors are used for measuring airborne concentrations of gases and vapours. Well known as a means of assessing alcohol consumption in roadside police checks, stain tubes are sealed glass tubes packed with chemicals which react specifically with the air contaminant being measured. In use, the tube is opened at the ends, a hand pump is attached and a standard volume of contaminated air is drawn through the tube. The chemical in the tube then changes colour in the direction of the airflow. The tube is calibrated so that

ENVIRONMENTAL MONITORING

the colour change corresponds to the concentration of the contamination.

The **main drawbacks** of grab sampling include inability to measure personal exposure by this method, except in the most general sense, and tube errors. These may arise because of the small volumes used, conditions such as temperature which affect some reactions in the tube chemical, and the possibility that the extent of the reaction may be influenced by the presence of other substances in the sampled air which may also cause a colour change in the tube. The accuracy of this method is not high, and it is best to use it to give a rough indication of the presence of a contaminant, with an estimate of the extent of contamination. It does not provide a time-weighted average result, and a single reading may not indicate a longer-term concentration.

Long-term sampling – This involves the taking of air samples for several hours, thus giving the average concentration at which the contaminant is present throughout the sampling period. Sampling may be done by attaching equipment to the operator so as to sample air entering the breathing zone (personal sampling), or by measuring at different points in the workplace (static or area sampling). Long-term sampling can be done by the use of long-term stain detector tubes which are connected to a pump. This draws air through the tube at a predetermined constant rate. At the end of the sampling period, the tube is examined and produces a value for the average level of concentration during the period.

The **main drawbacks** are as before, except that the accuracy of measurement of the sampled volume of air is improved by the use of a pump taking small samples over a long period.

For a few substances, direct measuring diffusion tubes are available, which do not require the use of a pump as diffusion is the means by which the sample of contaminant is collected.

More accurate results are obtained from operator personal sampling by means of **charcoal tube sampling**. This involves drawing air through a tube containing activated charcoal which absorbs the contaminant. The tube is then analysed in a laboratory to find the airborne concentration of the contaminant. Diffusion badges or monitors containing absorbents are becoming widely used. No pump is required; the method is reliable, versatile and accurate. Analysis is normally done in a specialist laboratory, so personal sampling generally suffers from delay in obtaining the results as compared with the use of stain detector tubes.

Dust sampling – The most widely-used technique is simple dust filtration, involving the use of a small pump to suck a measured quantity of air through a filtering membrane over a period of time. The sampling head containing the membrane is then removed from the pump and analysed in a laboratory.

Direct monitoring – Some instruments available commercially, and also able to be hired, can produce an immediate quantitative analysis of the level of a particular contaminant, or even a qualitative analysis of the air sample as a whole. The results are available on a meter or chart recorder. Infrared gas analysers are the most common type. This method allows the detection of the presence of short-term peak concentrations of contaminant during the work period, which is useful for working out control methods.

Hygrometers – These are instruments used for the measurement of water vapour in air. Although everyone is aware when the atmosphere becomes humid, people's ability to estimate humidity accurately is not good. Hygrometers can be very useful in measuring the humidity and comfort of the working environment.

Other measures – Measurement of other environmental hazards which may be encountered involves similar considerations and techniques, although the equipment required is usually more sophisticated. **Radiation** is measured by grab sampling using a Geiger counter; **microwave** energy can be measured by a meter as it is radiated, or its presence can be detected by the fluorescing of a rare earth in a vacuum tube – an ordinary fluorescent lighting tube can be used for the purpose if small enough. **Sound** energy is measured using a proprietary meter, as is **light** for quantity and colour temperature.

Measurement of wave and particle energy, including noise, normally requires special equipment, and special training to operate it correctly and to produce reliable and useful results. Simple equipment can be very useful in identifying the presence of a hazard, but should not be relied on totally in the development of controls.

An example is in the selection of personal hearing protection (see Part 3 Section 6), where although a simple meter can identify the broad extent of the hazard, an octave band analysis would be required in order to match the characteristics of the sound source with the attenuating capabilities of different hearing protection. Note that this matching of the protective equipment to the risk it will control and to the wearer is a requirement of many local and national laws and codes.

Interpreting the results

Interpretation of the results is a skilled task – it involves making judgments about the results and the norms and standards laid down. The interpretation will determine the control strategy (see the next Section).

Summary of techniques

For chronic hazards – continuous personal dose measurement, continuous measurement of average background levels, spot readings of contaminant levels at selected positions and times.

For acute hazards – continuous personal monitoring with rapid response, continuous background monitoring with rapid response, spot readings of background contaminant levels at selected positions and times.

For analysis of whether an area is safe to enter – direct-reading instruments. Particle qualitative and quantitative analysis can be carried out by direct-reading instruments, which are expensive.

REVISION

The main forms of environmental monitoring in the workplace are:

■ Grab sampling
■ Long-term sampling
■ Direct monitoring

ENVIRONMENTAL ENGINEERING CONTROLS

Introduction

Having established a potential for injury in the workplace, selection of one or more control measures is necessary. An integral part of the effectiveness of the control is the monitoring of the controls once in place. It is important to remember that engineering and designing the problems out must be the primary consideration. The use of personal protective equipment is low in the list of control measures to be considered as a single solution. The **safety precedence sequence** applies to these control measures, placing the need for human intervention lower on the scale of acceptability than 'hardware' solutions.

The following control measures can be used, in descending order of efficacy and priority:
- Substitution
- Isolation
- Enclosure of the process
- Local exhaust ventilation
- General (dilution) ventilation
- Good housekeeping
- Reduced exposure time
- Training
- Personal protective clothing and equipment
- Welfare facilities
- Health surveillance

The use of warnings (such as signs) may be regarded as an aid to these controls, not as a substitute. As they depend on the correct action being taken in response to the warning, they are not effective unless combined with other measures. It may be necessary to include warnings in order to comply with national or local regulatory requirements.

Types of control

Substitution of safer alternatives in procedures or materials is the first stage in the review of existing processes and procedures.

Isolation and enclosure of the process can be achieved by the use of physical barriers, or by relocation of processes and/or facilities.

Local exhaust ventilation (LEV) is achieved by trapping the contaminant close to its source, and removing it directly by purpose-built ventilation prior to its entry into the breathing zone of the operator or the atmosphere.

LEV systems have four major parts, all of which must be efficiently maintained:
1. Hood – the collection point.
2. Ducting – to transport the contaminant away.
3. Air purifying device – eg charcoal filters to prevent further pollution.
4. Fan – the means of moving air through the system.

The efficiency of LEV systems is affected by draughts, capture hood design and dimensions, air velocity achieved, and distance of capture point from the source. A major design consideration is that sucking air is very inefficient as an alternative to blowing it into a capture hood.

General or dilution ventilation uses natural air movement through open doors or assisted ventilation by roof fans or blowers to dilute the contaminant. It should only be considered if:
1. There is a small quantity of contaminant.
2. The contaminant is produced uniformly in the area.
3. The contaminant material is of low toxicity.

Good housekeeping lessens the likelihood of accidental contact with a contaminant. It includes measures to anticipate and handle spillages and leaks of materials, and minimising quantities in open use.

Reduced exposure time to a contaminant may be appropriate, provided that the possible harmful effect of the dose rate is taken into account, ie high levels of exposure for short periods of time may be damaging.

Training should emphasise the importance of using the control measures provided, and give an explanation of the nature of the hazard which may be present together with the precautions which individuals need to take.

ENVIRONMENTAL ENGINEERING CONTROLS

Personal protective clothing and equipment may be used where it is not possible to reduce the risk of injury sufficiently using the above control strategies. In that case, suitable personal protective equipment must be used (see Part 3 Section 6).

Welfare facilities allow workers to maintain good standards of personal hygiene, including regular washing and showering, and using appropriate clean protective clothing and equipment. The presence of adequate first-aid and emergency facilities minimises the effects of exposure to hazards.

Health surveillance may detect early signs of ill health. In some cases, this can be carried out by supervisors trained to recognise the effects of exposure to workplace materials, or otherwise by the use of trained nursing and medical staff and facilities.

Failure of controls

Once a control strategy has been devised and introduced, it is tempting to assume that there will be no further problems. A brief study of the possible ways in which things can go wrong will show that there are two broad areas where problems can occur – in the introduction phase and as a result of change:

Inadequate initial design because of inappropriate choice of the type of control system, lack of consultations between designers, users and workers, failures to foresee future demands on the system, and failure to consider the possible consequences of introducing the system (eg increased noise).

Inadequate installation because of incompetence, or lack of adequate instructions or specifications.

Incorrect use may be due to lack of training, supervision or poor ergonomic design – or all of these.

Inadequate maintenance resulting in blocked, damaged or removed parts, filters clogged or badly fitted, or worn fans.

Failure to anticipate changes which may include:
- The process itself
- The materials used
- The workers and supervisors concerned
- Work methods
- The local environment including operator adjustments and additions
- Regulatory changes such as exposure limits and LEV changes

REVISION

Eleven control strategies:
- Substitution
- Isolation
- Enclosure of the process
- Local exhaust ventilation
- General (dilution) ventilation
- Good housekeeping
- Reduced exposure time
- Training
- Personal protective clothing and equipment
- Welfare facilities
- Medical surveillance

Five causes of failure of controls:
- Inadequate initial design
- Inadequate installation
- Incorrect usage
- Inadequate maintenance
- Unanticipated change

NOISE AND VIBRATION

Introduction

Noise enables us to communicate, and can create pleasure in the form of music and speech. However, exposure to excessive noise can damage hearing. Noise is usually defined as 'unwanted sound', but in strict terms noise and sound are the same. Noise at work can be measured using a sound-level meter. Sound is transmitted as waves in the air, travelling between the source and the hearer. The frequency of the waves is the **pitch** of the sound, and the amount of energy in the sound wave is the **amplitude**.

How the ear works

Sound waves are collected by the outer ear and pass along the **auditory canal** for about 2.5cm to the **ear drum**. Changes in sound pressure cause the ear drum to move in proportion to the sound's intensity. On the inner side of the ear drum is the middle ear which is completely enclosed in bone. Sound is transmitted across the middle ear by three linked bones, the **ossicles**, to the **oval window** of the **cochlea**, the organ of hearing which forms part of the **inner ear**. This is a spirally-wound tube, filled with fluid which vibrates in sympathy with the ossicles. Movement of the fluid causes stimulation of very small, sensitive cells with hairs protruding from them and rubbing on a plate above them. The rubbing motion produces electrical impulses in the **hair cells** which are transmitted along the auditory nerve to the **brain** which then interprets the electrical impulses as perceived sound.

Hair cells sited nearest the middle ear are stimulated by high frequency sounds, and those sited at the tip of the cochlea are excited by low frequency. **Noise-induced hearing loss** occurs when the hair cells in a particular area become worn and no longer make contact with the plate above them. This process is not reversible, as the hair cells do not grow again once damaged.

How hearing damage occurs

Excessive noise energy entering the system invokes a protection reflex, causing the flow of nerve impulses

to be damped and as a result making the system less sensitive to low noise levels. This is known as threshold shift. From a single or short duration exposure, the resulting temporary **threshold shift** can affect hearing ability for some hours, but recovery then takes place. Repeated exposure can result in irreversible permanent threshold shift. The following damage can occur as a result of exposure to noise:

Acute effects

1. **Acute acoustic trauma** from gunfire, explosions; usually reversible, affects the ear drum, ossicles.
2. **Temporary threshold shift** from short exposures, affecting the cochlea.
3. **Tinnitus** (ringing in the ears) results from intense stimulation of the auditory nerves, usually wears off within 24 hours.

Chronic effects

1. **Permanent threshold shift** from long duration exposure; affects the cochlea and is irreversible.
2. **Noise-induced hearing loss** from (typically) long duration exposure; affects ability to hear human speech, irreversible, compensatable. It involves reduced hearing capability at the frequency of the noises that have caused the losses.
3. **Tinnitus**, as the acute form, may become chronic without warning, often irreversibly.

Presbycusis is the term for hearing losses in older people. These have been thought to be due to changes due to ageing in the middle ear ossicles, which causes a reduction in their ability to transmit higher-frequency vibrations.

Measurement of noise

The range of human hearing from the quietest detectable sound to engine noise at the pain threshold is enormous, involving a linear scale of more than 100,000,000,000 units. Measuring sound intensity on such a scale would be clumsy, and so a method of compressing it is used internationally. The sound intensity or pressure is expressed on a logarithmic scale and measured in **bels**, although as a bel is too large for most purposes, the unit of measurement is the **decibel (dB)**. The logarithmic decibel scale runs from 0 to 160dB.

A consequence of using the logarithm scale is that an increase of 3dB represents a doubling of the noise level. If two machines are measured when running separately at 90dB each, the sound pressure level when they are both running together will not be 180dB, but 93dB. To establish noise levels on this scale, several different types of measurement are used.

Three weighting filter networks (A, B and C) are incorporated into sound-level meters. They each adjust the reading given for different purposes, and the one most commonly used is the **A-weighted dB**. This filter recognises the fact that the human ear is less sensitive to low frequencies, and the circuit attenuates or reduces very low frequencies to mimic the response of the human ear, and attaches greater importance to the values obtained in the sensitive frequencies. Measurements taken using the A circuit are expressed in dB(A).

In most workplaces and most types of work, noise levels vary continuously. A measurement taken at a single moment in time is unlikely to be representative of exposure throughout the work period, yet this needs to be known as the damage done to hearing is related to the total amount of noise energy to which the ear is exposed.

A measure called L_{Eq} – **the Continuous Equivalent Noise Level** – is used to indicate an average value over a period which represents the same noise energy as the total output of the fluctuating real levels. L_{Eq} can be obtained directly from a sound-level meter having an integrating circuit, which captures noise information at frequent timed intervals and recalculates the average value over a standard period, usually eight

hours. It can also be calculated from a series of individual readings coupled with timings of the duration of each sound level, but this is laborious and relatively inaccurate.

Noise dose is a measure which expresses the amount of noise measured as a percentage, where eight hours at a continuous noise level of 90dB(A) is taken as 100 per cent. If the work method and noise output is uniform, and the dose measured after four hours is 40 per cent, then the likely eight-hour exposure will be less than 100 per cent. However, if the dose reading after two hours is 60 per cent, this will be an indication of an unacceptably high exposure.

$L_{EP,d}$ measures a worker's daily personal exposure to noise, expressed in dB(A). $L_{EP,w}$ is the measure of the worker's weekly average of the daily personal noise exposure, again expressed in dB(A).

Peak pressure is the highest pressure level reached by the sound wave, and assessments of this will be needed where there is exposure to impact or explosive noise. A meter capable of carrying out the measurement must be specially selected, because of the damping event of needle-based measuring which will consistently produce underreading. A similar effect can be found in 'standard' electronic circuitry.

Controlling noise

This can be achieved by:

Engineering controls – purchasing equipment which has low vibration and noise characteristics, and achieving designed solutions to noise problems including using quieter processes (eg presses instead of hammers), design dampers, making mountings and couplings flexible, and keeping sudden direction and velocity changes in pipework and ducts to a minimum. Operate rotating and reciprocating equipment as slowly as practicable.

Orientation and location – moving the noise source away from the work area, or turning the machine around.

NOISE AND VIBRATION

Enclosure – by surrounding the machine or other noise source with sound-absorbing material, but the effect is limited unless total enclosure is achieved.

Use of silencers – can suppress noise generated when air, gas or steam flow in pipes, or are exhausted to atmosphere.

Lagging – can be used on pipes carrying steam or hot fluids as an alternative to enclosure.

Damping – can be achieved by fitting proprietary damping pads, stiffening ribs or by using double skin construction techniques.

Screens – are effective in reducing direct noise transmission.

Absorption treatment – in the form of wall applications or ceiling panels (these must be designed for acoustic purposes to have significant effect).

Isolation of workers – in acoustically-quiet booths or control areas properly enclosed, coupled with scheduling of work periods to reduce dose will only be effective where there is little or no need for constant entry into areas with high noise levels. This is because even a short duration exposure to high sound pressure levels will exceed the permitted daily dose.

Personal protection – by the provision and wearing of earmuffs or earplugs. This must be regarded as the last line of defence, and engineering controls should be considered in all cases. Areas where personal protective devices must be worn should be identified by signs, and adequate training should be given in the selection, fitting and use of the equipment, as well as the reasons for its use.

Choice of hearing protection

Hearing protection should be chosen to reduce the noise level at the wearer's ear to below the recommended limit for unprotected exposure. Selection cannot be based on A-weighted measurement alone,

because effective protection will depend on the ability of the protective device to attenuate (reduce) the sound energy actually arriving at the head position. Sound is a combination of many frequencies (unless it consists of a pure tone), and it can happen that a particular noise against which protection is required has a frequency component which is not well handled by the 'usual' protection equipment. Therefore, a more detailed picture of the sound spectrum in question should be made before selection, checking the results obtained by **octave band analysis** against the sound-absorbing (attenuation) data supplied by the manufacturers of the products under consideration.

REVISION

Two types of damage:

- **Acute** = acute acoustic trauma, temporary threshold shift, tinnitus
- **Chronic** = permanent threshold shift, noise induced hearing loss, tinnitus

Eleven noise control techniques:

- Engineering
- Orientation/location
- Maintenance
- Enclosure
- Silencers
- Lagging
- Damping
- Screens
- Absorption treatment
- Isolation of workers
- Use of personal protective equipment

PERSONAL PROTECTIVE EQUIPMENT

Introduction

This Section discusses the methodology and practicalities of selecting and using personal protective equipment (PPE).

Personal protective equipment (PPE) has two serious general limitations. It does not eliminate a hazard at source, and it cannot be guaranteed to work for 100 per cent of wearers for 100 per cent of the time. If the PPE fails and the failure is not detected, the risk increases greatly. Where used, this equipment must be appropriately selected, and its use and condition monitored. Workers required to use it must be trained. For a PPE scheme to be effective, three elements must be considered:

Nature of the hazard – details are required before adequate selection can be made, such as the type of contaminant and its concentration.

Performance data for the PPE – the manufacturer's information will be required concerning the ability of the PPE to protect against a particular hazard.

The acceptable level of exposure to the hazard – for some hazards, the only acceptable exposure level is zero. Examples are work with carcinogens and the protection of eyes against flying particles. Occupational Exposure Limits can be used, bearing in mind their limitations.

Factors affecting use

There are three interrelated topics to consider before adequate choice of PPE can be made:

The workplace – What sorts of hazards remain to be controlled? How big are the risks which remain? What is an acceptable level of exposure or contamination? What machinery or processes are involved? What movement of objects or people will be required?

The work environment – What are the physical constraints? They can include temperature, humidity, ventilation, size, and movement requirements for people and plant.

The PPE wearer – Points to consider include:

1. **Training** – Users (and supervisors) must know why the PPE is necessary, any limitations it has, the correct use, how to achieve a good fit, and the necessary maintenance and storage for the equipment.

2. **Fit** – A good fit for the individual wearer is required to ensure full protection. Some PPE is available only in a limited range of sizes and designs.

3. **Acceptability** – How long will the PPE have to be worn by individuals? Giving some choice of the equipment to the wearer without compromising on protection standards will improve the chances of its correct use.

4. **Wearing pattern** – Are there any adverse health and safety consequences which need to be anticipated? For example, any need for frequent removal of PPE, which may be dictated by the nature of the work, may, in turn, affect the choice of design or type of PPE.

5. **Interference** – Regard for the practicability of the item of equipment is needed in the work environment. Some eye protection interferes with peripheral vision, other types cannot easily be used with respirators. Correct selection can alleviate the problem, but full consideration must be given to the overall protection needs when selecting individual items, so that combined items of equipment may be employed. For example, an air-fed helmet gives respiratory protection, and has fitted eye protection incorporated into the design.

6. **Management commitment** – The *sine qua non* of any safety programme, required especially in relation to PPE because it constitutes the last defence against hazards. Failure to comply with instructions concerning the wearing of it raises issues of industrial relations and corporate policy.

Types of PPE

The types of PPE have different functions, including eye protection, hearing protection, respiratory protection, protection of the skin, and general protection in

PERSONAL PROTECTIVE EQUIPMENT

the form of protective clothing and safety harnesses and lifelines.

Hearing protection

There are two main forms of hearing protection – objects placed in the ear canals to impede the passage of sound energy, and objects placed around the outer ear to restrict access of sound energy to the outer ear as well as the ear drum and middle and inner ear. It should be noted that neither of these forms of protection will prevent a certain amount of sound energy reaching the organ of hearing by means of bone conduction effects in the skull.

Earplugs fit into the ear canal. They may be made from glass down, polyurethane foam or rubber, and are disposable. Some forms of re-usable plugs are available, but these are subject to hygiene problems unless great care is taken to clean them after use, and unless they are cast into the individual ear canal, a good fit is unlikely to be achieved in every case. Even though some plugs are available in different sizes, the correct size should only be determined by a qualified person. One difficulty is that in a reasonable proportion of people the ear canals are not the same size.

Earmuffs consist of rigid cups which fit over the ears and are held in place by a head band. The cups generally have acoustic seals of polyurethane foam or a liquid-filled annular bag to obtain a tight fit. The cups are filled with sound-absorbing material. The fit is a function of the design of the cups, the type of seal and the tightness of the head band. The protective value of earmuffs may be lost almost entirely if objects such as hats or spectacles intrude under or past the annular seals.

Respiratory protective equipment (RPE)

There are two broad categories: respirators, which purify the air by drawing it through a filter to remove contaminants, and breathing apparatus, which supplies clean air to the wearer from an uncontaminated

external source. Most equipment will not provide total protection; a small amount of contaminant entry into the breathing zone is inevitable.

Four main types of respirator are available:

Filtering half-mask – a facepiece covers the nose and mouth, and is made of a filtering medium which removes the contaminant; generally used for up to an eight-hour shift and then discarded.

Half-mask respirator – which has a rubber or plastic facepiece covering the nose and mouth, and which carries one or more replaceable filter cartridges.

Full-face respirator – covering the eyes, nose and mouth, and having replaceable filter canisters.

Powered respirator – supplies clean, filtered air to a range of facepieces, including full, half and quarter-masks, hoods and helmets via a battery-operated motor fan unit.

NB: *Respirators do not provide **any** protection in oxygen-deficient atmospheres.*

There are three main types of breathing apparatus which provide continuous air flow (in all cases the delivered air must be of respirable quality):

Fresh air hose apparatus – which supplies clean air from an uncontaminated source, pumped in by the breathing action of the wearer, by bellows or an electric fan.

Compressed airline apparatus (CABA) – using flexible hosing delivering air to the wearer from a compressed air source. Filters in the airline are required to remove oil mist and other contaminants. Positive pressure continuous flow full-face masks, half-masks, hoods, helmets and visors are used.

Self-contained breathing apparatus (SCBA) – in which air is delivered to the wearer from a cylinder via a demand valve into a full-face mask. The complete unit is usually worn by the operative, although cylinders can be remote and connected by a hose.

PERSONAL PROTECTIVE EQUIPMENT

To make proper selection of any type of RPE, an indication is needed of its likely efficiency, when used correctly, in relation to the hazard guarded against. The technical term used in respiratory protection standards to define the equipment's capability is the **nominal protection factor (NPF)**. For each class of equipment, it is the Total Inward Leakage requirement set for that class, and therefore does not vary between products meeting the class standards.

Manufacturers will supply information on the NPF for their product range – it is the simple ratio between the contaminant outside the respirator – in the ambient air – and the acceptable amount inside the facepiece. Examples of typical NPFs are:

Disposable filtering half-mask respirator	4.5 to 50
Positive pressure powered respirator	20 to 2,000
Ventilated visor and helmet	10 to 500
Self-contained breathing apparatus (SCBA)	2,000
Mouthpiece SCBA	10,000

The NPF can be used to help decide which type of RPE will be required. What is needed is to ensure that the concentration of a contaminant inside the facepiece is as far below the OEL as can reasonably be achieved. The required protection factor to be provided by the RPE will be expressed as:

$$\frac{\text{Measured ambient concentration}}{\text{Occupational Exposure Limit}}$$

and this value must be less than the NPF for the respirator type under consideration. Other limitations may apply, including restrictions on the maximum ambient concentration of the contaminant based on its chemical toxicity, and its physical properties such as the Lower Explosive Limit.

In 1997, the term **Assigned Protection Factor (APF)** was introduced in the UK to describe the level of protection that can reasonably be achieved in practice in the workplace, given that workers have been appropriately trained and the RPE is properly fitted and working. Used in the same way as the NPF, the APF provides a higher margin of safety. A full discussion of the use of the APF is beyond the scope of this book.

Eye protection

Assessment of potential hazards to the eyes and the extent of the risks should be made in order to select equipment effectively. There are three types of eye protection commonly available:

Safety spectacles/glasses – which provide protection against low-energy projectiles, such as metal swarf, but do not assist against dusts, are easily displaced, and have no protective effect against high-energy impacts.

Safety goggles – to protect against high-energy projectiles and dusts. They are also available as protection against chemical and metal splashes with additional treatment. Disadvantages include a tendency to mist up inside (despite much design effort by manufacturers), lenses which scratch easily, limited vision for the wearer, lack of protection for the whole face, and high unit cost. Filters will be required for use against non-ionising radiation (see Part 3 Section 8).

Face shields – offering high-energy projectile protection, also full-face protection and a range of special tints and filters to handle various types of radiation. The wearer's field of vision may be restricted. The high initial cost of this equipment is a disadvantage, although some visors allow easy and cheap replacement of shields. Weight can be a disadvantage, but this is compensated by relative freedom from misting up.

Protective clothing

Provides body protection against a range of hazards, including heat and cold, radiation, impact damage and abrasions, water damage and chemical attack.

Head protection – is provided by two types of protectors: the safety helmet, and the scalp protector (also known as the 'bump cap') which is usually brimless. Their function is to provide protection against sun and rain, and against impact damage to the head. The ability of the scalp protector to protect against impacts is very limited, and its use is mainly to protect against bruising and bumps in

PERSONAL PROTECTIVE EQUIPMENT

confined spaces. It is not suitable for use as a substitute for a conventional safety helmet. Safety helmets have a useful life of about three years, which can be shortened by prolonged exposure to ultraviolet light and by repeated minor or major impact damage.

Protective outer garments – are normally made of PVC material and often of high-visibility material to alert approaching traffic. PVC clothing can be uncomfortable to wear because of condensation, and vents are present in good designs. Alternatively, non-PVC fabric can be used, which allows water vapour to escape, but garments made from this material are significantly more expensive.

Protective indoor garments – such as overalls and coats are made of polycotton, and some makes are disposable. If overalls are supplied, arrangements for cleaning must be made to prevent unhygienic conditions developing if the clothing is worn in circumstances where oils or chemicals are handled. Failure to keep the clothing clean and changed regularly may result in dermatitis or skin cancer formation. Aprons and over-trousers should be fire-resistant, and trousers worn during cutting operations require protection in the form of ballistic nylon or similar material. Clothing may limit movement, and become entangled in machinery – careful selection of type and manufacturer is required, together with necessary training about its proper use. This may involve rules concerning the buttoning of coats in the vicinity of rotating machinery. Wearing anti-static clothing is of major importance in reducing static electricity effects – local rules should be strictly followed.

Gloves – must be carefully selected, taking account of use requirements such as comfort, degree of dexterity required, temperature protection offered, and ability to grip in all conditions likely to be encountered – these factors being weighed against considerations of cost and the hazards likely to be encountered by the wearer. Resistance to wearing gloves can be found; it is often claimed that gloves impede work by reducing sensitivity in the fingers, and some users find that excessive sweating causes the gloves to become damp. It is important to change gloves frequently

where solvents and fuels are handled because they permeate many protective materials quickly. Gloves should not be used for longer than half the indicated breakthrough time.

The main types of material and their features are shown in Table 1.

TABLE 1: Good glove guide

MATERIAL	GOOD FOR
Leather	Abrasion protection, heat resistance
PVC	Abrasion protection, water and limited chemical resistance, good for people with latex allergy
Rubber	Degreasing, paint spraying
Cloth/nylon, latex coated	Hand grip
Natural rubber latex	Electrical insulation work (but this material is a recognised allergy risk)
Nitrile rubber, 0.4mm or thicker	Resistance to liquid fuels and solvents, most paints (but not toluene and acetate-based products), rust inhibitors
Chain mail	Cut protection

Footwear – is designed to provide protection for the feet, especially for the toes, if material should drop or fall to the ground. It should also protect against penetration from beneath the sole of the foot, be reasonably waterproof, provide a good grip, and be designed with reference to comfort. Steel toecaps are inflexible, and it is important to purchase the right size of footwear. Electrical insulation can be assisted by the correct footwear for the circumstances, and anti-static conducting shoes are essential where static effects need to be eliminated.

International Principles of Health and Safety at Work | Allan St John Holt

PERSONAL PROTECTIVE EQUIPMENT

Skin protection

Where protective clothing is not a practicable solution to a hazard, barrier creams may be used together with a hygiene routine before and after work periods. There are three types of barrier cream commonly found: water miscible, water repellent and special applications.

Safety harnesses

These are not replacements for effective fall prevention practices. Only where the use of platforms, nets or other access and personal suspension equipment is impracticable is the use of safety harnesses permissible. The functions of belts and harnesses are to limit the height of any fall, and to assist in rescues from confined spaces. In addition to comfort and freedom of movement, selection of this equipment must take into account the need to provide protection to the enclosed body against energy transfer in the event of a fall. Because of this, harnesses are preferable to belts except for a very limited number of applications where belts are required because of the movement needs of the work.

Harness attachments to strong fixing points must be able to withstand the snatch load of any fall. A basic principle is to attach the securing lanyard to a fixing point as high as possible over the area of the work, so as to limit the fall distance. Similarly, a short lanyard should be provided. Equipment which has been involved in arresting a fall should be thoroughly examined before further use, according to the manufacturer's instructions.

The CE mark

One of the definitions of 'suitable' PPE is that it must conform to relevant legal requirements. Within the European Union, workwear and other PPE which meets the relevant strict rules for products must be sold carrying the mark 'CE'. This stands for 'Conformité Européenne', and the letters show the item complies with necessary design and manufacturing standards based on several levels and classes of protection. The rules apply throughout the European Union, so that PPE which complies and bears the 'CE' mark can be sold in any Member State, as part of the harmonisation of standards.

There are three categories or levels of 'conformance' within the 'CE' mark system – basically, equipment is designated as being suitable for protection against low risks, medium risks and high risks. In some cases, PPE in the higher protection categories is subject to examination by an approved body before the mark can be displayed, and the category details will be displayed alongside the mark.

Workwear in the first **simple** category will protect against, for example, dilute detergents. Gloves capable of handling items at less than 50 degrees Celsius will also be in this category, and equipment capable of protecting against minor impacts. The manufacturer of products in this category can assess his own product and award himself the 'CE' mark to be shown on the equipment, but must keep a technical file.

In the second **intermediate** category, the manufacturer must submit a technical file for review, which holds details of the product's design, and claims made for it, and details of the quality system used by the manufacturer. The product itself is liable to be tested to ensure it can do what is claimed for it.

The third high risk or '**complex design**' category mostly covers hazards where death is a potential outcome of exposure. Products which can protect against limited chemical attack, ionising radiation protection, and respiratory equipment protecting against asbestos are examples of products in this group. Manufacturers must comply with all the requirements for the second category, and also submit to an EC examination annually or have a recognised quality system in place, such as ISO 9000.

REVISION

Usage factors:
- Fit
- Period of use

Allan St John Holt | International Principles of Health and Safety at Work

PERSONAL PROTECTIVE EQUIPMENT

- Comfort
- Maintenance
- Training
- Interference
- Management commitment

Types of PPE:
- Hearing protection
- RPE
- Eye/face protection
- Protective clothing
- Skin protection
- Safety harnesses

Introduction

Asbestos is the name given to a group of naturally-occurring mineral silicates, which are grouped because of their physical and chemical similarity and their consequent general properties. Asbestos is strong, inert, resilient and flexible – and, therefore, almost indestructible. It has been used in a wide range of products requiring heat resistance and insulation properties. In humans it has been claimed with varying degrees of certainty to be a factor in asbestosis, lung cancer, cancers of the stomach, intestines and larynx, and mesothelioma. There is no safe level of exposure to any form of asbestos; mostly, long periods of time pass before any effect on an individual can be diagnosed.

Asbestos produces its effects more because of the size, strength, sharpness and jagged shape of the very small fibres it releases than as a result of its chemical constituents, although these do also have relevance. The health hazards arise when these small fibres become airborne and enter the body, and when they are swallowed. The body's natural defence mechanisms can reject large (visible) dust particles and fibres, but the small fibres reaching inner tissues are those that are both difficult to remove and the most damaging. They are particularly dangerous because they cannot be seen by the naked eye under normal conditions, and they are too small (less than 5 microns in length) to be trapped by conventional dust-filter masks.

Asbestos is normally encountered in the demolition or refurbishment processes, but even simple jobs such as drilling partitions or removing ceiling tiles can disturb it. It is important to be aware that asbestos is normally present in a mixture containing a low percentage of asbestos in combination with filling material. Therefore, neither the colour nor the fibrous look of a substance is a good guide. The only reliable identification of the presence of asbestos is by microscopic analysis in a laboratory. The alternative to this is to adopt a default position of assuming that blue asbestos is present (which requires the strictest controls) and proceeding accordingly.

There has been much debate over whether it is better

to remove asbestos wherever it is found as a matter of course, or to leave that which is in good condition in place, recorded and monitored. Arguments other than safety, health and environmental ones have a place in the risk debate. Cost is an issue as is the fact that all the fibres are never controlled when asbestos is removed and the background level of asbestos in air would rise.

Common forms of asbestos

Crocidolite – usually known as blue asbestos. The colour of asbestos can only be an approximate guide, because of colour washes and coatings following application, and also because the colour changes due to heat either in the manufacturing process or following application of a product or chemical action on it. This is the type of asbestos considered by some to be the most dangerous, linked with a high cancer risk and particularly with mesothelioma – a specific form of lung cancer affecting the lining of the lungs and occasionally the stomach. The condition can take up to 25 years to develop following exposure. As with other forms of asbestos-induced cancer, even a minimal exposure may trigger the disease which is invariably fatal.

Crocidolite has been banned in practice in many countries for more than 30 years, but is still to be found in boiler lagging, piping, older insulation boards and sheeting. Asbestos lagging installed before 1940 has a high chance of containing a measurable percentage.

Amosite – brownish in colour unless subjected to high temperature, this form of asbestos is now considered as dangerous as crocidolite.

Chrysotile – white asbestos and the most common form, found in cement sheets, older proprietary ceiling compounds, lagging and many other products, and with all other forms of asbestos now banned from use. Prolonged exposure causes asbestosis, which is a gradual and irreversible clogging of the lungs with insolvent asbestos fibres and the scar tissue produced by the body's defence mechanisms trying to

ASBESTOS

isolate the fibres. Even short periods of exposure have been known to trigger lung cancer, especially in smokers.

Less common substances which fall within the legal definition of asbestos are fibrous actinolite, fibrous anthophyllite and fibrous tremolite (and any mixture containing any of the above).

Working safely with asbestos

Asbestos cement

The general principles to be followed are:
- Reduce the risk of breathing fibres by avoiding the need to do the work where reasonably practicable
- Segregate the area, considering use of a physical barrier such as an enclosure
- Post appropriate warning notices
- Keep the material wet while working on it
- Avoid using abrasive power and pneumatic tools, choosing hand tools instead
- Where power tools are used, provide local exhaust ventilation and use at low speed
- Wear suitable PPE and RPE
- Organise essential high-risk tasks such as cutting and drilling at a central point
- Minimise dust disturbance by choosing appropriate cleaning methods (not sweeping)
- Provide training and information for employees

Asbestos cement sheets

Cleaning by dry scraping or wire brushing should never be allowed. Water jetting can produce slurry which contaminates the area, and the process can cause the sheets to break. Use of surface biocides followed by hand brushing from a safe working platform is the method of choice.

Removal of asbestos cement sheets causes problems because of their potential height and fragility, and weathering which produces fibrous surface dust.

Basic principles to follow are:
- Do not allow anyone to walk or stand on sheets or their fixing bolts or purlins – they should be removed from underneath
- Take asbestos cement sheets off before any other demolition is done
- Do not break the sheets further
- Keep the material wet and lower it onto a clean and hard surface
- Remove waste and debris quickly to avoid further breakdown
- Do not dry sweep debris
- Follow safe waste disposal practice
- Consider background air sampling at the site perimeter to reassure neighbours as well as workers
- Conduct a final inspection to confirm removal of all debris and that a clean area has been left behind

Disposal of asbestos waste

Asbestos waste should always be consigned to a site authorised to accept it. Whether put into plastic sacks or another type of container, the container should be strong enough not to puncture and to contain the waste, be capable of being decontaminated before leaving the work area, and be properly labelled and kept secure on site until sent for disposal. The label design is often specified in national regulations and standards.

Large pieces or whole sheets should not be broken up, but transferred direct to covered trucks or skips, or wrapped in polythene sheeting before disposal. Smaller pieces can be collected and put into a suitable container. This should be double wrapped or bagged, and labelled to show it contains asbestos. Dust deposits are removed preferably using a Type H vacuum cleaner. Outer surfaces of waste containers should be cleaned off before removal.

Acknowledgement: The publishers acknowledge with thanks the permission and co-operation given by Blackwell Science Limited in allowing reproduction of selected material from the author's *Principles of Construction Safety.*

RADIATION

Introduction

Energy which is transmitted, emitted or absorbed as particles or in wave form is called **radiation**. Radiation is emitted by a variety of sources and appliances used in industry. It is also a natural feature of the environment. Transmission of radiation is the way in which radios, radar and microwaves work.

The human body absorbs radiation readily from a wide variety of sources, mostly with adverse effects. All types of electromagnetic radiation are similar in that they travel at the speed of light. Visible light is itself a form of radiation, having component wavelengths which fall between the infrared and the ultraviolet portions of the spectrum. Essentially, there are two forms of radiation, ionising and non-ionising, which can be further subdivided.

Ionisation and radiation

All matter is made up of **elements**, which consist of similar **atoms**. These, the basic building blocks of nature, are made up of a **nucleus** containing **protons** and orbiting **electrons**.

Protons have a mass and a positive charge.

Electrons have a negligible mass and a negative charge.

Neutrons have a mass but no charge.

If the number of electrons in an atom at a point in time is not equal to the number of protons, the atom has a net positive or negative charge, and becomes **ionised**.

Ionising radiation is that which can produce ions by interacting with matter, including human cells, which leads to functional changes in body tissues. The energy of the radiation dislodges electrons from the cell's atoms, producing ion pairs (see below), chemical-free radicals and oxidation products. As body tissues are different in composition and form as well as in function, their response to ionisation is different. Some cells can repair radiation damage, others cannot. The cell's sensitivity to radiation is directly proportional to its reproductive capability.

Ionising radiation

Ionising radiations found in industry are alpha, beta and gamma, and X-rays. Alpha and beta particles are emitted from **radioactive** material at high speed and energy. Radioactive material is unstable, and changes its atomic arrangement so as to emit a steady but slowly diminishing stream of energy.

Alpha particles are helium nuclei with two positive charges (protons), and thus are comparatively large and attractive to electrons. They have short ranges in dense materials and can only just penetrate the skin. However, ingestion or inhalation of a source of alpha particles can place it close to vulnerable tissue, so essential organs can be destroyed. **Beta particles** are

TABLE 1: Radiation sources and hazards

RADIATION	EMITTED FROM	EXAMPLES OF HAZARDS
Radio-frequency and microwaves	Communications equipment, catering equipment, plastics welding	Heating of exposed body parts
Infrared	Any hot material	Skin reddening, burns, cataracts
Visible radiation	Visible light sources, laser beams	Heating, tissue destruction
Ultraviolet	Welding, some lasers, carbon arcs	Sunburn, skin cancer, ozone
X-rays and other ionising radiations	Sources, radiography and X-ray machines	Burns, dermatitis, cancer, body cell damage

RADIATION

fast-moving electrons, smaller in mass than alpha particles but having longer range, so they can damage the body from outside it. They have greater penetrating power, but are less ionising.

Gamma rays have great penetrating power and are the result of excess energy leaving a disintegrating nucleus. Gamma radiation passing through a normal atom will sometimes force the loss of an electron, leaving the atom positively charged – an **ion**. This and the expelled electron are called an **ion pair**. Gamma rays are very similar in their effects to **X-rays**, which are produced by sudden acceleration or deceleration of a charged particle, usually when high-speed electrons strike a suitable target under controlled conditions. The electrical potential required to accelerate electrons to speeds where X-ray production will occur is a minimum of 15,000 volts. Equipment operating at voltages below this will not, therefore, be a source of X-rays. Conversely, there is a possibility of this form of radiation hazard being present at voltages higher than this. X-rays and gamma rays have high energy, and high penetration power through fairly dense material. In low density substances, including air, they may have long ranges.

Common sources in industry of ionising radiation are X-ray machines and isotopes used for non-destructive testing (NDT). They can also be found in laboratory work and in communications equipment.

Non-ionising radiation

Generally, non-ionising radiations do not cause the ionisation of matter. Radiation of this type includes that in the electromagnetic spectrum between ultraviolet and radio waves, and also artificially-produced laser beams.

Ultraviolet radiation comes from the sun, and is also generated by equipment such as welding torches. Much of the natural ultraviolet in the atmosphere is filtered out by the ozone layer, but a sufficient amount penetrates to cause sunburn and even blindness. Its effect is thermal and photochemical, producing burns and skin thickening, and eventually skin cancers. Electric arcs and ultraviolet lamps can produce a photochemical effect by absorption on the conjunctiva of the eyes, resulting in 'arc eye' and cataract formation.

Infrared radiation is easily converted into heat, and exposure results in a thermal effect such as skin burning, and loss of body fluids. The eyes can be damaged in the cornea and lens which may become opaque (cataract). Retinal damage may also occur if the radiation is focused, as in laser radiation. This is a concentrated beam of radiation, having principally thermal damage effects on the body.

Radio-frequency radiation is emitted by microwave transmitters including ovens and radar installations. The body tries to cool exposed parts by blood circulation. Organs where this is not effective are at risk, as for infrared radiation. These include the eyes and reproductive organs. Where the heat of the absorbed microwave energy cannot be dispersed, the temperature will rise unless controlled by blood flow and sweating to produce heat loss by evaporation, convection and radiation. Induction heating of metals can cause burns when touched.

Controls for ionising radiation

The intensity of radiation depends on the strength of the source, the distance from it and the presence and type of shielding. Intensity will also depend on the type of radiation emitted by the source. Radiation intensity is subject to the **inverse square law** – it is inversely proportional to the square of the distance from the source to the target. The dose received will also depend on the duration of the exposure. These factors must be taken into account when devising the controls. **Elimination of exposure** is the priority, to be achieved by restricting use and access, use of shielded enclosures, and written procedures to cover:
- Use, operation, handling, transport, storage and disposal of known sources
- Identification of potential radiation sources
- Training of operators
- Identification of operating areas

146

- Monitoring of radiation levels around shielding
- Monitoring of personal exposure of individuals, by dosimeters
- Medical examinations for workers at prescribed intervals
- Hygiene practice in working areas
- Wearing of disposable protective clothing during work periods
- Clean-up practice
- Limiting of work periods when possible exposure could occur

Controls for non-ionising radiation

Protection against **ultraviolet radiation** is relatively simple (sunbathers have long known that anything opaque will absorb ultraviolet light); that emitted from industrial processes can be isolated by shielding and partitions, although plastic materials differ in their absorption abilities. Users of emitting equipment, such as welders, can protect themselves by the use of goggles and protective clothing – the latter to avoid 'sunburn'. Assistants often fail to appreciate the extent of their own exposure, and require similar protection.

Visible light can, of course, be detected by the eye which has two protective control mechanisms of its own – the eyelids and the iris. These are normally sufficient, as the eyelid blink reflex has a reaction time of 150 milliseconds. There are numerous sources of high-intensity light which could produce damage or damaging distraction, and sustained glare may also cause eye fatigue and headaches. Basic precautions include confinement of high-intensity sources, matt finishes to nearby paintwork, and provision of optically-correct protective glasses for outdoor workers in snow, sand or near large bodies of water.

Problems from **infrared** radiation derive from thermal effects and include skin burning, sweating, and loss of body salts leading to cramps, exhaustion and heat stroke. Clothing and gloves will protect the skin, but the hazard should be recognised so that effects can be minimised without recourse to personal protective equipment.

Controls for **laser** operations depend on prevention of the beam from striking persons directly or by reflection. Effects will depend on the power output of the laser, but even the smallest is a potential hazard if the beam is permitted to strike the body and especially the eye. Workers with lasers should know the potential for harm of the equipment they work with, and should be trained to use it and authorised to do so. If the beam cannot be totally enclosed in a firing tube, eye protection should be worn which is suitable for the class of laser being operated (classification is based on wavelength and intensity). Work areas should be marked so that inadvertent entry is not possible during operations. Laser targets require non-reflecting surfaces, and much care should be taken to ensure that this also applies to objects nearby which may reflect the laser beam.

Toxic gases may be emitted by the target, so arrangements for ventilation should be considered. It is also necessary to ensure that the beam cannot be swung unintentionally during use, and that lasers are not left unattended while in use.

Equipment which produces **microwave** radiation can usually be shielded to protect the users. If size and function prohibits this, restrictions on entry and working near an energised microwave device will be needed. Metals, tools, flammable and explosive materials should not be left in the electromagnetic field generated by microwave equipment. Appropriate warning devices should be part of the controls for each such appliance. Commercially-available kitchen equipment is now subject to power restrictions and controls over the standard of seals to doors, but regular inspection and maintenance by manufacturers is required to ensure that it does not deteriorate with use and over time.

General strategy for the control of exposure to radiation

In addition to the previous specific controls, the following general principles must be observed:
1. Radiation should only be introduced to the workplace if there is a positive benefit.

RADIATION

2. Safety information must be obtained from suppliers about the type(s) of radiation emitted or likely to be emitted by their equipment.

3. Assessments of risks should be made in writing, noting the control measures in force. All those affected, including employees of other employers, the general public and the self-employed must be considered, and risks to them evaluated. They are then to be given necessary information about the risks and the controls.

4. All sources of radiation must be clearly identified and marked.

5. Protective equipment (see 7 below) must be supplied and worn so as to protect routes of entry of radiation into the body.

6. Safety procedures must be reviewed regularly.

7. Protective equipment provided must be suitable and appropriate, as required by relevant regulations. It must be checked and maintained regularly.

8. A radiation protection adviser should be appointed with specific responsibilities to monitor and advise on use, precautions, controls and exposure.

9. Emergency plans must cover the potential radiation emergency, as well as providing a control strategy for other emergencies which may threaten existing controls for radiation protection.

10. Written authorisation by permit should be used to account for all purchase, use, storage, transport and disposal of radioactive substances.

11. Workers should be classified by training and exposure period. In some jurisdictions, especially the European Union, those potentially exposed to ionising radiation should be classed as 'persons especially at risk'.

REVISION

Two forms of radiation:
- Ionising – alpha and beta particles, gamma rays, X-rays
- Non-ionising – ultraviolet, infrared, visible light, lasers, radio-frequency, microwaves

Introduction

Ergonomics is the applied study of the interaction between people and the objects and environment around them. In the work environment, the objects include chairs, tables, machines and workstations. Ergonomics looks at more than just the design of chairs, though. A complete approach to the work environment is the aim, including making it easier to receive information from machines and interpret it correctly.

Careful ergonomic design improves the 'fit', and promotes occupational wellbeing. It also encourages employee satisfaction and efficiency. Ergonomics is concerned with applying scientific data on human mental and physical capabilities and performance to the design of workplaces, hardware and systems. Usually, the ergonomic design emphasis is on designing tools, equipment and workplaces so that they and the job fit the person rather than the other way around.

A combination of techniques is normally used. These include:

Work design – incorporating ergonomics into the design of tools, machines, workplaces and work methods. These topics are not mutually exclusive.

Organisational arrangements – aimed at limiting the potentially harmful effects of physically demanding jobs on individuals. They may be concerned with selection and training, matching individual skills to job demands, job rotation methods and work breaks. Studies carried out by the Swedish construction employment and insurance organisation Bygghälsan with employees and manufacturers have shown that considerable gains in productivity can be associated with optimising working conditions using ergonomic solutions. Bygghälsan investigated musculoskeletal disorders in the necks and shoulders of construction workers. A survey showed that almost half of all construction workers work more than 10 hours a week with their arms above shoulder level, leading to increased risk of problems in the neck and shoulders. Sickness absences due to these problems increase for individuals over 30 in all trade categories in the industry, indicating that work-related problems in the neck and shoulders manifest themselves after 10 to 15 years of exposure.

It is impossible to eliminate totally the need to work with the hands above shoulder height, and so Bygghälsan looked at alterations in the way the work was organised, work methods, improved equipment and techniques to make the work easier. One of the discoveries made was that the use of micropauses – very short breaks – reduced muscular load and resulted in faster work. Screws were tightened into a beam at eye level, and those who took a 10-second pause after every other tightening did the work 12 per cent faster than those who did not. Interestingly, the workers themselves thought it took longer to carry out the work with micropauses than without.

Designing work and work equipment to suit the worker can reduce errors and ill health – and accidents. Examples of problems which can benefit from ergonomic solutions are:

- Workstations which are uncomfortable for the operator
- Hand tools which impose strain on users
- Control switches and gauges which cannot be easily reached or read
- Jobs reported to be found excessively tiring

Anthropometry

Anthropometry is the measurement of the physical characteristics of the human body. People vary enormously in basic characteristics such as weight, height and physical strength. A car built for the 'average' passenger may require tall people to bend at uncomfortable angles, while smaller people may not be able to reach the controls.

Designers use information on variations in size, reach and other physical dimensions to produce cars and other objects which most people can handle comfortably and conveniently.

This has particular application in the design of workplaces and work equipment. Including these

ERGONOMICS

measurements in system design assists in the process of making man and machine more compatible, and produces considerable benefits to industry because of improvements in efficiency, quality and safety.

Anthropometry is concerned with measurements of body movement as well as static dimensions, and includes the discipline of **biomechanics**, which studies the forces involved in movements. Knowledge of all these factors is combined to make improvements in workplace design – seating, for example, and work equipment, where the knowledge assists in the design of appropriate machine guards.

The 'average' person

Ergonomic designers usually try to meet the physical needs of the majority of a population. For any dimension, usually 10 per cent of the population will fall outside the range used. For example, the height of a workstation will only be wrong for the shortest five per cent and the tallest five per cent – the range is five to 95 per cent.

The designer will have to make deliberate compromises of this kind. It is not possible to produce a single size to fit everyone. Information about the design will enable purchasers to make informed decisions about equipment so that it meets the physical needs of the workforce.

Some ergonomic issues

Display screen equipment

Over the past twenty years, display screen equipment (DSE) has been claimed to be responsible for a wide variety of adverse health effects, including radiation damage to pregnant women. Medical research shows, however, that radiation levels from the equipment do not pose significant risks to health. The range of symptoms which is positively linked relates to the visual system and working posture, together with general increased levels of stress and fatigue in some cases.

In the European Union, **repetitive strain injury (RSI)** arising from work activities is now known with other musculoskeletal problems as **work-related upper limb disorders** (see below). One difficulty with 'RSI' has been that ill health is not necessarily due solely to repetitive actions, and is not limited to strains. The physical effects of DSE work range from temporary cramps to chronic soft tissue disorders, such as carpal tunnel syndrome in the wrist. It is likely that a combination of factors produces them. They can be prevented by action following an analysis of the workstation as required by the EC Directive, together with an appreciation of the role of training, job design and work planning.

Eye and eyesight defects do not result from use of DSE, and it does not make existing defects worse. Temporary fatigue, sore eyes and headaches can be produced by poor positioning of the DSE, poor legibility of screen or source documents, poor lighting and screen flicker. Staying in the same position relative to the screen for long periods can have the same effect.

Fatigue and stress are more likely to result from poor job design, work organisation, lack of user control over the system, social isolation and high-speed working than from physical aspects of the workstation. These factors will also be identified in an assessment, and through consultation with the workforce.

Epilepsy is not known to have been induced by DSE. Even photosensitive epileptics (who react to flickering light patterns) can work safely with display screens.

Facial dermatitis has been reported by some DSE users, but this is quite rare. The symptoms may be due to workplace environmental factors including low humidity and static electricity near the equipment.

Pregnancy is not put at risk by DSE work, but those worried about the dangers should be encouraged to talk with someone aware of current advice – this is that DSE radiation emissions do not put unborn children, or anyone else, at risk.

Work-related upper limb disorders

'Upper limb disorders' is a label that refers to a wide range of conditions caused or aggravated by work. In the USA, the term 'cumulative trauma disorders' covers the same phenomena. From the neck to the fingertips, underlying changes in anatomy produce symptoms including pain, restriction of movement, and reduction in strength or sensation. Not all upper limb disorders (ULDs) are related to work. Jobs with a high level of manual work and restrictions on posture are likely to have a significant percentage of sufferers from ULDs. These jobs include assembly and processing line working, cleaners and hairdressers.

An ergonomic approach encourages taking into account all relevant parts of the system of work, and encourages participation. Work over long periods that is repetitive and involves awkward or static postures and/or high levels of applied manual force should be specially assessed.

Hand-arm vibration

Some pieces of work equipment have characteristics that can have lasting and damaging effects on users. Regular exposure to high levels of vibration from tools can lead to permanent injury and functional impairment. Hand-guided and hand-fed powered equipment and hand-held power tools used as a regular part of a job are potential causes of hand-arm vibration – examples are road-breaking hammers, lawnmowers and grinders. The permanent injuries that can result from the use of this equipment range from numbness and tingling in the fingers through pain and loss of grip strength, and loss of the sense of touch. These effects are known collectively as hand-arm vibration syndrome (HAV). The most well-known form of HAV is vibration white finger (VWF).

The most effective control to prevent HAV is to specify low-vibration equipment (if its use at all is justified). Manufacturers are required to provide information on vibration levels, but this needs to be interpreted and may not be reliable in terms of actual exposure under field conditions. Poor maintenance is also a factor; machines with worn parts are likely to vibrate. The use of special gloves is rarely a substitute for low-vibration equipment – they are not likely to reduce the amount of vibration reaching the hands significantly. Changes in work practices can be effective, such as the use of jigs and holders at grinding machines.

Where HAV risks cannot be eliminated, health surveillance should be provided. Use of a questionnaire to gather information can be productive. It should establish the daily amount of use for each type of equipment, and ask people to report symptoms of fingers going white on exposure to cold, tingling or numbness following equipment use, hand and arm joint and muscle problems, and difficulties with fine gripping. Health surveillance should include regular health checks, and should itself be supervised by a medical practitioner.

PART 3 SECTION 9

INTERNATIONAL HEALTH AND SAFETY LAW

INTRODUCTION

PART 4
Compliance

INTERNATIONAL HEALTH AND SAFETY LAW

Introduction

The remainder of this book is mostly devoted to a review of the principles of European Union-led action on health and safety at work. This is in marked contrast to what may be called 'the American model'; an understanding of the basic differences in approach may be of assistance to international readers. Apart from these two chief legal systems, the standards of the Geneva-based International Labour Organisation (ILO) provide the minimum basis for compliance in jurisdictions not owing other historical or cultural allegiance.

Historical perspective

Until 1970 there was a broad agreement between governments on their regulatory approach to health and safety at work. National laws prescribed in lesser or greater detail the minimum standards which employers must achieve at their workplaces – although some workplaces were deliberately excluded because of perceived low risk, difficulty of enforcement, and industry and local traditions.

But, in 1970, the United States introduced a new legal regime in the Williams Steiger Act, better known as OSHA. This was, and is, a comprehensive statute which is essentially prescriptive – it contains full details of the means of compliance and control for a huge variety of circumstances and hazards. Later enactments followed the same prescriptive course.

In the United Kingdom, a review of existing legal controls carried out by the Robens Committee resulted in the introduction in 1974 of the Health and Safety at Work etc Act. This measure contained relatively little by way of prescription and relied instead on the achievement of "reasonably practicable" standards of health and safety at work and elsewhere, on the part of both the employer and those in control of premises.

This was in contrast to the UK's earlier, highly specific and prescriptive rules which were destined to be progressively replaced by requirements introduced under the new system, which referred to guidance and codes mostly offered as examples which the employer and others could choose to follow in the pursuit of "reasonably practicable" control measures. Many felt that the new law would lead to lowered standards. Time has shown that the increased flexibility offered by this approach conferred benefits not previously available, although the lack of a 'rule book' is still complained of by some groups.

The balance was redressed to some extent by the European Community, now the European Union, which required the United Kingdom as a Member State to provide more specific rules in compliance with the various health and safety directives introduced from the mid-1980s. Later Sections of this Part examine the central Framework Directive, and the way in which it was implemented in the United Kingdom, as an illustration of the current European approach to health and safety legislation.

The role of government

Where there is little social or economic reason for the employer to take positive action to prevent workplace injuries and ill health, experience shows that these actions will only be taken where there is a firm leadership role taken by national government, backed by appropriate sanctions which are seen as significant by those they may affect. What are the components of such a role?

Six major elements can be distinguished:
1. **Setting of appropriate standards for health and safety at work**. This requires a government to have available a pool of knowledge, skills and experience to enable the most appropriate legislation for the community to be devised, and revised as needed. Many governments have successfully borrowed legislation piecemeal from other nations; unfortunately some of what is borrowed may not 'fit' the new wearer, and even borrowed material needs revision over the passage of time. These are reasons why the local knowledge pool is needed.
2. **Enforcement of those standards through the legal system**. Among the many elements

of an enforcement programme is, at the least, an adequate number of trained and competent inspectors or regulators, whose duties extend to the planned and random inspection of workplaces covered by the legislation, the investigation of incidents and complaints, and the conduct of proceedings as necessary following such inspections and investigations. For financial reasons, and because of tradition, health and safety enforcement is often to be found within the framework of a department of labour, whose inspectors are also concerned with policies and enforcement of other aspects of the working environment including wages and conditions. As a result, the time and skills of these inspectors may well be stretched to accommodate specialist knowledge of health and safety matters.

3. **Advice to employers, workers and the public on appropriate control measures, and the issue of explanatory publications.** Development of information resources in hazard controls, risk assessment techniques, and collection of injury data produces inputs into an information system which will be able to offer answers to problems within the community and to monitor the national measures in force.

4. **Uniformity of approach.** There must be an appropriate means of dealing with those who deliberately avoid compliance with national laws, which is seen to be fair. Similarly, the penalties imposed should be appropriate to the offence and at a common level for the same offence committed in different places and environments. The level of penalty should be such that it offers an incentive to comply with the law, and sufficient so that there is no economic advantage to be gained by failure to comply, followed by a willingness to accept the resulting penalty. Equally, there must be some relation between national control measures and those of other international trading partners and other countries with broadly similar economies and standards. This will be significant for multinational employers.

5. **Setting targets for future improvement.** Government moves to improve future national performance can include requiring the formal assessment of risk as a part of the planning process, making designers responsible for the provision of information about their designs and the future maintenance or dismantling of buildings, plant and equipment, and the publication of injury and ill health data and other results set against future targets. It is self-evident that governments that do not carry out a progressive assessment of the impact of measures on the lives and wellbeing of the workforce are seen as paying lip-service to the common international goal of reduction in the numbers of workplace accidents of all kinds.

6. **Fostering co-operation between the parties involved – workers, worker representatives, management and government.** In many countries, legislation provides for joint consultation and information exchange on matters related to workers' safety and health. Experience in many countries shows that the potential for the contribution to good practices which can be made by workers is often undervalued, and those given consultation on their own safety and health are more likely to co-operate with the measures put in place to protect them. Equally, legislation which has the support of these major elements is more likely to be effective than that which is developed in isolation.

The big picture – Sustainability

As the world moves into a new century and a new millennium, there is a growing recognition that 'health and safety' is but one of the facets of organisational control that must be mastered, not in isolation but together with others. Earlier concepts of loss control and risk management developed in response to the realisation that the protection of assets of organisations, states and even cultures is necessary to ensure survival. Now, the umbrella of 'sustainable development' has been raised to cover all of the dynamic elements of modern society.

INTERNATIONAL HEALTH AND SAFETY LAW

One definition of sustainable development that has received general acceptance is 'development that meets the needs of the present without compromising the ability of future generations to meet their own needs'. Thus, occupational health and safety is a part of sustainable development at the simplest level, because failure to achieve an adequate standard and to limit risks will compromise the very existence of the future generation. Sustainable development is linked most closely with environmental concerns. A more refined definition puts the concept as a dynamic process that 'enables all people to realise their potential and improve their quality of life in ways which simultaneously protect and enhance the Earth's life support systems'.

Among multinational organisations especially, the sustainable development concept is becoming the main focus of action to demonstrate sensitivity towards their impact on the 'global village'. Criteria are being developed which measure progress towards satisfying not only their shareholders but also social and environmental performance. As yet, there is little sign of agreement on what should be achieved, or indeed how to do it. However, the trend is towards integration of activity in these areas, such that environmental and quality management are increasingly being linked with health and safety management. Partly, this is because the central features of their management systems are the same and there are likely to be economies of scale to be made as a result. Examination of the major international standards for these topics (ISO 9000, 14000 and OHSAS 18000 series) shows that their many common features enable the same management structures to be used.

Within the European Union (EU), the sovereignty and right of each Member State to pass laws on safety and health – or any other subject – is not affected: by agreement, the Member States harmonise their regulatory activities by proposing and discussing regulatory action in the European forum, resulting in directives which contain the principles and objectives to be attained by national legislation in each Member State. There is also a timetable for the implementation of the legislation, which must be sufficient to ensure compliance with the minimum standards set out in each of the directives.

There are major differences between the Member States in the organisation and administration of their national laws, in procedures including enforcement, and in terminology. These differences will be significant for health and safety practitioners working in each of the countries, and for employing organisations with operations in more than one country. There are differences in enforcement practices and standards, in the ability and knowledge of the enforcing authorities and their staff, and differences in legal systems and penalties applied. Consistency in these areas is an important goal for the EU.

National needs vary the extent to which internal legislation in Member States exceeds, extends or varies the directives. For example, in general, United Kingdom laws made in response to directives on health and safety at work exceed the directives' minimum standards because they apply to the self-employed as well as employees, employers and other duty-holders.

This Part does not discuss the Directives on Product and Machinery Safety, which impose standards on products and equipment rather than on people and systems. There are considerable links between the two fields. Only one example of a directive is given in detail, followed by a summary of the legislation introduced in the United Kingdom in order to comply with it, for illustrative purposes.

European courts

The European Court of Justice, sitting in Luxembourg, adjudicates on the law of the European Union, and its decisions are binding on Member States' national courts by reason of the European Communities Act 1972. It gives rulings regarding the interpretation and application of provisions of European Union law referred to it by Member States. A single judgment is given, from which there is no right of appeal. Any decisions it makes are enforceable throughout the network of courts and tribunals within each of the Member States.

The European Court of Human Rights enforces the agreed Community standards on the protection of human rights and fundamental freedoms.

The European Union system

Administration of the EU is carried out through a network of four bodies:

The Commission, led by a Board of Commissioners of representatives from each Member State. The Commission administers the law throughout the EU. Proposals for future legislation originate from the Commission in the form of directives, sent for approval to the Council of Ministers.

The Council of Ministers is composed of members of government from each Member State, and is responsible for decision-making within the EU.

The European Parliament is formed of representatives elected from constituencies from within Member States, and consults on and debates all proposed legislation.

The European Courts – see above.

Making health and safety legislation in the EU

Proposals for health and safety legislation are made either under Article 100A (now Article 95) or Article 118A (now Article 138) of the Treaty of Rome. The original Article 118A has been completely reworded

EUROPEAN LAW

as Article 138. Following consultation in international committees and Council working groups, proposals are generated by the Directorates Generale, of which DGV is the one most often associated with health and safety matters. These are submitted to the Commission, which submits in turn its proposals to the Council of Ministers. Consultation follows with the European Parliament and the Economic and Social Committee, both of which issue Opinions on the proposals after voting.

The Commission receives the Opinions and may modify its proposals as a result although it is not required to do so. The proposals then go to the Council of Ministers. Health and safety matters are normally proposed under Article 138 of the Treaty, and in these cases the relevant Council is the Labour and Social Affairs Council. The Council discusses the proposal, and votes using the qualified majority vote system to adopt a Common Position.

The Common Position is the official starting point for the European Parliamentary process. The Parliament can reject a Common Position. Where this happens, it can only be adopted after a unanimous vote by the Council. The European Parliament can approve a Common Position either directly, or indirectly by taking no decision on it. In the latter case, the proposal is automatically adopted by the Council of Ministers. The third possibility is that the European Parliament proposes amendments to the Common Position. This forces a resubmission, starting back at the Commission and ending at the Council where a unanimous vote is required in order to insert amendments proposed by the European Parliament and not supported by the Commission.

Elements of European law

Apart from the general provisions of the Treaty of Rome, which is signed by all Member States, there are three elements or instruments of European law:

European Regulations passed by the Council of Ministers, which are adopted immediately into the legal framework of each Member State; *unlike*

Directives, which set out objective standards to be achieved but allow Member States to decide on how their own individual legal frameworks will be altered to adopt them. In the UK, the most common method of implementation of directives is by statutory instrument.

Decisions are reached in cases which are taken to the European Courts, and affect only the company or individual concerned.

The *Official Journal of the European Communities* publishes the instruments at different stages of their development.

THE FRAMEWORK DIRECTIVE (89/391/EEC)

Introduction

The European Directive No 89/391/EEC, known as the 'Framework Directive', is the measure dealing generally with 'the introduction of measures to encourage improvements in the safety and health of workers at work'. The European Parliament adopted four resolutions in February 1988 which specifically invited the Commission to draw up a framework to serve as a basis for more specific directives covering all the risks connected with health and safety at the workplace. This Directive was the result of that invitation, and its structure is typical of directives in general.

This Section summarises the Framework Directive (FD) and outlines its structure. The next Section follows its implementation within the United Kingdom as an example of how the general requirements were taken up by a Member State and passed into specific laws within the allowed time period for implementation.

Preliminary

The reasons for the presence of the FD are set out in a series of paragraphs, each beginning with the word "Whereas", summarised as follows:

- The FD is founded on the requirement of the former Article 118A of the Treaty of Rome, by which the Council must use the directive system to adopt minimum requirements for encouraging improvements, especially in the working environment, to guarantee a better level of protection of the health and safety of workers
- The FD does not justify any reduction in existing levels of protection already in place in Member States
- Workers can be exposed to the effects of dangerous environmental factors at the workplace during the course of their working life
- The former Article 118A of the Treaty of Rome required that directives must not impose constraints holding back the creation and development of small and medium-sized undertakings

- Member States have a responsibility to encourage improvements in worker safety on their territory, and taking these measures can also help in preserving the health and safety of others
- Member States have different legislative systems on health and safety at work which differ widely and need to be improved, and national provisions in this field may result in different levels of protection and allow competition at the expense of health and safety
- The incidence of accidents at work and occupational disease is still too high and measures ensuring a higher level of protection are to be introduced without delay
- Ensuring improved protection requires the contribution and involvement of workers and/or their representatives by means of balanced participation to see that necessary protective measures are taken
- Information, dialogue and balanced participation must be developed between employers and workers and/or their representatives
- Improvement of workers' safety, hygiene and health at work is an objective which should not be subordinated to purely economic considerations
- Employers must keep themselves informed of technological advances and scientific findings on workplace design and inform workers accordingly
- The FD applies to all risks, especially those arising from chemical, physical and biological agents
- The Advisory Committee on Safety, Hygiene and Health Protection at Work is consulted by the Commission on the drafting of proposals in this field

General provisions

Article 1 states the object of the FD as the introduction of measures to encourage improvements in the safety and health of workers at work, to which end it contains general principles and implementation guidelines and is without prejudice to existing or

Allan St John Holt | International Principles of Health and Safety at Work

THE FRAMEWORK DIRECTIVE (89/391/EEC)

future Community/Union or national provisions which are more stringent.

Article 2 states the scope of the FD applies to all sectors of activity both public and private, but not to specified public services activities such as the armed forces or police, where the objectives of the Directive must be followed as far as possible.

Article 3 contains definitions of the following terms: worker, employer, workers' representative, prevention.

Article 4 requires Member States to take the necessary steps to ensure their laws extend the Directive's provisions to employers, workers and their representatives, with adequate controls and supervision.

Employers' obligations

Article 5 describes general duties of employers to ensure safety and health of workers in every aspect related to the work. These are duties which cannot be delegated to workers or third parties. An option is given to Member States to exclude or limit employers' responsibility where occurrences are due to unusual and unforeseeable circumstances beyond the employers' control, and to exceptional events where the consequences could not have been avoided despite exercise of all due care.

Article 6 sets out the general obligations of employers. These include the general principles of prevention, the need for co-operation with other employers sharing a workplace, not involving workers in the financial cost of any measures taken, worker instruction and capability assessment, and the assessment of risks.

In **Article 7** the employer is required to designate one or more workers to carry out protection and prevention activities, who must be allowed time to do this and not be placed at any disadvantage because of these activities. If there are no competent persons in the undertaking, the employer must enlist competent external services or persons. These persons must be given access to information required to be made available by Article 10. All designated workers must be sufficient in number and ability to deal with the organising of health and safety measures appropriate to the undertaking, the hazards there and their distribution throughout the entire undertaking. Member States must define the necessary abilities required to do this, and how many such people will be designated. They can also define those undertaking(s) where size and activities indicate that the employer who is competent can take personal responsibility for carrying out the activities referred to.

Article 8 covers first aid, firefighting and evacuation of workers, and the concept of serious and imminent danger. The employer must designate personnel required to implement the chosen measures in these areas. Workers who are assessed as being potentially exposed to serious and imminent danger of the risks involved must be identified and given information about the risks and the steps to be taken concerning stopping work and proceeding to a place of safety. In general, workers must not be asked to resume work where a risk of serious and imminent danger remains. When, because of such a risk, workers leave a dangerous area, they must be protected against any harmful or unjustified consequences. Actions of workers in this context do not place them at any disadvantage unless they acted carelessly or there was negligence on their part.

Various additional obligations are given in **Article 9**, including a requirement for the employer to be in possession of risk assessments including those facing particular groups of workers, and a record of accidents resulting in a worker being unfit for work for more than three working days.

Article 10 obliges employers to provide a wide range of information on identified risks and preventive and protective measures to workers, outside employers of workers sharing or using common workplaces, persons appointed under Article 7, and workers' representatives. They are also entitled to accident reports and summaries, and information provided by regulatory agencies.

Worker participation and consultation is to be

THE FRAMEWORK DIRECTIVE (89/391/EEC)

guaranteed under **Article 11**. Consultation is to be in advance and in good time. Such consultation is to be held on any measure which substantially affects safety and health, designation of workers under Articles 7 and 8, information provision under Articles 9 and 10, appointing of external services or persons under Article 7, and planning and organising of training referred to in Article 12. Workers must be given the right to ask for and propose appropriate measures to mitigate hazards, must be allowed time off with pay to exercise their rights and functions and to liaise during inspection visits by the enforcing authority, and may not be placed at a disadvantage because of their activities in relation to this Article.

Article 12 deals with the training of workers. This is to be provided by the employer on recruitment, on changing jobs, and following introduction of new technology or new equipment. Training takes the form of information and instructions specific to the job or workstation, and must be repeated where necessary, especially when changed or new risks are identified. The employer is also to ensure that workers from outside undertakings have received appropriate instructions on the risks to be found during activities in the employer's undertaking. Worker representatives with a specific role in protecting health and safety of workers are entitled to appropriate training.

Generally, no training under this Article is to be at the workers' own expense, and must take place during working hours.

Workers' obligations

Workers' own obligations under **Article 13** are to, as far as possible, take care of their own health and safety and that of others who might be affected by their acts at work in accordance with training and instructions given by the employer. The Article details that workers must make correct use of the means of production and the personal protective equipment supplied to them, use supplied safety devices correctly and not change or remove any devices fitted to structures or equipment, and co-operate with their

employer and other employees with health and safety responsibilities. They must also inform their employer immediately about any work situation which they reasonably consider to be dangerous and about any shortcomings in protection arrangements.

By **Article 14**, health surveillance may be received by any worker wishing it, appropriate to the risks incurred at work. Such surveillance may be provided as part of a national health system. Particularly sensitive risk groups are to be specifically protected (**Article 15**).

Individual directives

Article 16 binds the Council to adopt individual directives in the areas listed in the FD Annex, which without prejudice provide more stringent or specific requirements. It also allows for amendment of the FD and these other 'daughter' directives. The areas specified in the Annex are:

- Workplaces
- Work equipment
- Personal protective equipment
- Work with visual display units
- Handling of heavy loads involving risk of back injury
- Temporary or mobile construction sites
- Fisheries and agriculture

Oversight

A mechanism is prescribed in **Article 17** for taking account of needs for technical adjustment, harmonisation, new findings and technological progress, and international regulatory changes as far as they affect the FD or the 'daughter' directives. In this, the Commission will be assisted by a representative committee.

Action

The final **Article 18** details the date by which the Member States must bring into force their provisions

THE FRAMEWORK DIRECTIVE (89/391/EEC)

necessary to comply with the Directive. This was 31 December 1992. The texts of national laws in place to cover the requirements must be lodged with the Commission. Every five years, Member States are to report their consulted comments on the practical implementation of the provisions of the Directive. The Commission then submits a report to the Council, Parliament, and the Economic and Social Committee.

THE MANAGEMENT OF HEALTH AND SAFETY AT WORK REGULATIONS 1999

Introduction

These Regulations (MHSWR) implement most of European Directive No 89/391/EEC of 29 May 1990, the Framework Directive, and also Council Directives 91/383/EEC dealing with the health and safety of those who are employed on a fixed term or other temporary basis and 94/33/EC on the protection of young people. The Regulations supplement the requirements of the Health and Safety at Work etc Act 1974; they extend the employer's general safety obligations by requiring additional specific actions on the employer's part to enhance control measures.

Originally issued in 1992, the MHSWR were enlarged and extended in 1994, and renumbered, updated and reissued at the end of 1999. The MHSWR do not cover all of the matters mentioned in the Directives, partly because some of them are dealt with elsewhere, and partly because existing provisions are considered to cover the points adequately. Examples include first aid, use of personal protective equipment and firefighting.

It should be noted that, in the UK, breaches of health and safety laws such as these are criminal offences tried by courts, and thus subject to penalties even where no physical injury has occurred. Employers and employees alike can be charged with offences. Imprisonment is a potential consequence of a limited number of offences against the main Act, the Health and Safety at Work etc Act 1974.

For the first time in UK regulations (as opposed to the Health and Safety at Work etc Act 1974 which also contains it), the MHSWR provide that a breach of a duty imposed by these Regulations generally does not confer a right of action in any civil proceedings (Regulation 15). Exceptions to this are Regulations in respect of 'young persons' and risks to new and expectant mothers (Regulations 16(1) and 19). The Regulations do not apply to the master or crew of a seagoing ship, or to their employer in respect of the normal shipboard activities of the crew.

Inevitably, there are some overlaps between these more general regulations and subject-specific ones such as the Manual Handling Operations Regulations 1992. Where these general duties are similar to specific ones elsewhere, as in the case of general risk assessments and those required by other specific regulations, the legal requirement is to comply with both the general and the specific duty. However, specific assessments required elsewhere will also satisfy the general requirement under the MHSWR for risk assessment as far as those operations alone are concerned. The employer will still have to apply the general duties in all work areas.

Because they provide the detail lacking in the Health and Safety at Work etc Act 1974, a knowledge of the MHSWR is important for every employer. There are specific requirements for risk assessments to be made, for training, and for dealing with other employers, to name only three of the significant areas requiring action by employers. They also include the development of arrangements which need to be written into the health and safety policy.

Requirements of the Regulations

Regulation 1 contains the date of commencement and relevant definitions. The latter include:

Child – in simple terms, a person who is not over compulsory school age.

Young person – a person who has not reached the age of 18.

New or expectant mother – an employee who is pregnant, who has given birth within the previous six months, or who is breast-feeding.

Regulation 2 disapplies the MHSWR to the master and crew of a seagoing ship, and most of the 'young persons' requirements in respect of 'occasional or short-term working involving either domestic service in a private household' and work 'not regarded as harmful, damaging or dangerous to young people in a family undertaking'. No definition is offered of 'family undertaking'.

THE MANAGEMENT OF HEALTH AND SAFETY AT WORK REGULATIONS 1999

Regulation 3 requires every employer and self-employed person to make a suitable and sufficient assessment of the health and safety risks to employees and others not in his/her employment to which his/her undertakings give rise, in order to put in place appropriate control measures. It also requires review of the assessments as appropriate, and for the significant findings to be recorded (electronically if desired) if five or more are employed. Details are also to be recorded of any group of employees identified by an assessment as being especially at risk.

With regard to young persons, an employer shall not employ a young person unless a risk assessment has been made or reviewed in relation to the risks to health and safety of young people, taking into account in particular:

- The inexperience, immaturity and lack of awareness of risks of young people
- The fitting-out and layout of the workstation and workplace
- The nature, degree and duration of exposure to physical, chemical and biological agents
- The form, range and use of work equipment and the way in which it is handled
- The organisation of processes and activities
- Risks from special processes which are listed

Regulation 4 requires any preventive and protective measures that the employer takes to be implemented on the basis of Schedule 1 to the Regulations. In practice, it can be assumed that existing measures, particularly those required by other regulations, will be regarded as complying with the Schedule, which is couched in rather general terms overall.

Regulation 5 requires employers to make appropriate arrangements, given the nature and size of their operations, for effective planning, organising, controlling, monitoring and review of the preventive and protective measures. If there are five or more employees, the arrangements are to be recorded.

Regulation 6 requires the provision by the employer of appropriate health surveillance, which has been identified by the assessments as being necessary.

Adequate numbers of 'competent persons' must be appointed by employers under **Regulation 7**. They are to assist the employer to comply with obligations under all the health and safety legislation, unless (in the case only of sole traders or partnerships) the employer already has sufficient competence to comply without assistance. This Regulation also requires the employer to make arrangements between competent persons to ensure adequate co-operation between them, to provide the facilities they need to carry out their functions, and to give specified health and safety information (on temporary workers, assessment results, and risks notified by other employers under other regulations within the MHSWR). Regulation 7 repays study, because it sets out clearly what is required of the competent person and the appointment arrangements, including the Regulation 7(8) 'preference' for internal appointment(s) of competent person(s) rather than of person(s) such as consultants not actually within the employer's employment.

Regulation 8 requires employers to establish and give effect to procedures to be followed in the event of serious and imminent danger to persons working in their undertakings, to nominate competent persons to implement any evacuation procedures, and to restrict access to danger areas. Persons will be classed as competent when trained and able to implement these procedures. For example, one effect of this Regulation is to require fire evacuation procedures with nominated fire marshals in every premises.

Regulation 9 directs that any necessary contacts with external agencies are in fact arranged.

Regulation 10 requires employers to give employees comprehensible and relevant information on health and safety risks identified by the assessment, the protective and preventive measures, any procedures under Regulation 8(1), the identities of competent persons appointed under that Regulation, and risks notified to the employer by others in shared facilities and other third parties as required by Regulation 11.

Regulation 10 also contains two paragraphs on the employment of children and young persons as defined above. The first of these requires that, before

THE MANAGEMENT OF HEALTH AND SAFETY AT WORK REGULATIONS 1999

employing a child, an employer must provide a parent of that child with comprehensible and relevant information on assessed health and safety risks, any preventive and protective measures employed, and details of any third-party risks notified to the employer under Regulation 11. The second paragraph defines the word 'parent' in terms of people who have parental rights (in Scotland) and parental responsibility (in England and Wales).

Regulation 11 deals with the case of two or more employers or self-employed persons sharing a workplace temporarily or permanently. Each employer or self-employed person in this position is to co-operate with any others as far as necessary to enable statutory duties to be complied with, reasonably co-ordinate his/her own measures with those of the others, and take all reasonable steps to inform the other employers of risks arising out of his/her undertaking.

Regulation 12 covers the sharing of information on workplace risks. It requires employers and the self-employed to provide employers of any employees, and every employee from outside undertakings, and every self-employed person, who is working in their undertakings, with comprehensible information concerning any risks from the undertaking. Outside employers, their employees and the self-employed must also be told how to identify any person nominated by the employer to implement evacuation procedures.

Regulation 13 requires employers to take capabilities as regards health and safety into account when allocating work tasks. Adequate health and safety training must be provided to all employees on recruitment, and on their exposure to new or increased risks because of: a job or responsibility change; introduction of new work equipment or a change in use of existing work equipment; the introduction of new technology; or the introduction of a new system of work or a change to an existing one. The training must be repeated where appropriate, take account of new or changed risks to the employees concerned, and take place during working hours.

Regulation 14 introduces employee duties. They

must use all machinery, equipment, dangerous substances, means of production, transport equipment and safety devices in accordance with any relevant training and instructions, and inform their employer or specified fellow employees of dangerous situations and shortcomings in the employer's health and safety arrangements.

Regulation 15 covers temporary workers. Employers and the self-employed have to provide any person they employ on a fixed-term contract or through an employment agency with information on any special skills required for safe working (and any health surveillance required) before work starts. The employment agency must be given information about special skills required for safe working, and specific features of jobs to be filled by agency workers where these are likely to affect their health and safety. The agency employer is required to provide that information to the employees concerned.

Regulation 16 requires specific risk assessment of the work of new and expectant mothers and the taking of appropriate measures as a result, including variation of working hours or conditions where reasonable to do so and effective against the risks, up to suspension from work where necessary. **Regulation 17** requires the employer to suspend new and expectant mothers from work 'for as long as is necessary' for their health and safety, either when night work is involved, or when a medical certificate indicates that this should be done. In both cases, the employee's rights to alternative work and remuneration are protected by the Employment Rights Act 1996 and earlier legislation.

Regulation 18 permits the employer to apply his/her knowledge of the medical condition of those people who may be affected by Regulations 16 and 17. For Regulation 16 to apply, the employer must have received written notice from the employee that she is pregnant, breast-feeding or has given birth within the preceding six months. Failure to produce a medical certificate where one is required or other specified failure to show that the provisions apply, may disapply them. Cases where the employer either knows the person is no longer a new or expectant mother, or

THE MANAGEMENT OF HEALTH AND SAFETY AT WORK REGULATIONS 1999

cannot establish whether she remains so, also disapply the provisions.

Regulation 19 is set in the most general terms, and contains a duty on employers to ensure that employed young persons are protected while at work from any risks to their health or safety which result from their lack of experience, lack of awareness of risks or any lack of maturity (paragraph 1). In particular (paragraph 2), young persons cannot be employed to do work beyond their physical or psychological capacity, or which involves:

- Harmful exposure to toxic, carcinogenic or other chronic agents of harm to human health
- Harmful exposure to radiation
- Risks of accidents which, it can reasonably be assumed, cannot be recognised or avoided by young persons because of lack of experience or training, or because of their insufficient attention to safety
- A risk to health from extreme heat or cold, noise or vibration

In deciding whether the work will involve such harm or risks, employers must pay attention to the results of their risk assessments (which are required by Regulation 3). Paragraph 3 does not prevent the employment of a young person who is not a child, where this is necessary for training, or where the young person will be supervised by a competent person and where any risk will be reduced to the lowest level that is reasonably practicable. These provisions are without prejudice to any other provisions or restrictions on employment arising elsewhere.

The Home Secretary can invoke national security where necessary to exempt various armed forces from the MHSWR by **Regulation 20**.

Regulation 21 denies the employer a defence in criminal proceedings because of any act or default by an employee or a competent person appointed by him/her. Breach of the MHSWR cannot be used to give a right of civil action (**Regulation 22**), with the important exceptions of Regulations 16(1) and 19.

Regulations 23–30 deal with procedural matters including application of the Regulations outside Great Britain, amendments and revocations. The consequential amendments are listed in an extensive Schedule 2.

Readers should note that the foregoing attempts only to summarise a complex set of Regulations, which should be studied in the original (together with the accompanying Approved Code of Practice) for full details and an interpretation to ensure accuracy.

THE INTERNATIONAL LABOUR ORGANISATION

The International Labour Organisation (ILO) is a UN body with a number of functions. One of these is to establish and maintain international standards on labour and social issues. These are issued in the form of **Conventions** and **Recommendations**. Guidance material is also available in codes of practice and reference manuals. Full details of significant ILO publications on all kinds on health, safety and environmental matters can be found at www.ilo.org/public (most documents can be downloaded free of charge).

About 70 of the Conventions and Recommendations deal with occupational health and safety. The conventions are open to be ratified (agreed to) by UN Member States, and once they have been ratified, binding obligations to comply are accepted. The text of each Convention states the means by which its provisions are expected to be applied. Those Member States ratifying the various Conventions are obliged to report regularly on progress, and complaints can be made by various organisations representing workers and employers as well as governments of other ratifying Member States where non-compliance is alleged. Conventions that have not been ratified have the status of Recommendations.

In the case of Recommendations, Member States have no specific obligations other than to notify their existence to their legislatures and to report on what happens as a result. Both Standards and Recommendations are used frequently as models for legislation or amendments and also by labour and employer organisations to support their points of view.

Codes of Practice and **Guidelines** are frequently published, having been drawn up at tripartite meetings of experts and following approval by the ILO Governing Body. The reader's attention is drawn particularly to *Guidelines on Occupational Safety and Health Management Systems*, which was sent to the Governing Body on 13 June 2001. The document's development and arguments about its contents are detailed in a report that can be obtained from the ILO website (see above) through the SafeWork section.

ILO documentation falls into four wide categories:
- Guiding policies for action
- Protection in given branches of economic activity
- Protection against specific hazards and risks
- Measures of protection

Examples of significant Conventions and Recommendations in each category are as follows:

Guiding policies for action

Occupational Safety and Health Convention 1981 No 155 and Recommendation No 164 – describe the progressive application of comprehensive prevention measures; also establish the responsibility of employers for making work and equipment safe and without risks to health, and the rights and duties of workers.

Occupational Health Services Convention 1985 No 161 and Recommendation No 171 – establish that occupational health services have primarily preventive functions advising employers and workers on maintaining a safe and healthy work environment.

List of Occupational Diseases Recommendation 2002 No 194 – gives a proposed list of occupational diseases, and commentary on the recording and notification of occupational accidents and diseases.

Protection in given branches of economic activity

The Safety and Health in Construction Convention 1988 No 167 and Recommendation No 175 – contain basic principles and measures to promote safety and health of construction workers. The Safety and Health in Mines Convention 1995 No 176 and Recommendation No 183 – cover risks unique to mining and apply to all mining activities both on the surface and underground, and to the preparation of extracted material.

Protection against specific hazards and risks

The Chemicals Convention 1990 No 170 and

THE INTERNATIONAL LABOUR ORGANISATION

Recommendation No 177 – international attempt to improve national measures and harmonise standards. Call for a coherent national policy of chemical safety from labelling and classification to control of all aspects of chemical use.

The Asbestos Convention 1986 No 162 and Recommendation No 172 – put forward organisational, technical and medical measures to protect workers.

Some of these have a long history, showing the early involvement of the ILO in what are now standard protective measures and regimes:

- Anthrax Prevention Recommendation 1919 No 3
- White Lead (Painting) Convention 1921 No 13
- Benzene Convention 1972 No 136
- Guarding of Machinery Convention 1963 No 119

Measures of protection

Early examples of landmark international codes promulgated by the ILO include:

- Maternity Protection Convention 1919 No 3 (last revised as No 183 in 2000)
- Underground Work (Women) Convention 1935 No 45

INDEX

INDEX

INDEX